OBSESSED

A SURVIVOR'S QUEST TO FIND JUSTICE FOR THE LOST BOYS OF NEW ENGLAND

DAVID McGRATH

WILDBLUE
PRESS

WildBluePress.com

OBSESSED published by:
WILDBLUE PRESS
P.O. Box 102440
Denver, Colorado 80250

WILDBLUE PRESS is registered at the U.S. Patent and Trademark Offices.

ISBN 978-1-964730-25-7 Hardcover
ISBN 978-1-964730-26-4 Trade Paperback
ISBN 978-1-964730-24-0 eBook

Cover design © 2024 WildBlue Press. All rights reserved.

Interior Formatting and Book Cover Design by Elijah Toten
www.totencreative.com

OBSESSED

CONTENTS

DEDICATIONS

This book is dedicated to FBI Special Agents Laura Schwartzenberger and Daniel Alfin, who were shot and killed while serving a child pornography warrant in the town of Sunrise, Florida, on February 2, 2021. Alfin and Schwartzenberger worked tirelessly to keep children safe in this new world of the internet. We are all indebted to them.

To my two boys, who never stopped bugging me for extra snacks during the writing of this book.

And to my Friend Kevin Linehan, who is the rarest of all friends: the one who tells you the truth even when you don't want to hear it.

Author's Note

It all started when I caught a cold. It's one of those colds that's mostly just annoying, like a pesky mosquito that keeps landing on your arm while you're fishing and trying to enjoy a beer.

I was up late. My head felt like it was in a vice. My face was sore and my sinuses were so tight, it felt like my head could snap off. My wife was pregnant with our first son, the aptly named Gunnar. She was fidgeting back and forth, changing positions and experiencing the kind of fitful sleep you might have when an invader takes over your body, saps your energy, takes all your nutrients, and makes itself at home. It was about 2 a.m. and I was mindlessly flipping through the channels and stumbled on a documentary on HBO: *Have You Seen Andy?*

Director Melanie Perkins was the childhood friend of a ten-year-old boy named Andy Puglisi who disappeared from Higgins Memorial Pool in Lawrence, Massachusetts, on August 21, 1976. The documentary chronicled that day in 1976 and the circumstances of Puglisi's disappearance. Puglisi's body was never found. The documentary outlined how there were five sex offenders identified at the pool the day Andy disappeared. Watching that documentary and seeing his picture struck a chord in me. It reminded me of myself. *I* had a secret I had been carrying my whole life. I had carried it through my teenage years, into my long military career, and even into graduate school.

I am a victim of childhood sexual abuse.

This story is not about me nor is it about who victimized me. He is long gone. This story is about the dark forces that some unfortunate, vulnerable children encounter. I was victimized. I felt ashamed, angry, and worried about what was coming around every corner. I could not have normal relationships. It was not until I met my wife at thirty and had a couple of little boys myself that I finally got my life straight. Straight enough to get into school and set my course for the rest of my life: identifying and stopping these predators.

Predators do not turn into wolves at midnight, nor do they walk around frothing at the mouth with large fangs. There is no identifying mark they must alert the public. They are completely anonymous. They melt into the community. They masquerade as teachers, clergymen, and, in this case, a janitor. The only people who ever see this side of them, their honest side, are their victims.

Sometimes, like me, they live to tell the tale. Sometimes they don't. The main suspect in Andy Puglisi's disappearance is a man named Wayne Chapman. The first time I saw Chapman's booking photo after a morning of Googling, I knew I had to find out everything there was to know about this man. He had the most vacant black eyes. There was just nothing there. I embarked on a five-year journey to learn everything I could about where Chapman came from and what factors led him to Higgins Memorial Pool in August 1976. If Andy's case were simply a murder, I would have quietly put the Puglisi family in my prayers and moved on with my life. What I found was much more sinister.

Chapman participated in an early ring of child pornographers and distributors. He had some infamous friends as well. He networked in the same circles as child killers Nathaniel Bar-Jonah and Charles Pierce. They did prison time together, commiserating on how they would do things differently should they be released. The three even committed crimes together, the breadth of which will probably never be known. That probability is what bugs me the most. These men and their crimes were mostly lost to history.

I needed to expose it. We can never forget. This book has heavy subject matter, but it's important. The scary truth is, statistically speaking, there is a Wayne Chapman in your neighborhood right now. If I can raise awareness and possibly help identify the next Chapman, then all the research, late nights, and typing would have been worth it. My entire life has been dedicated to identifying and stopping predators like Wayne Chapman.

I do not go into graphic detail on crimes, just general outlines. I sincerely hope this book sheds some light on a very dark time in New England. Child pornography, child sex rings, and even child murder were prevalent. The National Man Boy Love Association (NAMBLA) sprouted up in Massachusetts at this time. I wanted to know what factors created Chapman and those like him. I answer these questions to the best of my research here. I tie Chapman and his cohorts to other missing children from that timeframe all over the country. I also introduce you to a few lesser-known child predators who were active and connected to Chapman during the 1970s and 1980s.

Wayne Chapman, now in his seventies, is free today. His window overlooks a school in Rocky Hill, Connecticut. I will explain how he was released and what he did behind the walls for many decades at the Massachusetts Treatment Center for the sexually dangerous. I expose the child sex ring that operated in Revere, Massachusetts, from 1973 to 1977.

I must warn you: there are no happy endings in this book. It may make you angry; it may make you lose all hope in humanity. I can only hope that it opens your eyes a little bit to the world around you and that we remember the children whose innocence was dashed due to the existence of men like this. It is my sincere hope, dear reader.

—Some random laundromat, 2019

KEY PLAYERS

WAYNE CHAPMAN: Child predator and the main suspect in the 1976 disappearance of ten-year-old Andy Puglisi. Chapman was civilly committed for life after being convicted of raping two young boys in Lawrence, Massachusetts, in 1975. Chapman admitted to more than one hundred victims, including Andy Puglisi, and started offending at age seven.

NATHANIEL BAR-JONAH: Born David Brown in Worcester, Massachusetts, in 1957. Bar-Jonah is the main suspect in the disappearance of ten-year-old Zachary Ramsay of Great Falls, Missouri. Bar-Jonah was convicted of the attempted murder of two young boys in Shrewsbury, Massachusetts, in 1977, and was sentenced to eighteen to twenty years in Bridgewater State Hospital.

ALBERT MINTZ: Providence, Rhode Island, Sex Crimes detective from 1968 to 1978. Mintz investigated Chapman while Chapman was living in Providence in the mid-1970s.

CHARLES PIERCE: Carnival worker and notorious child killer. Pierce served decades behind bars with Bar-Jonah and Chapman. Pierce's body count is unknown. When asked to identify how many children he killed, Pierce stated, "There are just so many." Convicted in 1980 of murdering Michelle Wilson, a thirteen-year-old Boxford, Massachusetts, girl.

EUGENE WEIR: Sex offender from Cumberland County, Maine. Friend of Chapman since the early 1970s.

RICHARD PELUSO: Sex offender from Massachusetts. Peluso was a self-employed advertiser who ran a child sex ring from 1973 to 1977 on Mountain Avenue in Revere, Massachusetts. Peluso was sentenced to fifteen to twenty-five years in prison for child rape and trafficking after the sex ring was busted in 1977.

FRANK DAMIANO: Sex offender from Massachusetts who pled guilty to twenty-three indictments of rape and unnatural sexual intercourse with children under sixteen.

CHILDREN MISSING FROM NEW ENGLAND IN THE LATE 1960s AND 1970s

ANDY PUGLISI: A ten-year-old boy who disappeared from the Higgins Memorial Pool in Lawrence, Massachusetts, in 1976. Last seen with Wayne Chapman and another man.

DAVID LOUISON: A five-year-old boy who disappeared from Brockton, Massachusetts, in 1974. David's body was found in a steamer trunk in 1980.

ANDREW AMATO: A four-year-old boy who disappeared from Webster, Massachusetts, in September 1978. Andrew disappeared near Route 395 which touches the Webster, Massachusetts, Rhode Island, and Connecticut borders. Andrew has never been found.

KURT NEWTON: A four-year-old boy who went missing from Coburn Gore in Maine in 1975. Kurt had been at a campground with his parents; his body had never been found.

LEIGH SAVOIE: A ten-year-old boy who went missing from Revere, Massachusetts, in April 1974. Leigh was known to shine shoes at the Suffolk Downs Racetrack in Revere and was never seen again.

DOUGLAS CHAPMAN: A three-year-old boy who went missing in 1971. Douglas was last seen playing in a sand pile near his home in Alfred, Maine. Douglas's father believed a local sex offender, who has since died, murdered the boy. Douglas has never been found. He is of no relation to Wayne Chapman.

INTRODUCTION

Albert Mintz needed a shower. He'd been working sex crimes for eight long years. Dealing with all the politics in an incredibly corrupt city tends to wear you down. Al had been working the case of a man suspected of sex crimes and had gone to New York to interview the suspect. He was starting to get a handle on what exactly he was dealing with. He had seen the man's picture many times and noted the vacant, dark eyes on a face that looked normal human, even. The suspect's eyes were jarring; Al could not stop looking at them.

The suspect's name was Wayne Chapman. Chapman had somehow ended up in Al's city on Linwood Avenue, right in the heart of Providence, Rhode Island. It would be a long time before Al understood how a man from Upstate New York ended up there. None of that mattered to Al right now though. He had received a cable from the New York State Police with a picture that had a background Al recognized.

The picture was of a young boy in front of a Labrador retriever statue. Al recognized the statue from Roger Williams Park in his city. After that cable, he immediately started tailing Chapman. Looking through his trash, following his 1965 Dodge van, Al knew Chapman lured children with the guise of a lost dog. Wayne would loiter in public parks, stalking children. Waiting for the right moment to spring the lost dog routine on them and ask children for help finding it. Only there was no dog. It was an isolation technique meant to prey on a very basic instinct we're born with and don't shed until we get a bit older and wiser, a bit more jaded.

Al booked and interviewed Chapman and then wanted to get away. He needed to eat, shower, see his kids, and try to put some distance between his thoughts and Wayne Chapman. Al lived on the very last street in Rhode Island in the small town of Gloucester. One step in either direction or you'd be in Connecticut. It was about 7:20 p.m. at that point and he had been going since 6 a.m. His wife was a hell of a cook, and he was looking forward to eating one of her meals. His stomach barked at him and his head pounded like John Bonham on the kick drum. But Al Mintz was so disturbed by Chapman that he had to do something. He grabbed a copy of Chapman's booking photo. He was sure, almost one hundred percent, that his kids had never seen Wayne Chapman. Hell, he lived a good bit from Providence's bustle, where he assumed Chapman mostly operated. His neighborhood was the rural type that if you parachuted in, you would have thought you were in Montana.

Al stepped through his back screen door and found his kids hanging around the dinner table in the kitchen. The aroma of the spaghetti his wife had cooked still hung in the air. It was hot that day. Al had sweat nearly entirely through his collared shirt under his blue suit. He grabbed the young children's attention and gathered them around. He pulled the picture from his leather briefcase and showed them the grainy booking photo of the disheveled man with vacant eyes. He asked them if they recognized this man from anywhere at all.

Had they seen him at a park? How about at school? It was not common practice for detectives to show booking photos to their kids, but Al was a father first. He was so unnerved by the man he spent all day with that he needed to know. He needed confirmation from his kids that they had never laid eyes on the man who disgusted yet fascinated him.

His kids looked at each other and one piped up, asking, "Isn't that the guy with the lost dog?"

Chapter 1:
Jamestown 1960s

When I knew I had to write this book, I felt the need to start from the beginning and get out on the ground. I immediately started in Jamestown, New York. I spent ten days there and visited Wayne Chapman's childhood home and high school. I searched the archives with an excellent research assistant named Ashley Senske. Ask the people from Jamestown and they will tell you, "Nothing happens here." The most common reply I got when I prompted, "Tell me about Jamestown," is that it is a random, forgettable city in a random, forgettable area of Upstate New York. It's roughly four hundred miles from the hustle and bustle of Manhattan, situated between Lake Erie on its north side and the Allegheny National Forest to the south. The city is indeed nothing to write home about, but the surrounding scenery is quite nice. Jamestown has some celebrity claims to fame: Lucille Ball and NFL commissioner Roger Goodell. It produced what we now know as the automatic voting machine with the lever on the side.

In the 1960s and 1970s, Jamestown's biggest employer was the Coca-Cola bottling plant on Washington Street. On June 23, 1923, in the tiny town of Chautauqua, Arthur Howard Chapman was born to Howard and Mildred Chapman.

Arthur was a typical Depression-era baby born to hard-working parents in a hard-working town. Arthur was a hardscrabble kid whose father was a drinker and a World War I veteran. There was nothing I could find through years of research that indicated Arthur was abused or had anything other than a normal, 1920s-type childhood. He often spoke about the good times he had with his father fishing on Chautauqua Lake. Arthur eventually graduated high school and rose to the challenge that a lot of able-bodied eighteen-year-old men faced in 1941 by enlisting in the United States Marine Corps.

On December 7, 1941, Japan attacked the United States Naval Station at Pearl Harbor in Hawaii. The next day, the United States declared war on Japan and the war machine started. Men like Arthur and hundreds of thousands of others were either forced into duty or enlisted willingly. 1941 was a hectic and unstable time for world peace. Adolf Hitler, the evil, unhinged chancellor of Germany, invaded Russia in what is known as Operation Barbarossa. Hitler was also taking British cities by force by what was known as the Blitz. Arthur had to have known when he arrived for basic training at Parris Island, South Carolina, in late 1941, that when he graduated, he would probably be shipped right to the frontlines.

Sometime in the middle of the night on August 7, 1942, the 1st and 2nd Marine Divisions arrived at Guadalcanal in the Pacific Theater, code named Operation Watchtower by US forces. The battle in the Pacific raged on from that August day until February 1943. The objective was to seize Guadalcanal and use it as a strategic base for the rest of the war effort and in other theaters. Guadalcanal was a key piece of real estate for the Allies, which was under the Japanese Imperial Army's control. The Japanese, who controlled the island since the spring of 1942, were outnumbered nearly three to one by the Allied powers.

On the night of August 8 the following morning, the Japanese Imperial Army defeated a small force of Allied soldiers at the Fourth Battle of Savo Island (Tassafaronga).

Eleven thousand marines initially descended on the island, forming a defensive perimeter near Lunga Point and the airfield. One of those eleven thousand marines was Private Arthur Chapman. He and his mates eventually drove the Japanese off the island, forcing the Imperial Army to evacuate in December 1942.

Arthur and his mates of the 1st Marine Division fought hard in the canal. He was awarded a Purple Heart for wounds in battle. He was a made man, coming home in 1945 a conquering hero at the end of World War II. Arthur's parents, Mildred and Howard, welcomed their son home, who was twenty-two years old in early 1946.

Arthur immediately set his sights on a young lady who attended the community chapel in Jamestown. Elizabeth Anderson graduated from Jamestown High School the same year Arthur arrived for boot camp at Parris Island. Elizabeth, daughter of Arthur and Edith Anderson, was a beautiful, shy, and well-liked member of the class of 1941. Immediately after connecting at the local chapel, Arthur and Elizabeth struck up a love affair. She was taken with his good looks and charm, and why not? He came from a good family, was a World War II hero, and was a handsome, God-fearing man. Even if he did like to drink a little bit at the local AMVETS, she could handle him. At no point in their early relationship before children did Elizabeth detect that Arthur may have had a dark side.

Their early relationship revolved around attending mass at the community chapel. Elizabeth had worked at Bigelow's Department Store as a clerk since high school And Arthur soon found work as a long-distance truck driver for Furniture Express, a long-since-closed furniture company. Arthur would spend late nights at the AMVETS, and call home to "Betty," as he affectionately called his wife. She was always there to pick him up after a long night. Sometimes, Arthur would verbally abuse Elizabeth after these drunken nights, often berating her in the post's parking lot and the car. She let it fall off her shoulders. *At least he didn't get behind the wheel and drive,* she thought.

Around late 1946, Elizabeth started taking sleeping pills. Eventually that turned into a full-fledged problem with barbiturates and her addiction to pills would last for decades. On her best day, Elizabeth could be aloof and absent-minded. On her worst day, she would stay in bed. After the kids were born, when she was up and functioning, she was a good, attentive parent. However, those days were few and far between. Her being an absentee mother yielded the opportunity for Arthur to verbally and physically abuse his kids without intervention. Young Betty and Arthur talked about marriage in 1946. Arthur figured Elizabeth was loyal, always quick to say it was okay when he had his drunken nights and violent outbursts.

In February 1947, Arthur and Elizabeth were pregnant and on March 23, 1947, they were married, as it was taboo in those days for unwed parents to have children. In early June, they found out they were having a baby boy. The expectant mother and father readied their life for their new addition, setting up their apartment. Arthur continued working as a long-haul trucker and Elizabeth quit her job at Bigelow's in preparation to become a stay-at-home mom.

In November 1947, on a cold, windy day, they welcomed their first son, whom they christened Wayne. Wayne's early days were hectic, as they are for any new family. By all accounts, Elizabeth assimilated quite well to motherhood. She was a natural, doting mother and the Chapmans were quite taken with their new son. They quickly settled into the new routine of Elizabeth tending to the baby and Arthur working long hours, hauling trucks up and down the Eastern Seaboard. Arthur was rarely home, with days away from home becoming weeks. The pay was good but Arthur was largely absent as a trade-off so he could provide for his wife and child. As time went on and Wayne started teething, Arthur became increasingly more agitated with the baby screaming at all hours of the night. He would insist Elizabeth get out of bed to tend to the screaming child; he had few precious moments at home to rest and hated having baby Wayne interrupt those few moments he had in his bed.

As Wayne grew into a toddler, his relationship with his mother strengthened. Wayne was the center of her universe. Around the time Wayne was about three years old, Arthur's alcoholism started to consume the family. Since returning from the war, Arthur has been a functioning alcoholic and his lifestyle didn't help; the miles were beginning to take a toll on him. He drank on the road, often falling asleep during his rest breaks at different truck stops around the country. When Arthur got off the road, he would drink all day at the local AMVETS and the Samuel Derby Post, where he was a member. He would sit around with his fellow WWII veterans and drink and exchange stories about the Pacific, reminiscing of a time not so far past yet seemed like forever ago.

When Arthur arrived home at night, his relationship with Elizabeth was cold. They simply didn't know each other much anymore. Arthur was so distant, literally and physically. The only thing holding them together was their son. Young Wayne witnessed his father's explosive temper, seeing him physically abuse his mother. Arthur could also be cruel to Wayne. Around age four, Wayne had the same issues many children his age go through. He was a habitual bedwetter. Wayne would go to any length to cover up his bedwetting when his father was home. He would hide his sheets in their Linwood Avenue backyard.

Unfortunately for Wayne, he could not hide for long.

On one particularly bad night, in the dead of winter, Wayne messed up the bed badly. Arthur heard Wayne creeping around the house at a late hour and got out of bed to investigate. He found Wayne, minus his underwear, running around the house with dirty, stained sheets. Arthur immediately ordered Wayne to go out the backdoor in the middle of the night in the dead of a northeast winter to stand in the snow. Wayne would later recount the cruelty of the event.

Clad in nothing but a nightshirt, the four-year-old shivered in the darkness in a mound of snow about seven inches deep. Wayne was only allowed to come in to warm up when he assured his father the bedwetting would stop. Wayne would never look at his father the same again. Elizabeth scolded Arthur for his disciplinary tactics, but she tended to look the other way regarding her husband's cruelty as her addictions ran her life by this point. It was mostly the downers. She loved her sons and was a good mother, but for the most part, she was impaired. Arthur's behavior became increasingly more erratic each time he stopped home for a quick layover.

During one alcohol-induced fight, Wayne witnessed his father push Elizabeth down the stairs of their home. Young Wayne cowered in the corner, his hands over his ears, waiting for the fight to settle. He would often hear his parents fighting in the driveway of their home. Arthur would be in the driver's seat of the family car, heading out to drink at the Post, and Elizabeth would be yelling in the window. During one such occasion, Arthur accelerated and ran over his wife's foot, all while young Wayne watched in horror from the front window.

Yet to the outside world, Arthur was known as an upstanding citizen. He was very active in the community. Most of the tight-knit community on Linwood Avenue knew him well. He was always seen working on his truck in the driveway. He was an avid fan of auto racing and never missed the opportunity to chat as he sat on the front porch of his home. Arthur was an avid people watcher and was easy to talk to. He would regale the neighbors with stories of fighting in Guadalcanal. He was a member of the local Neighborhood Watch and volunteered a lot of his off time to the local church. The Allen Park Community Church counted on Arthur to run fundraisers for families in need, where he dutifully did whatever was asked of him.

Something about Wayne and Arthur's relationship flipped as Wayne navigated adolescence. Their relationship would become less violent as Wayne got older. Arthur just had no interest in him. His idea of quality time with his eldest son was having Wayne join him at the bar while he drank. Often, Wayne would sit out in the locked car, no matter the season, as his dad drank all afternoon and into the evening. Wayne had little idea what shape his dad would be in when he walked out of the bar.

Elizabeth was still his supportive, doting mother through it all. She was understated and quiet. Wayne described himself as a "mama's boy." She was also active in the church. What Elizabeth could never have known, however, was that something else was brewing inside her son. Something sinister. Something that would take nearly two decades to fully come to light. Around the time Wayne was four or five years old, some neighborhood girls cornered him and allegedly made him disrobe so they could look at him. Chapman recalled no sexual contact in this incident.

Maybe it can be chalked up to kids just experimenting or maybe like a lot of his later recollections, it was not true at all. Chapman recounted that this event was the one that got him "thinking along this track." Even at that age, he had many bouts with what he would later call "nerves" due to his dysfunctional home life.

Around age eight, young Wayne Chapman was already having problems in school. He would later confess he was being bullied. Chapman would often skip class to hide under a local bridge close to school. He was already in a bevy of special classes. He was given many IQ tests over the course of his life, scoring somewhere between 67-85, though he was not a very memorable student, nor did he pay close attention to his hygiene, which would be a problem most of his life. Administrators and students were concerned about young Chapman's vacant state. He seemed to always be in his head. So deep into his thoughts, he sometimes couldn't be bothered to change his clothes regularly. The fantasies in Chapman's head were already completely overwhelming him.

Wayne Chapman was already fantasizing about boys his age. He had not yet acted on those fantasies, instead transferring his anger. He would torture animals. He would lock cats in boxes in the woods and monitor the boxes as the cats slowly starved, or use bricks to crush the cats and watch them bleed out. He would have fantasies about fondling his classmates but become so enraged over not having the opportunity to act on it that he would take it out on the neighborhood pets. By about fourth grade, Chapman was already examining other boys' bodies; even his younger brothers were not off limits. He seemed to be dominated and consumed by his fantasies. Unable to stop, he exhibited next to no self-control. This indiscretion would be a common theme throughout his life.

There was one person in Wayne Chapman's life who recognized that he needed some professional intervention. His Uncle Willard confided to his brother Arthur that maybe his son should see a psychologist. An incident had turned Willard's antenna up—Wayne made his younger brother disrobe so he could examine his body. Willard felt that was reprehensible behavior for a seven-year-old. Arthur agreed that the behavior was concerning, but he was old school and didn't believe in seeing psychologists. He figured Wayne would grow out of it. Maybe enlisting in the Marine Corps one day would straighten him out. Either way, Arthur was often way too intoxicated to recognize his son's problematic behavior.

Uncle Willard was unnerved by Wayne's vacant eyes and disturbing behavior. He ignored Arthur's rebuff and took his nephew to see Dr. Morgan, a psychologist in town. The doctor asked Willard to complete a questionnaire about Wayne's home life and behavior. Willard answered truthfully that Chapman had problems keeping his hands off boys his age and the incident where he made his younger brother undress. Dr. Morgan and Willard talked privately after the doctor interviewed Chapman; they agreed that he was homosexual, immature, and not very bright. His low IQ affected his behavior—maybe he was not capable of understanding why his behavior was inappropriate. Either way, Willard came away from the appointment dissatisfied.

Dr. Morgan was a bit unnerved by Chapman, who was quite open about his sexual preoccupations. He talked openly with the psychologist about his curiosity to examine young boys' bodies. He confided that he might need some help, and he had tried to keep his mind off young boys by focusing on his Christian values and being more active in the church. Dr. Morgan noted that Chapman should be having regular intense therapy sessions to deal with his anger towards boys his age and his fantasies. However, he would never see the inside of Dr. Morgan's office again.

After arriving home from Dr. Morgan's office, Willard made another impassioned plea to his older brother: keep a close eye on that boy. Willard was so shaken by being in Chapman's presence the entire day, that his voice almost trembled as he spoke. Arthur would respond by calling Chapman a "queer." Arthur hoped that someone else would straighten Chapman out, like a drill sergeant at Parris Island. Much like Arthur had been. Arthur was so deeply alcoholic that he could not help mending his broken son. He simply kept his distance and retreated into the bottle. Chapman would later talk about how much he hated his father. I suspect that Chapman believed the feeling was completely mutual. They were like two trains passing in the night when Arthur was home.

Elizabeth tried to help her son by centering his life on Christianity and encouraging him to be active in the church. At age fifteen, he held it together enough to be a youth volunteer at the Weakland Chapel in Jamestown. Chapman was very involved in church activities and was well-liked. He would later lean on this Christianity while incarcerated. Chapman was so dedicated that in 1962, Reverend Bixby Crichton awarded him the Youth of the Year Fellowship award. He was even pictured in the local newspaper, *The Jamestown Journal*. In an article from June 9, 1962, Chapman is pictured with a plaque that has a Bible verse etched in the center. To the outside world, he was just a good, old Christian boy spreading the good word in his community with perfect attendance in Sunday school. He always held the door open for a woman and was happy to help carry older neighbors' groceries. By this time, he was already exploring sex with older men.

Often, his mother would take Chapman shopping with her when Arthur was out of town working. During one excursion, he and Elizabeth went by cab. The cab driver chatted Chapman up and eventually invited him to his apartment. He obliged and eventually, they had a semi-romantic relationship that lasted a few meetings. The meetings were often unfulfilling for him because he had little interest in older men. He had even less interest in women of any age. By sixteen, Chapman had had it with school and quit, eventually leaving home. He often stated later that he went to live with his paternal grandmother because she needed someone to help her. The truth is his father had had his fill. If he wasn't going to attend regular classes, then he couldn't stay under Arthur's roof. The last thing Arthur wanted was to have his oldest son hanging around the house more often.

Wayne Chapman was essentially told to pack up and leave and he was ready to go out on his own where he could be free to hang around at local schoolyards and playgrounds. He was over his father and mother hassling him. He had already tried to seduce his youngest brother, who was only four years old at the time; he was completely out of control. He needed to roam, hunting and stalking his prey. At this point in some predators' development, the need to be released from normal life's shackles is strong. Chapman would have felt boxed at his parents' home. Unable to live out his fantasies, the situation could have turned violent, even that early on. Young Chapman would eventually reveal himself too soon to a victim.

One person who was particularly interested in him moving out was Chapman's next-door neighbor, James Bender, who would cross paths with Chapman years later while Bender was deputy director of the Massachusetts Department of Corrections and Chapman was an inmate at Bridgewater Treatment Center. Unfortunately, I could not connect with Bender to discuss this book, but it's been recounted by those who have talked to Bender that he was so enamored with his former neighbor he considered writing a book of his own, chronicling Chapman's crimes.

It did not take Chapman too long before he found work at the old Coca-Cola bottling, but he never kept a job for long. He gave his coworkers the creeps with his bizarre behavior and vacant eyes. His poor hygiene cost him jobs as well. After getting hired at Sunnybrook Farms, the staff tired of Chapman quickly. The family farm is a mainstay of the community and still stands today. He worked there for mere days when the owner fired him; he showed up to work disheveled with uncombed and unwashed hair and he smelled horrible. The staff and patrons could not stand to be near him. He would also often disappear, especially after he discovered pornography shops in Buffalo and Toronto with child porn readily available.

Chapman had been on his own for months and was oh-for-two with jobs. His inner tension was growing. On his third try, he washed dishes in a local hospital's kitchen. It was there that he had another experience with a different man a bit older than him. A hospital orderly came to him and they had an encounter. Again, Chapman felt unfulfilled.

He had little interest in men his age, never mind someone older. The orderly would mostly talk to Chapman about sex and he would confide his sexual desires to the orderly.

For a few months, Chapman washed dishes at the hospital and even assisted in a bit of janitorial work. He loved being left alone to clean up the bathrooms and wash the floors. The job was almost solitary. He would sneak into an unoccupied latrine and look at his collection of photos. He would set them up next to the toilet and stare intently at the images; sometimes even talking to them. Chapman would also make regular trips to the hospital's incinerator in the basement where they burned old body parts and stray animals, like rats and mice that were pests to the staff and patients. Chapman loved the idea of operating the incinerator and would have loved to have a key to operate it. He would have taken great delight in burning up animals, having always had a thing for taking out his anger on unsuspecting pets. Chapman did not last long at the hospital. He wouldn't be hanging out in Jamestown much longer and was about to spread his wings. He took note of how easy it was to be a janitor; everyone left you alone. It was like no one wanted to talk to you. He preferred it that way. *Perhaps*, he thought, *he would make a career of it someday*.

One person, however, saw Wayne Chapman for what he truly was—Ford W. Peterson.

Chapman had been following way too close to Peterson's farm tractor and they collided at a stop light on Water Street in the Frewsburg neighborhood. Chapman thought Ford had stopped intentionally. He exited his vehicle with his arms flailing and threatened Ford. Patrolman Robert Payne was tasked with calming the situation. Eventually, he cited Chapman for driving too closely and having bald tires. Chapman was irate that he had been blamed for the extensive damage to both vehicles. He had to go to court eventually and pay a one-hundred-dollar fine. Ford kept his eye on the Chapman boy from that day on. He knew there was something wrong there.

CHAPTER 2:
PENNSYLVANIA 1965

1965 was a turbulent year for the United States. Twelve hundred Viet Cong soldiers ambushed the 173rd Airborne Brigade members in Operation Hump. This furthered American bloodshed in an increasingly unpopular war in Southeast Asia. "I Can't Help Myself" by the Four Tops and "(I Can't Get No) Satisfaction" by the Rolling Stones traded places as the top songs on the Billboard charts.

That year started well for Wayne Chapman; he achieved the dream of most young people nearing eighteen—he obtained his driver's license and was now mobile. That meant danger for the children of Jamestown, New York, or just about any other state he had enough gas to reach. In the late fall of 1965, Chapman's fantasies began to take over his life.

He would later admit he simply could not control himself much after his first offense. Chapman was fixated on stalking and luring young children, hanging around the park benches and schools. There were also some conflicting reports at the time that he may have been peeping in windows at night and had voyeuristic tendencies. He never admitted to doing it. I think that he would do whatever it took to get his rocks off. Nothing is off limits to a man who doesn't have a moral compass.

During the lead up to Thanksgiving 1965, Chapman was falling deeper into his sexual fantasies. Instead of looking forward to dinner with family, he was buying a bevy of pornography and stalking children. His father, Arthur, had all but disowned his firstborn son by then. Chapman's brothers found him odd and barely knew him. The younger Chapman boys had no idea what to make of their big brother. He seemed to have no control over his actions or his words. His brothers, like their father, retreated into alcoholism. His mother, Elizabeth, knew he had problems. She held out hope that Wayne would grow out of whatever had a hold on her son.

Those hopes were dashed that Thanksgiving. Chapman had his eye on a pair of young blue-eyed, blond-haired boys he had been stalking at the local park. He watched the boys for hours from his perch on a bench where the boys played with friends after school. Chapman preferred fair-haired boys and these two were the perfect victims. Just after the holiday, he isolated the boys and assaulted them. He would later use a ruse to lure his victims, like pretending to be a police officer or asking children to look for his lost dog, promising money to any child who could help him locate the fictitious pet. He didn't use this guise to assault these two boys. The facts of the assault are unclear and lost to time.

I have gathered that Chapman lured the boys into wooded areas to assault them. When the boys fought back, he disrobed them and burnt their clothes. He could be incredibly sadistic if the assault did not go the way he'd planned or if a victim angered him enough. It hardly ever started that way. Chapman was sadistic but not a sadist. This scenario would play out a fair amount in his later crimes.

The boys managed to get away and immediately contacted the police, who knew Chapman. It was not hard to put the facts together from the boys' description of Chapman and his vehicle. He was arrested at his home on 78 Linwood Avenue. His mother was horrified. Thankfully, his father was on the road; by this time, Arthur was driving for Crossett Incorporated, retiring from there in 1982. Chapman didn't bother lying to the police. He wouldn't start constantly lying to the police until much later after more hardened pedophiles and killers schooled him.

Chapman was far too deep into his head and fantasies to work out alibis or concoct cover stories for his crimes. He had a low IQ. He did not have the capability until much later to work out a defense. It was an embarrassing scene as law enforcement dragged Chapman away from his family home. At just eighteen years old, he was about to embark on a rather lengthy police record. He was immediately charged with corrupting the morals of minors and was released on one hundred dollars bail on November 29, 1965. Elizabeth was beside herself with anger and sorrow. Her firstborn was sick; Wayne needed serious help before he ruined another child's life—or his own. He would eventually be ordered to undergo a psychiatric evaluation.

No records of a 1965 evaluation exist; it's unclear if Chapman had any contact with psychologists or saw the inside of a medical facility that year or the following year. Chapman mostly skated on the 1965 charge. He was free to brood and delve back into consuming large amounts of pornography available to him at the sex shops in Jamestown and surrounding areas. He was very mobile at the time as well. Committing assaults in Jamestown was completely off the table now. He was not a very bright man, but he knew enough to not commit crimes in his parents' town. The heat was on in the sleepy little village; he was on law enforcement's radar. Chapman could no longer waste his days watching kids play at local parks or park his vehicle outside an elementary school. He must be a ghost.

Chapman's activities in late 1965 and all of 1966 are completely unknown. He was living and breathing, so he was offending somewhere.

Chapman could not control his sexual urges; he was a ticking time bomb and a danger to any child in whatever community he landed. Who he encountered is also unknown. A few years later, he would connect and operate with like-minded pedophiles in the New England area. I imagine Chapman is associated with local pedophiles in Jamestown or nearby. One thing about fixated pedophiles is that they know they are the pariahs of society. The need to connect with like-minded individuals is strong and has played out in many cases.

Wayne Chapman was no different. People navigate to their tribe—even sex offenders.

***

1967 brought Wayne Chapman many troubles, all self-induced. After he got heat in Jamestown, he traveled up and down the East Coast. He would visit sex shops and pornography stores in Virginia, Massachusetts, Ohio, Rhode Island, and Pennsylvania. He did his best to make connections with other predators in as many states as possible. He would often chat up other men who hung around parks and school playgrounds, watching the children from a distance. Eventually, this routine would bear fruit and earn Chapman a best friend. For now, though, in 1967, Chapman was focused on isolating another boy for another assault.

In June, he was haunting the streets of Oil City, Pennsylvania. Chapman was a coward and completely uninterested in using physical force to lure a boy if he could help it. The 1965 assaults went sideways on him because the boys caught on to him and fought back. He was hoping to gain the boys' trust first, then spring his true intentions on the unsuspecting victims. On this hot summer day in June, he was stalking in Oil City, something he loved to do. He felt like a secret agent trawling the streets with a secret he would only reveal to his victims. Chapman would chat with kids all over Oil City neighborhoods. In that era, "stranger danger' was not as prevalent as it is today. Parents were not nearly as educated on the dangers their kids face from evil men like him as they are now. We simply didn't have the awareness back then.

Kids would leave the house after breakfast on their bikes and not return until dinner. It was a prime period for predators. Chapman took advantage of that. He fixated on a boy in Oil City. He loved this stalk. It was far from home and nobody in this little town nearly sixty miles from his last crime had any idea who he was or the danger he posed. He immediately concocted a story to isolate the target from his friends. Chapman met the boy at a park surrounded by a dozen kids playing and eagerly enjoying their summer vacation and asked the boy if he had a way to make some extra money, like a paper route. The boy said no. He knew he had piqued the child's interest. He explained that he could get the young boy a paper route that would start as soon as tomorrow. It was late in the day and hot, and the boy's friends were around.

Chapman knew he should postpone the crime until the next morning in a rare moment of

restraint. That night, he slept in his van close to the meeting spot and went over the details of the assault in his head. He hoped the boy would show up on time. Everything needed to happen the way he saw it in his head. Most nineteen-year-olds Chapman had gone to high school with were now attending college. Maybe some were drafted or enlisted to serve in Vietnam like Chapman's father, Arthur, had done during the beginning of World War II. Chapman, however, was sleeping in his van with no air conditioning on a brutally hot June night, counting down the hours until his victim would arrive to start the non-existent job he'd promised.

Chapman awoke that morning soaked with sweat. It did not bother him much though. He never worried about his hygiene. He hardly ever brushed his teeth or showered. He was a singularly focused being. He could not be bothered with trivial things like body odor or dental care. His only focus was satisfying his sexual appetite. The boy arrived just a little bit late on his bike. The young man was in good spirits and hoping to make a little bit of money to buy some baseball cards or perhaps save for a car. Chapman had other ideas. He was there for the meeting to irrevocably smash this boy's psyche and create lifelong pain, all for his own selfish, sexual gratification.

At this point in the story, you probably want to reach in and grab the boy, explain to him the danger he is facing, and pull him to safety. I have played this scenario out in my mind a million times while researching this case. I would lie awake at night and fantasize about taking the boy to safety and doing the world a favor by disposing of Wayne Chapman. I would never advocate for violence, however. I do not recommend ever physically confronting anyone. The visceral reaction to this story is understandable to me and frankly appreciated.

At this point, he told the boy to take a walk with him into the woods. If the young man's senses were starting to tingle, Chapman did not recognize it yet. Again, most young people would trust an adult; it is extremely hard to envision this scenario playing out today. This young boy may have even told his parents that he was meeting a man for a job and they may not have objected.

The man and the young boy chatted as they strolled. The morning was beautiful. The sun was out and the birds were chirping. After Chapman believed they were deep enough in the woods, he started asking the boy pointed sexual questions. The boy continued to press Chapman on the job's specifics, ignoring all his questions. He asked when they would arrive to see about the paper route and Chapman pressed with his line of questions about the boy's sexual history. The twelve-year-old boy was starting to understand what was happening—there was no job and he was in grave danger. He immediately started to walk in the opposite direction of the weird older man with the bizarre questions.

Chapman sped up and turned the boy around to ask more pointed questions. His breathing became more pronounced. The boy pushed Chapman with all his might and ran off. Chapman became enraged; he chased the boy down and administered a brutal beating. Nobody could hear the boy's cries over the sounds of the birds and dense forest. Chapman eventually tore the boy's shirt off and placed it in the boy's mouth, who immediately started gagging. The young man tasted the t-shirt fabric the entire time. Taste is one of the senses tied closest to memory. You may not remember the décor of that great Italian restaurant but you will always remember the taste of the delicious sauce they used on the chicken Parmigiana.

The young man from Oil City would forever remember the taste of that t-shirt. It haunted him for the rest of his life. The young man's fight-or-flight was activated, and he was able to summon the strength to break loose. Chapman was breathing heavily at this point and his arms were exhausted from holding down the struggling boy. The young man high-tailed it out of the woods as soon as he could break free. Chapman did not have the strength to chase him down. He gave up the chase and let the boy go. He knew he had limited time before the young boy would get home and tell his parents.

The boy exited the wood line screaming at the top of his lungs. Nearby, adults and kids were alerted to the commotion. The boy's abrasions struck the adults first on the scene. It looked like he had fought in the woods. The adults assumed it was with another child or maybe even a group of children. Perhaps the boy was jumped by a group of older boys who had been a problem in the neighborhood. The young, shirtless boy was trying to catch his breath long enough to explain that an older man had asked to meet him near the woods. The man had promised him a job and had flipped out on him in the woods and started asking him questions. The man then pushed him to the ground and tried to choke him with his t-shirt. One of the adults called 911 and told them an adolescent was there, covered in bruises, with a disturbing story about a man in the woods.

Meanwhile, Chapman was trying to collect his thoughts. He thought for sure the boy would be contacting the police immediately. The boy was hysterical, after all. Would he be able to describe Chapman adequately? Had he gotten a good enough look at his van? Chapman had no time to waste on these questions. He had to get the hell out of Oil City and manage to get out of there before the local police could catch up. He was undeterred by the screaming boy and the brutal scene in the woods. Unfortunately for Chapman and fortunately for the young boys of Titusville, Pennsylvania, the young boy *could* recall and adequately describe Chapman's 1965 Dodge van to the police. Long before we had the national Amber Alert system or online capabilities, in these situations, law enforcement in Oil City had to issue a teletype to be on the lookout for a man trying to befriend children or offering them employment.

Chapman took a long drive to calm his nerves. He felt like he had dodged a major bullet. He was ready to put Oil City in his rearview mirror. He slept overnight in his van, another brutally hot night. He arose the next morning in Titusville, a twenty-two-minute drive and some fifteen miles from Oil City. He felt secure in his distance from Oil City authorities to continue trawling for children. Chapman thought maybe he could just snap some pictures. He always kept a camera in the right pocket of his button-up shirt, always ready to take pictures of unsuspecting victims. It was not enough to assault these children; he wanted to make sure he had photo keepsakes from his travels. It was unclear if he was trading pictures of these children with other pedophiles in 1967, but later, he was a major player in a crude, early child pornography ring.

Chapman found a treasure trove of potential victims on this warm June day in Titusville. With the memory of yesterday's assault behind him, he immediately struck up conversations with a few young boys at a local park. In a stroke of luck for the children involved, a patrolman surveyed the scene. He found it odd that an older man would be hanging around, chatting up the children. The officer decided to question Chapman, who immediately fell apart under the slightest bit of police pressure. After law enforcement called in his vehicle and license plate, word came back that the man who was wanted for a brutal assault, just fifteen miles away the day prior, was standing right there in Titusville Park among children.

Chapman was booked into jail on North Franklin Street and was now a ward of the State of Pennsylvania. He elected not to call home when he was given his one phone call from the jail that night. Instead, he stewed in his cell alone. He eventually did one of the few good deeds in his rotten, worthless life: pleaded guilty to the two charges levied against him. He was sentenced to one to two years in the county workhouse and began his first prison sentence on June 20, 1967. As inmate number 91480, he performed hard labor eight to ten hours a day. Of all the inmates I could find on the county's handwritten sign-in register for the timeframe Chapman was sentenced, he was the only one charged with a sex crime, the lone sex offender in the workhouse. He was stuck in there with deadbeat dads and violent fugitives.

Later in life, he would find like-minds in prison, but not so much here. He would serve in the Allegheny County workhouse for a total of one year and five months. Fellow inmates chastised him but he worked as hard as he had ever worked in his life. Chapman was not exactly the picture of health and strength; even at age twenty, he thought the manual labor would about kill him if the other inmates didn't get him first. He was involved in a few scuffles during his first real prison stint. He was called "queer" and he was smacked around a couple of times. Nothing too serious happened—surely not enough to scare him into going straight when he would rejoin the rest of the world.

Chapman had a reprieve in August 1967 from life in the labor camp. Due to a court order and the conditions of his sentence, he was sent to Warren State Hospital for an evaluation. When he arrived on August 31, 1967, the doctors and staff noticed Chapman's nervousness and lack of hygiene. He displayed symptoms of anxiety and depression. He complained of frequent insomnia, headaches, and recurring bouts of shortness of breath. During the evaluations at Warren, he admitted to offending in his early teens, disrobing small boys, and examining their bodies. He readily admitted he knew when he committed these crimes that he would be caught but stopped short of admitting that he belonged behind bars.

Instead, he started to focus on the thing inside him that drove him to commit these crimes against children. This was the first time that he would push his religious beliefs hard. He began pontificating to every examiner who would listen that his focus in life was to be a "good Christian." He would continue to lean on Christianity to bail him out of various jams for the rest of his life. With the help of God and his Christian faith, he said he'd be able to control these impulses and put his days of offending behind him. Time would reveal the absurdity of this statement.

Examiners concluded that Chapman had major guilt over his offenses. He also fixated on his hatred for his father, Arthur. The psychologists noted that he had a schizophrenic reaction and was incredibly paranoid. Nevertheless, the doctors did not ask to keep him longer nor did they recommend he be under intense supervision when he was released. He was simply shipped back to the Allegheny County workhouse. For the remainder of his sentence, he worked the long, hard hours, mostly in the prison's western block—scrubbing floors, cleaning bathrooms, and even cleaning toilets. He was beside himself with joy when he was told he would be released on parole.

At the end of his nearly year-and-a-half sentence, Wayne Chapman was released to Venango County on November 25, 1968, weighing one hundred and seventy pounds. At 2:23 p.m., after signing the discharge register, he was officially paroled. From the time he was paroled until his next offense in Pennsylvania in August 1971, he had little contact with law enforcement.

This period represents a bit of dead space in his offending record. Had he stopped? Did he become ill? Maybe he had served enough hard times and brought enough embarrassment to his family to finally realize the error of his ways and seek professional help. The real story behind this dead space is quite simple: Chapman had run into a bit of luck for the first time in his pathetic existence. He would not, and simply could not, stop offending. In this dead space, he would up the ante.

Wayne admitted to more than one hundred victims. My guess, just by the numbers, is that it's probably much higher than that. He was a machine programmed for only one mission: his sexual gratification. He simply did not have the propensity to care about his victims. Young boys were just objects. How they felt and the way their lives were affected by his abuse was just collateral damage to him.

In the summer of 1969, Chapman struck again. The details of the crime are incredibly murky and the boy in question was never found. He confessed that somewhere in New York State he lured a ten-year-old boy into the woods and raped him. The boy fought back and bit Chapman in a very private area. Chapman became enraged. In this incident, he gagged and tied the victim to a tree and simply walked away. He confessed to this unreported crime many times over the years. He was never prosecuted for it. No young man ever came forward and no body was ever found.

I believe the story, however. Wayne Chapman would not confess to anything unless it was true.

Later in life, he became a compulsive liar, especially about his crimes. He did not have the smarts nor was he cute enough to play cat and mouse, confessing to assaults that didn't happen to throw off the police. If he admitted to it, he did it. There is no more detail or event in this book that I researched more than this confession. I scoured records for years in New York State for missing boys trying to match story details to a specific boy. As of this publication, no one has ever come forward claiming to be the little boy Chapman spoke about in this confession. My only hope is that the little boy who encountered him that day got loose from his bindings and ran home to safety. I have dreamed of that scenario at least a thousand times in my research. I pray he got the help he needed to overcome that incredible situation he found himself in with this monster masquerading as a kind adult.

I know. I was that boy in another time and place.

Chapman was now emboldened having gotten away with the New York State rape. Because police hadn't come for him even weeks later, he figured the boy probably died out there. He thought the animals probably got to the child's body, likely chewing him up. He figured the boy would be unrecognizable to anyone who may be walking through the woods. Chapman was sure he was in the clear.

During this time, he was still making regular trips upstate to Buffalo and even crossing into Canada to go to cities like Toronto to consume pornography that catered to his dangerous psychological disorder. He enjoyed going to new towns and networking or just walking around feeling free from law enforcement's prying eyes that were surely on him back in Jamestown. He would sometimes partake in the local gay scene. He hardly had any interest in grown men his age. He was singularly interested in young boys. In 1969 and 1970, Chapman visited Virginia, Ohio, Maine,

Connecticut, and Rhode Island. In Maine, he met a man named Eugene Weir. Eugene's mother owned a farm in Cumberland County. He loved to visit the farm. Chapman and Eugene struck up quite the friendship.

Eugene was easy to talk to and Maine was beautiful. *It was quiet*, Chapman thought. There was space. Lots of room for privacy. Eugene and his family would throw a lifeline in Chapman's direction nearly five decades later.

Around Christmastime 1971, Chapman was back in his old Pennsylvania haunts. Now, he was nearly eighty miles away from Titusville, in Smethport. He was trawling for victims again and was now using the ploy of searching for a lost dog to isolate boys from their friends. On this day, he walked up to a group of boys and asked them for help finding his lost dog "Scott." He told the kids he had a daughter about their age at home and she would be upset if Old Dad came home without her precious mutt. He would offer money to the kid who would be the day's hero and find the lost pup for three or five dollars; it didn't matter. There was no money and there was never a dog.

On December 6, 1971, Chapman successfully isolated a boy with this ruse and destroyed his life forever. He sexually assaulted the child in a wooded area right there in Smethport. After he finished, he whipped out his camera from his right pocket and took photos of the boy. At this point, Chapman was a prolific producer of child pornography. He used his crimes not only to gratify his despicable sexual urges but also to make sure he had photo evidence for trading around.

Little is known about how Chapman was caught for this assault. Yet again, Pennsylvania authorities booked him and placed him immediately in custody. He pled guilty to his crimes, never bothering to try to lie in the early days. Almost always, he would immediately admit his guilt. Chapman would launch right into his diatribe about how he had dark forces inside him and he needed help to drive them out. He would explain that he was a good Christian and he was hopeful that with God's help, he could defeat his demons. Incredibly, he was not jailed for these crimes. Instead, Chapman was placed on "indefinite probation, under the condition he seeks psychiatric help." From December 1971 to March 1973, he was under intense psychiatric care yet still managed to attempt to lure a little boy into the woods by showing the boy pornography. He was ultimately unsuccessful in this attempt and was again immediately arrested and admitted to Gowanda State Hospital on March 18, 1973.

In 1973, Gowanda State Hospital was located on about five hundred acres off Wheater Road in Erie County, Pennsylvania. By the early seventies, the population had exploded at the hospital. Drug laws kept the correctional facility connected to the hospital overflowing with new inmates. When Chapman had his initial intake on March 18, the hospital staff was aghast by how freely he spoke about his crimes. The staff was used to having to draw criminal details out of offenders; no such dance needed to happen with him. He was more than happy to acknowledge he was the aggressor in all his sexual assaults. Gowanda staff noted that he never mixed with other patients, mostly keeping to himself. Staff observed that Chapman basically lived inside his mind and was completely preoccupied with his sexual deviancy. When he lived behind the walls of a psychiatric treatment center or a prison, he almost always spent most of his time plotting. He would think through how he could better commit crimes and avoid the hassle of police interference. It wouldn't be long before he would meet a few criminal mentors and his openness about his crimes would stop dead in its tracks.

Wayne Chapman was released from Gowanda on April 8, 1973. The staff reported in his discharge packet that Chapman was mostly "UNCOOPERATIVE." He was diagnosed with pedophilia. His condition was described as "UNCHANGED" at discharge.

Now is a good time to pause, because I am sure, dear reader, you are thinking exactly what I am thinking at this point—should someone have stepped in and asked the obvious question: how is this guy getting out of here? When you look at the totality of his offenses leading up to April 1973, it would be hard to imagine this sick young man getting his life together and melting into anonymity or, better yet, becoming a productive member of society. He was punished for assaulting young children, getting out and immediately offending again, and not behind closed doors, with little to no regard for consequences. Chapman would do hard time and get right out and commit assault in broad daylight. He ate dinner to have more energy to stalk victims. He slept so he could be well-rested to commit more crimes. He breathed to abuse young children. How was this not completely apparent to every psychiatric professional he ever came across? Why was he freed again?

If one such person stepped in and made the obvious point I just posed, I could not find them anywhere in his massive psychiatric files. Nobody was championing locking this guy up forever or committing him for an indefinite amount of time. On April 8, 1973, Wayne Chapman walked out of Gowanda and into his mother Elizabeth's waiting vehicle. However, Elizabeth could not look at her firstborn child objectively. She was holding out hope Wayne would reconnect with God and straighten his life out. But Chapman would use Christianity when it helped his cause in conversations with police, and hospital and prison staff. There was no *God* in his vernacular. He was much more like the Devil, the arch nemesis of all that is good.

In 1967, while in the workhouse, a prison guard gave Chapman some life advice he took to heart. The guard told the sexual deviant that when he got outside the prison walls, he should get married and live a normal life, maybe even think about a career. This guard saw him as a young man who had a chance of being saved. Of course, Chapman could not live a normal life. Instead, he skewed the advice a little bit, figuring he better find someone to shack up with to give the outside world the impression he was a normal kind of guy. *It may be easier to commit crimes*, he thought. He may even get easier access to children. In 1971, he did just that.

It bears repeating here: he was born a pedophile. He had no interest in adults. He could not perform sexually with any woman and had absolutely no idea how to interact with someone in an actual relationship. The details of how he met his wife are a bit unclear, but in 1971, Chapman married a forty-three-year-old woman (to his twenty-three years). How they met or the circumstances around the nuptials are unknown. Horrifyingly enough, this woman was the mother of two young boys, ages eleven and fourteen. In reports I obtained, he stated that he married to try a normal life on for size. He specifically "wanted to marry a woman with children to test" himself.

His newfound heterosexual lifestyle failed miserably, of course. At one point, Chapman and his new family ended up living in sunny Florida, and his activities while there were not well known. I have researched missing and abused children's cases from 1971 to 1974 in Florida when he could have been there, but I think he was quiet. The only lives he destroyed were those of his new stepsons'. The only reason Chapman married a woman twenty years his senior was because of her young children. He did not even try to have sex with his new bride and she was often angry at his inability to perform. Chapman lied on psychiatric exams over the decades that his sex life with his wife was good. I know better. There is no chance Chapman could have ever performed with this woman. He would lie to evaluators to keep up the bullshit story that he was a normal, functioning human being capable of normal behavior. Evaluators would later note that he was angry about his wife's sex drive. She wanted it all the time and he, of course, couldn't oblige. He was there for one reason: to groom her children for sexual abuse.

Chapman's new stepsons were on to him early. They hated him. The two boys would often throw things at him and beg their mother to send this creep back to wherever she found him. He was weird. He asked inappropriate questions and he always wanted to lay on the couch with them, even sleep in their beds. Chapman sexually abused both boys, often groping the eleven-year-old while he slept. He would make aggressive advances on the fourteen-year-old. Married life and the white sandy beaches of Florida did not curb his behavior. Of course, it never could; he was rotten to the core. How Chapman exited the situation in Florida is not clear. I assume he performed his go-to move when things got too hot. He simply disappeared. Amazingly, Chapman's wife never filed a criminal complaint about the assaults. The boys, to my knowledge, never came forward either. He never faced consequences for abusing those two boys. I know the scenarios happened, however, because he confessed to them.

Incredibly, Chapman and his wife never divorced. Even after he was committed for life in 1977, she remained loyal to her husband. His wife would often accept calls from him while he was incarcerated at MCI Shirley and the Massachusetts Treatment Center for sexually dangerous. As late as 2015, Chapman stated that he and his wife had a weekly conversation. What became of his stepsons is unclear; nor is it clear if his wife had any idea about the abuse.

Chapman's marriage and Florida activities remain a mystery to me. Did the ability to abuse his stepchildren quench his thirst for abusing boys? Or were there other victims in the Sunshine State? I took multiple Florida trips in the research for this book, at one point I laid some roots and rented a house in Marion County for nine months. All I can ascertain at this time is I believe Chapman and another notorious pedophile from the Florida area may have more victims there and I believe that's another investigation for another time. I hope I can be a part of it.

Either way, I hope the young men got help for what they had to endure under their new stepfather's rule. Any child who got in this monster's path was either a potential victim or being actively victimized. He was singlehandedly destroying generations of children and he was about to move again.

CHAPTER 3: PROVIDENCE 1975

On September 1, 1975, an AC-130 gunship lifted off from Eglin Air Force Base in the beautiful Florida Panhandle. Eglin is known for its beautiful scenery and the white-sand beaches in nearby towns, like Destin and Panama City. This mission was not ordinary for the gunship's crew, which included a lead pilot, a lieutenant colonel, and second-in-command, a captain. This flight was the first of its kind in the United States: a military aircraft was tapped to use the gunship's thermal imaging to look for a missing child in Northern Maine's dense woods.

The plane lifted off from the Pensacola side of the airbase at night so the imaging equipment could work. The crew would be looking for heat signatures in the thick brush. As the bird banked to the north, the heading the pilot entered 2-2-0 in his compass. The mission was "cleared hot."

***

By Labor Day weekend 1975, Ron and Jill Newton had been married for eight years. The Newtons had what they thought was an idyllic life; they had a son and a daughter. All their hard work and savings were about to pay off. The family was planning to purchase their first home. The Newtons decided to blow off some steam with a Labor Day trip to the Chain of Ponds, a beautiful, secluded campground situated just between Eustis, Maine, and the Canadian border. Their son, Kurt, was a handsome little boy with blond hair and fair skin. Just four years old.

On Sunday, August 31, 1975, the Newtons got up early. Kurt was shaking off a cold and surprisingly slept in until about 9 a.m. Kurt immediately got dressed in corduroy pants and a heavy sweatshirt. He put on a light jacket emblazoned with pictures of baseballs and bats and helped his dad gather some firewood. They made a fire in the chilly Maine morning. They cooked a hearty egg, ham, and potato breakfast over the campfire. After breakfast, Ron decided to cut more firewood. Their supply was getting low and the cold could grip Maine very early and very quickly. Jill decided to wash the kids' muddy sneakers. The rain had been early and was often in Northern Maine that year and the puddles were treacherous. The kids never seemed to miss them either. Ron grabbed the dull axe he often used to cut firewood and took off into the dense forest. That is where time began to stand still.

Neighbors recall hearing four-year-old Kurt pedaling his tricycle and faintly yelling for his dad, "Daddy! Daddy!" Ron did not hear his son screaming for him over the sound of his Ford Bronco. It was in that moment that every parent's worst nightmare comes true: with one parent distracted and the other gone, the little boy disappeared out of sight into the deep undergrowth, gone without a trace.

Kurt was sighted just a few minutes later by twelve-year-old Lou Ellen Hanson, who was out for a stroll around the campsites. She had been up enjoying the Labor Day weekend with her parents and recognized Kurt as the cute kid from the adjoining campsite.

She called out to Kurt, "Do your parents know where you are?"

Kurt didn't reply. He pedaled on, not even aware of Lou Ellen's presence.

Lou Ellen said that encounter haunted her for years. She would play it back in her mind. Returning to the place in her dreams as an adolescent, she chases Kurt down and returns him to safety. That's the best part of dreams—you can rewrite the story with the happiest endings, like dough that you can mold. I know the feeling. My deepest sympathies lie with Lou Ellen Hanson. There is no way she could have ever known the dark forces that waited for Kurt.

The road he was pedaling down only lasted about another quarter mile. It would eventually fork. If Kurt went left, he would have reached another campground and a sketchy bridge that passes over a stream that runs fast some days. If he went right, he would have had a straight path for about a mile, then he would have encountered dense forest that even his father's Bronco would have had problems getting through. In a bizarre twist, Jack Hanson, Lou Ellen's father, who was an unofficial groundskeeper of the campsites, would find Kurt's tricycle at the edge of the woods. It sat like a parked vehicle kept out of the way of traffic. It was perfectly nestled in the wood line. Jack tossed the tricycle into the campground's dump at the top of the hill. Jack assumed a camper had discarded the bike.

After hanging the newly washed sneakers for drying, Jill went to round up her kids. She assumed Kurt had gone to chop wood with Ron, so when Ron rounded the corner without Kurt, she immediately began to panic like only a parent can when their child is unaccounted for. Ron and Jill immediately ran from campsite to campsite asking campers if they saw the blond-haired boy pedaling on a tricycle. When Duane Lewis arrived around 4 p.m., he figured Kurt would be home by nightfall. Duane, the veteran game warden, had nearly one hundred successful searches under his belt. He understood the psychology of kids who are lost in the woods. Eventually, they break. They find a tree, somewhere to anchor themselves, and usually cry. Kids don't have the wherewithal to keep going deeper, and in some cases, farther away. They are mentally and physically incapable.

After hours of searching and still no Kurt, helicopters from the warden's office were immediately gathered and a search plane from the Maine game warden's office also came on station. Duane took to the skies, immediately getting on the chopper's PA system and calling to Kurt in a soft voice. "Kurt, I am up in the helicopter, follow me back to the camp. Mommy and Daddy are waiting for you. Do not sit down. Walk towards the helicopter. Don't be afraid. I will take you back to camp."

Duane repeated himself again and again. He said it so many times that he could recall word-for-word what his script was four decades later. After word got out in Manchester, Maine, the Newtons' hometown, Chain of Ponds was completely overrun by friends and neighbors assisting in the search. Traffic jams ensued and people abandoned their vehicles to walk to the campsite. Ron and Jill forever appreciated the community rallying around their golden-haired boy.

By nightfall, the temperature in the dense forest of Northern Maine had dropped to well below freezing. Jill was beside herself in agony thinking about what her young son must have been thinking. She didn't want Kurt to think he was abandoned out there. "Momma is coming, Kurt," she said over and over to herself. It became Jill's mantra as she navigated the never-ending brush.

As the search continued, the weather deteriorated further. Dark, thick fog descended on the searchers. The constant drizzle kept everyone in a state of cold and wet. Eventually, more than a thousand people joined the search. Business folks. College students. Food and water donations trickled in from many counties over. One thing was incredibly apparent to everyone who joined the search: Ron Newton was a man of incredible endurance. Any parent reading this can feel Ron's immense pain. At one point during the search, Ron rolled an ankle in the ever-thickening undergrowth. His ankle was immediately swollen and discolored. Ron was ordered to sit on the sidelines and rest, but he wouldn't have it. He had a Grade 3 sprain, and it never healed right. Years later, Ron would stab at that sore ankle, a reminder of the injury he suffered in a deep gully. Ron was awake the entire search, but eventually, Ron's friends had to lace his endless cups of coffee with downers.

Still, he kept going, constantly repeating, "It's on us" to find Kurt.

Even Maine's governor, James Longley, arrived on September 4, to offer support to the Newtons. Longley was so moved by the search party's dedication, most of whom were perfect strangers to the Newtons, that he would later call that day "the most impressive experience I have ever had." The search officially ended on September 12, after a two-day extension of resources Longley approved. In the waning hours of the search, volunteers busied themselves by putting up missing posters of Kurt deep in the vast woodlands. Hunters would be pouring in from all over the country soon, the Newtons wanted to warn them to report anything and everything they saw that might relate to their missing son. No detail should be overlooked. The Newtons stayed in the brush for a while. Ron even bought a second-hand snowmobile to navigate the inevitable Northern Maine snowfall.

At some point, the Newtons had to transition from finding their baby boy to the inevitable question: "What became of Kurt?"

Police acknowledged that there was no evidence Kurt was abducted but they needed to do their due diligence. Local law enforcement interviewed everyone who stayed or visited the campsite on that fateful weekend. Police administered polygraph tests to folks they deemed suspicious. Nothing materialized from the questioning. There was a story of a camper who said she saw a station wagon driving around the campground. No tire tracks were found on the little-used country roads. Another rumor circulated about a bear that had been let loose from a local animal sanctuary and had been wreaking havoc on campsites. Trackers found no evidence of bear droppings, unable to corroborate the claims. Police broadcast Kurt's photo to the entire country, and even Canada, by teletype. A generation would walk into post offices and supermarkets and see Kurt Newton's face staring back at them. Sightings of Kurt often sprouted up from around the country and even abroad. The Newtons had some close calls. At one point, they were sure a little boy who appeared in New Orleans was their son. The boy answered with a name that vaguely sounded like Kurt's.

It turned out it wasn't Kurt, of course. Little Kurt Newton never came home. Nothing was ever found of Kurt either. Not a single shred of clothing was ever discovered.

The same goes for little Douglas Chapman (no relation to Wayne) of Alfred, Maine. Douglas disappeared from the front of his family's home on June 2, 1971. Bloodhounds traced young Douglas' scent to an apple orchard, then to an abandoned field adjacent to a main road. Police immediately suspected foul play and eliminated family members by way of polygraph tests. Little Douglas' father was convinced that his son had been abducted and killed by a local sex offender. In a little town with less than two thousand people, I obtained a list of all area sex offenders in 1971 from a former Maine State Trooper who remained interested in the two cases, decades after retirement. A violent, registered sex offender did live nearby, just 1.8 miles away. I will not name this person. My investigation is ongoing into Kurt and Douglas' disappearances. However, I would not be one bit surprised if one or both disappearances are connected to Wayne Chapman.

By 1971, Chapman had already visited Maine many times. He had a network of friends there and had a place to stay on a big farm. Many years later, Al Mintz, the lead detective on Chapman's criminal activity in Rhode Island, would tell me stories of how Chapman would reminisce about meeting boys on campsites in Maine. Chapman trusted Al, who had a way of getting people to tell him things they wouldn't otherwise divulge. Al could shave away your outer shell and leave you bare and exposed.

Chapman often spoke to Al about a boy he met near a waterfall or a bridge. In vivid detail, he described the campsite and the stream that ran through it. I took a pilgrimage up to Alfred in York County in 2014. I had to see the sights for myself and imagine what Chapman could have been describing. Less than three miles away from Douglas' childhood home is a place called Great Falls. It's a breathtaking sight—beautiful white water cascading over the rocks. I imagined this could have been what Chapman described. He likely hadn't forgotten the sights or the soothing sound of the rushing water. I know I never will. Al took note to check on missing boys in Maine. His conversations with Chapman took place in 1976. Al left the Providence Police Department in 1978. It wasn't until he and I met some four decades later that we started to possibly piece together the breadth of Chapman's crimes in Maine.

He was cooling his heels a little in late 1971, his messy stay in Florida with his wife still fresh in his mind. He was looking for new beginnings. I will describe, to the best of my knowledge, here, how and most importantly why, Chapman ended up living on Linwood Avenue in Providence, Rhode Island. This question, the *why*, haunted me for years. Through all my research and investigations, I could never quite figure out why a serial pedophile like Wayne Chapman ended up driving nearly eight hours from Jamestown to arrive in the capital city of the smallest state in the union. He didn't have to look far to find a place to stay; this certainly was not his first time in the city.

Providence is known for a few things. Of all those things, corruption is probably number one, two, and three. From the late 1950s until the early 1990s, Providence was a hotbed of organized crime, once the hub of New England

Mob boss Raymond L.S. Patriarca. In 1938, the Providence Board of Public Safety named Raymond "Public Enemy #1." He ruled the New England crime scene with an iron fist. In 1956, Raymond moved all Mob-related activities to Providence. He mostly worked out of the National Cigarette Service Company on Atwells Avenue near the historic Federal Hill neighborhood. Patriarca was the judge, jury, and executioner for every business in Providence whether legal or illegal. He expected his kickbacks and he was not a very patient man. Even famous mobster (and future FBI Most Wanted fugitive) James "Whitey" Bulger never dared to cross into Providence. Whitey stayed in his little world, that small stretch of island in South Boston.

In Providence, the fish rotted from the head. It all started with Mayor Buddy Cianci, who served from 1974 to 1984. With an administration fraught with scandals, Buddy, the first Republican to run Providence in decades, had a major flair for drama and never met a reporter he wouldn't talk to. Buddy ended up in the middle of a bizarre love triangle in late 1984. A contractor from nearby Cranston became romantically involved with his then estranged wife. Buddy found out and confronted the man, giving him a brutal beating. There have been plenty of unconfirmed reports and plenty of rumors about Buddy's Mob ties and the brutal assault. I walked the streets of Providence for years conducting research for this book and the common theme among locals is that Buddy brought a few low-level mobsters when he was the man in charge, and he had the mobsters carry out his dirty work.

Regardless, Mayor Cianci was found guilty of the assault and received a suspended five-year sentence. A special law, which Buddy ironically tried to eradicate the year prior, prohibited convicted felons from serving as mayor was coming back to bite him; he was out as mayor in late 1984. Buddy would have an incredible run after his conviction and ousting, and he would later become mayor of Providence again and do a stint in federal prison. After losing a race for yet another term as mayor, he died of colon cancer in 2016 and would lie in state for two days at Providence City Hall. His Mob ties were long rumored; his later convictions revealed that Buddy was, at the very least, Mob-friendly in the 1970s, and, at worst, completely in bed with La Cosa Nostra.

How does this relationship relate to a pedophile like Wayne Chapman? Nothing happened in Providence in those days without organized crime approving or taking a cut of the money, especially the production and distribution of child pornography. Chapman had long been traveling the East Coast, indulging in sex shops and frequenting adult bookstores since he became mobile in late 1965. When he committed brutal assaults on young boys, he was always careful to take pictures of the boys he victimized. Sure, he loved having the keepsakes from his crimes, but he was much more interested in the currency the pictures provided. Chapman came to Providence because it was a lucrative place to be a low-level producer and distributor of child pornography. Providence was geographically perfect, an easy hop to Boston, a mecca of sex shops. All he had to do was head north on Interstate 95, fight traffic for forty minutes, and he would be in Downtown Boston. It was also far enough away from the prying eyes of law enforcement in Jamestown and Pennsylvania. He felt free for the first time in a very long time.

Leigh Savoie, a ten-year-old boy from Revere, Massachusetts, was secretly hoping to buy his mother an Easter present. Leigh had been stuck at home lately. He had been falling behind in school and his mother grounded him. Leigh was having that age-old struggle we all must face in math class. Leigh was running out of time. Easter was coming. On April 7, 1974, Leigh pleaded with his mother Dolores to let him head over to Suffolk Downs Racetrack and resume his young career as a shoe shiner. He had been hustling the shoeshine racket for a bit, polishing the shoes of businessmen and wise guys, cigar and cigarette smoke thick in the air.

Dolores couldn't say no to her son she nicknamed "Lee-Lee." She acquiesced and Leigh headed out to make some money for the anticipated Easter holiday. When Leigh left his home on State Road, it was the last time Dolores would ever see her son. Leigh's shoeshine kit was found at a small restaurant next to the Beachmont MBTA station located on Winthrop Avenue in Revere. The restaurant's owner later explained to Dolores that Leigh had dropped it off on the way to Suffolk Downs. The racetrack was located just one mile from Beechmont.

When Leigh didn't return home, Dolores filed a missing person's report later that evening. Larry Malta, a detective with the Revere Police Department, immediately went to work. The investigation was wide in scope. Trainers, jockeys, and even security guards at Suffolk Downs were interviewed. Leigh's schoolmates were counseled and interviewed. Larry was trying to get a feel for what was going on in Leigh's life in the lead-up to his disappearance. A teletype was sent to local and national police departments regarding Leigh. They mentioned the unique t-shirt Leigh was wearing the day he disappeared which featured the phrase "TRY IT, YOU'LL LIKE IT," which was a popular jingle in Alka-Seltzer and Life Cereal commercials in the early 1970s.

The investigation dragged on with no suspects and seemingly no movement. As time went on, rumors circulated that Revere Police had lost the Savoie files completely. The details, even forty-seven years later, are very scant. In the fall of 1974, the City of Revere was again shaken by a brutal attack on a young boy. On the afternoon of September 16, a nine-year-old boy left his family home to meet up with three of his buddies. The boys met up at the Suffolk Downs in Revere, connecting at the gate that looks at Wally Street.

The young boys were doing what many young boys did in that era: they were hustling for money. It was very common for Revere boys that age to sell programs outside for that day's races.

At approximately 5:30 p.m., a white, four-door Oldsmobile pulled to the boys and the driver motioned them to come over to the driver's side window. The boys "shot the shit" with the man for approximately fifteen minutes about everything from the Red Sox's chances to the weather. Eventually, the man offered the boys an opportunity to make a few bucks. The mysterious man offered up ten bucks to the boys to split if they would come wash his car. If two of them came, they would have to split it. One boy was chosen for the job and climbed into the passenger side of the man's car. The man made small talk with the nine-year-old as he wheeled across Revere over towards East Boston and Annavoy Street that intersected the beach close to the approach path for airplanes landing at Logan Airport.

As they arrived at the beach, the man told the boy to take a walk down the clearing that led to the surf. The path was littered with tall weeds and made perfect cover for the assault. The man ordered the boy to perform a sexual act on him and threatened to kill him if he refused. It wasn't until the next morning; that a young East Boston resident found the young boy clinging to life in the tall weeds adjacent to the beach. The boy was taken to an area hospital where he lay in a coma for five weeks. He was littered with injuries that were consistent with being hit by a blunt force object with nails in it. The police theorized he was beaten with a board.

As the boy lay in the hospital a week later, police took the other boys out into the community to find the white Oldsmobile the assailant was driving. It didn't take long to find the vehicle, which was registered to Kenneth Magnasco, a young local whom witnesses saw hanging around the scene the next morning when the boy was being loaded into an ambulance. Multiple civilians testified that Magnasco and his white Oldsmobile were spotted driving around the beach area the night of the attempted murder and the next morning. Magnasco was arrested and charged with attempted murder and armed assault. At trial, a young boy whom Magnasco sat for accused the defendant of molesting him; the boy's statements about Magnasco's abuse and the effect it had on. The nine-year-old's friends also testified that Magnasco was the man who struck up the conversation with them at Suffolk Downs. Magnasco was convicted of the assault and attempted murder of the young boy, who made a full recovery.

In 2021, amid the COVID-19 pandemic, I found the nine-year-old boy, now a much older man, on Facebook. We talked for hours over weeks about the assault and how it may have connected to Leigh Savoie's disappearance. The man remains convinced that Magnasco was also the man who attacked Leigh Savoie months prior and is a strong advocate for the missing boy. He periodically checks in on the Revere Police cold case unit to see where they are at on the case. In one of our last conversations, the man quipped to me that he never did get those ten dollars that Magnasco promised him. It was the same self-deprecating, dark humor I had grown up with in Boston. It was comforting. I wish the man (who asked his name not to be used here) a lot of peace. As for Magnasco, my attempts to track him after his incarceration went nowhere. As far as I could find, Ken Magnasco kept his nose clean after prison.

***

Wayne Chapman was very active already in the New England area in April 1974. He was convicted of rape and was a major suspect in the murder of a boy in Lawrence, Massachusetts, not far from Revere. Chapman likely knew the area.

Also, consider this: In 1977, just three years after Savoie's disappearance and the brutal beating of the other young boy, a sex ring involving young boys was discovered and subsequently busted (much more on this later). A local advertising executive and pedophile ran the sex ring on Mountain Avenue in Revere, two miles from Suffolk Downs Racetrack and 2.2 miles from Leigh Savoie's residence. Leigh was also Chapman's typical victim type. In later interviews with police and examiners, Chapman would often state that he preferred blue-eyed, blond-haired boys. He was well schooled in lying to police by the mid-70s to throw them off his trail and his story about preferring fair-haired kids was likely a ploy. If you look at his actual victimology, Chapman's ideal victim had darker skin and hair. Like Leigh and Andy Puglisi. Looking at Leigh, I cannot help but see parallels to Chapman's known victims. In my semi-educated opinion, Wayne Chapman should be the number one suspect for any missing boy it can be proven he was geographically close to who fits the profile. Leigh Savoie does. Leigh's face was plastered on missing children's flyers for years. And forty-seven years later, we are no closer to finding out what happened to him. It's cases like Leigh's, and mothers like his, that keep me going. If there is breath in my lungs, I will talk about Leigh and champion his case.

Wayne Chapman got quickly to work in Providence. He rented the third floor of a nine-bedroom, three-bath, triple-decker on Linwood Avenue. Linwood was centrally located. If you took a left out of Chapman's old driveway, you would be on Cranston Street, where an old check-cashing service once stood, and Cranston Meat Market, a timeless butcher shop where residents would wait in line into the street to get the day's fresh cuts. I have walked the stretch of road from his former apartment at least a hundred times and have tried to imagine what the streets were like in the early to mid-1970s. I tried to envision the sites Chapman would take in as he drove around, stalking prey, while his stash of self-produced pornography sat on his dashboard.

It was around this time that I first shelved this project. I was leaving work early to research Chapman's crimes and would go to Providence every day and ask questions. A professor in my undergraduate program once told me the best way to get the straight story was to get on the ground and ask questions. People will tell you much more when they think there is no paper trail, unlike sending an email or text message. That professor was so right. People tell you so much when they think the conversation only exists at that moment. No digital trail.

Most of my Providence research took place in 2014 and 2015. I was leaving work, or sometimes not even showing up, and heading over to the city in the morning and asking around. During that time, when I looked in the mirror, I realized I wasn't shaving. My beard was completely unkempt and I hadn't cut my hair in ages. My wife was concerned about me. She had little idea what I was doing. She knew I had an interest in the case, but she didn't understand how deep I was. She assumed I was battling severe PTSD from my last brutal deployment to Afghanistan a few years prior, which I certainly was. I would stay up all night and research any and every connection Chapman made in life. I would hunt down all his known associates and scrutinize every move in their lives. This book is the byproduct of all those late evenings and early mornings. In the end, I decided to keep going. I don't have to imagine the horror a young boy like Andy Puglisi felt when he realized he was in grave danger. I lived it.

That is the point of my entire work—speak for those who can no longer speak and make sure no one ever forgets.

Chapman immersed himself in the local pornography scene. Sex shops and adult bookstores were abundant in Providence. Providence, to this day, is run by the adult entertainment industry. The city has more strip clubs and sex shops per capita than any big city in the United States; it was no different in the 1970s. Pornography was big to Chapman—it was his business, after all. Sometimes he would head out to the woods in neighboring Massachusetts communities. Just a fifteen-minute drive he could leave city life behind and find suburban areas like Seekonk and Swansea.

Sometimes Chapman would go east down I195 and end up in the waterfront community of Fall River. I don't believe he ended up in those communities by chance. He had connections there—either someone who provided intelligence about where he could locate victims or a friend who would help him. Nothing was happenstance. He would go out into the woods of those communities and spread his pictures out on the ground, sometimes leaving pictures on the trails and lying in wait. This was well before kids were glued to YouTube or social media and would have to find their adventures outdoors. Chapman preyed on that. He would lay out his horrific materials hoping kids would come by, and at the very least be curious.

After Chapman got oriented, he figured he better find some gainful employment close to home. He remembered the relatively easy, solitary workplace environment janitors had at the Jamestown hospital. He looked at hospitals in the greater Providence area. All he had to do was make a left onto Cranston Street and catch North Main Street, which runs near the Emergency Room on Summit Avenue. I have scoured the Earth for information from former employees about Chapman's activities while employed at the hospital. Not a single former employee could seem to recall anything memorable about him. I was looking for any sliver of information that would have shed some light on his activities. He melted into the background, like most janitors. Most people have heard the urban legend about the creepy janitor who doubles as a sadistic psychopath. Chapman was exactly that. It was not until the full breadth of his crimes came to light that hospital employees and administrators began asking questions about the janitor who worked the 3 p.m. to midnight swing shift. *Was he not vetted? Had they done a criminal history check?*

The staff at that time was completely unnerved and more shocking rumors were to come.

It was around that time that flyers started to circulate in Providence about a 4-H club. 4-H is designed for youths from all areas of the country to come together and learn by doing. Club members are taken out by volunteers and taught about leadership and community. Volunteers included high school gym teachers, coaches, and even clergy members. After Chapman got wind of the local 4-H club, he began to distribute flyers in the neighborhood. While he officially volunteered, he also operated outside of that to lure and groom victims. Just like getting married to a woman with kids, Chapman's entire social life centered around getting close to and eventually grooming potential victims.

Providence Police Detective Al Mintz eventually found one of these flyers, which was amateur and poorly worded, and by the time he saw the flyers, he was much too late. Parents had already contacted the number on the flyers, and some of their children were lured to the third-floor apartment on Linwood Avenue. The victims noted the sophisticated camera equipment he kept in his apartment. One victim later spoke of Chapman's professional-looking darkroom located in the rear bedroom. He would use this dark room to develop pictures of his victims. He couldn't exactly drop that type of material off at CVS and come back in an hour to get it. Just think of what you had to do in the 1970s to pick up a new hobby. There was no Internet then, so you couldn't Google "how-to" videos. Chapman would have needed hands-on instruction. The low-IQ janitor was likely given a crash course on how to develop film and operate professional camera equipment to carry out the crimes.

One victim was a man who grew up with an alcoholic mother in hardscrabble Providence. His mother was delighted when her little boy, just seven years old, befriended Chapman and was subsequently invited to 4-H outings. He would take the boy and other disadvantaged kids out to the kids' museum and Lincoln Woods State Park. Lincoln Woods was the summer highlight for the 4-H members. The crew would go to the river and raft. Chapman would often tie the raft to a rock and let the kids float on the water while other kids waited their turn.

While the kids in his care were on the water tied down, he would show the kids waiting patiently on the shore pictures from his porn stash, systematically separating the kids he desired by keeping them off the rafts. He would often park his van in the brush just overlooking the woods and bring kids into the back and abuse them. A generation of young, disadvantaged Rhode Island kids was destroyed in that van in the woods. On my last visit to Lincoln Woods, which sits just minutes from a Rhode Island State Police barracks that has been there for decades, I took note of just how easy it would have been to park a vehicle in the brush that borders the lake and remains hidden.

Victims from that 4-H period would often report that Chapman was more than eager to show off his ever-growing stash of pornography. He would show off his photos to gauge the children's interest and sometimes make threats. One victim came forward decades later and reported that Chapman would show him pictures of what he was sure were deceased children. He would threaten the young boy with pictures of boys hogtied to trees and gagged. He had been raping this boy for months. The young boy took the threats to heart. He kept quiet for decades because of the horrible images he saw from that stash. Chapman also told the boy he would kill the boy's entire family if he ever talked about the rapes.

At this point, Chapman wasn't the spectacularly dumb pedophile who immediately admitted guilt. He was a far more sinister predator who would do whatever it took to avoid being caught. When Chapman was off duty from the hospital and the 4-H club, he would often visit Roger Williams Park. Chapman loved the sprawling 4.8-acre lot just north of downtown Providence. Chapman would offer kids a buck or two to pose in front of the many statues that adorned the pathways of the park. His Roger Williams photos would materialize a few years later during a traffic stop in New York and set off a firestorm in the Providence Police Department.

Chapman was active in the local coastal communities and in July 1974, he approached some local boys. He was looking for his daughter's lost dog. He told the kids his daughter was about their age and she would be upset if the dog went missing. Two of the three boys made a decision that would haunt them for the rest of their lives. They decided it was better they went home and asked permission to leave with the man. The third boy stayed. Chapman got lucky. It saved him from having to ask the boys to split up. That was his modus operandi. Prey on the kids' vulnerability.

I think of my kids, who are now seven and two. I think about what they would do if they were told this exact story. Knowing my seven-year-old, I think he would rush to help. Chapman knew this youthful compunction. He took the boy into the woods to look for the dog, and the boy later noted in his statement how Chapman seemed relaxed, even whistling as they walked. The man the boy knew as "Jim" explained to the boy that he had two children. He explained to the nine-year-old that he worked in a bookstore that sold dirty books.

Once they got away from civilization, Chapman overpowered the boy and pushed him down to the ground, making him undress. He sexually assaulted the boy and took his camera out of his right pocket to snap pictures of the naked boy. Chapman likely developed the film later in his darkroom on Linwood Avenue. Afterward, he told the boy to get dressed and then divulged a half-truth to the young man.

Chapman told the victim his picture would be featured in *Playboy* magazine. He took the boy's picture because he was a cog in the child pornography production machine, which had grown to a multi-million-dollar business even in the early 1970s. Chapman was a foot soldier, if you will, who was set loose on society with marching orders: find kids, take advantage of them, and leave with photo or video evidence. Chapman did not reveal this assault until 1976. It's unclear whether the little boy immediately went to his parents or the police. If you are one of his victims and are reading this book, my contact information is on the last pages. Reach out to me, day or night. I know the feeling and I will always be here to listen.

This specific offense happened in the little town of Dartmouth, Massachusetts, a town about forty minutes away from Chapman's apartment. Did he simply show up in these towns randomly? Probably not. He had to have known people in these communities that he terrorized. He didn't wake up in the morning and throw darts at the map. He went to places he was comfortable in, and he likely received intelligence on which areas were good to spot children. Places close to wooded areas where you could isolate them and set up camera equipment. More than likely, there was a semi-sophisticated network of pedophiles that shared trade secrets about the best "cruising" spots.

***

I have scoured the archives in Dartmouth looking for known pedophiles that lived in the area during the time Chapman was active. There are a few incredibly interesting names. I looked for offenders who offended over many decades, the ones who seemed untreatable. The types I figured would be low enough to interact with the likes of Wayne Chapman. I zeroed in on two men whom I will not name here. I believe these two men, or at least one of them, could have had connections to Chapman. Remember, these men have a strong need for validation, and they will flock to one another. I feel they at least crossed paths until I can prove otherwise.

The investigation continues.

***

Chapman also struck in communities that were home to infamous predators. He molested two boys in the hometown of alleged cannibal and serial pedophile Nathaniel Bar-Jonah. There has been much speculation about the friendship between Bar-Jonah and Chapman. I will attempt to put it in perspective here.

Nathaniel Bar-Jonah was born David Brown in Worcester, Massachusetts, in 1957. His first offense was at age seven when he tried to strangle a young female neighbor in his basement. At age twelve, he sexually assaulted his first young male victim. At fourteen, he allegedly tried to murder two boys by luring them to a cemetery, only to be thwarted when one boy wisely persuaded the other not to go.

In March 1975, Bar-Jonah dressed in police garb and forced an eight-year-old into his mother's vehicle. Luckily, an alert neighbor saw the abduction and contacted local authorities to describe the car. Police scrambled every resource to pursue the stolen vehicle. When a young patrolman found a vehicle matching that description parked conspicuously on a busy corner, the officer investigated further. When Bar-Jonah exited the vehicle at gunpoint, law enforcement found the child bloodied and beaten. The child had urinated and defecated all over the vehicle and was near death.

Bar-Jonah was placed on probation and was in Hartford, Connecticut, just weeks later dressed again in his police uniform. He abducted a little girl with a short haircut that he mistook for a boy. When he realized he had made a mistake, he beat the little girl mercilessly. Eventually, he ran his mother's car up on a sidewalk, opened the door, and dumped the little girl on the sidewalk. A civilian nearby saw the car ride up on the sidewalk and noted the vehicle's plate number. Bar-Jonah was arrested for the brutal assault, which left the little girl convulsing in shock. Incredibly, Bar-Jonah's probation officer in Massachusetts was not notified about the Hartford case. In late 1976, he was released from his probation period in Webster with a letter thanking him for his "cooperation."

On September 24, 1977, Nathaniel Bar-Jonah put on a black jacket with the letters *FBI* sewn on the right breast pocket and headed over to nearby Shrewsbury. He loitered outside the White City Cinemas on Turnpike Street waiting for kids to exit the movie theater and used his FBI agent ruse to get two young boys inside his mother's car. He drove the boys to a wooded area about two miles away and handcuffed them.

The morbidly obese Bar-Jonah clocked in at nearly four hundred pounds in 1977 and used his weight to suffocate the boys by jumping up and down on their chests. He thought the boys were dead after his torture and assaults and left one boy in the wooded area while he drove off with the other. Amazingly, the abandoned young victim regained consciousness and immediately ran for help giving a detailed description of the assailant's car. Bar-Jonah was quickly arrested and was ultimately convicted of attempted murder and sentenced to eighteen to twenty years in prison, the maximum sentence in Massachusetts. Eventually, he was classified as a sexually dangerous person and was transferred to the Massachusetts Treatment Center for the sexually dangerous. He lived on unit A-1 with Chapman for many years before he was released in July 1991, which will be covered later.

One of the biggest mysteries of the entire Wayne Chapman saga is whether he and Bar-Jonah could be placed at the same place and the same time before they were at the treatment center in Bridgewater. I know Chapman and Bar-Jonah had at the very least crossed paths on the outside. Pedophiles know their behavior is completely repugnant to nearly all of society. Like any other group, they tend to find one another and remain close. The mere fact that Chapman would confess to police that he was active in Webster during the time Bar-Jonah lived there is enough.

There are two hundred and ninety-four towns and fifty-seven cities in Massachusetts. Do you think it was a coincidence that Chapman ended up committing crimes in Bar-Jonah's neighborhood? I don't think there was a chance. It was likely that just like the Dartmouth assaults, Chapman had a good idea of where to find kids. He had someone on the inside. The intelligence network was usually dead on.

I have never seen photo evidence nor printed evidence that Bar-Jonah and Chapman were ever together in the same place and time outside of treatment. I think they were careful not to have one another's names in each other's hefty address books. The men often wrote letters back and forth while at different institutions. They offered each other kind words, even advice on each other's cases. I doubt they struck up that kind of friendship as they crisscrossed the Massachusetts criminal justice system. The circumstantial evidence is overwhelming.

Chapman was prolific in 1974. He admitted to picking up a boy somewhere in Western Massachusetts and in the Worcester area. I believe he would have been comfortable there, Bar-Jonah's birthplace. They may have even prowled together and watched kids from park benches as some authors have suggested.

Chapman had aborted two assaults when one boy told him that his father was a policeman. That spooked him enough to let the child go. Another young boy recognized Chapman as the man who asked him to look at some pornography the summer before. He had gotten around so much that he was brazen enough to return to the same haunts, but that habit came with a price. He was there to produce his pictures and keep the machine running, not get jammed up by the cops. He had a peculiar accent that was unforgettable. It was almost like a country twang. Slow and deliberate. He also had the most peculiar eyes. When he was a younger man, they were dark like holes, like the old William Shatner mask made famous by Michael Myers in John Carpenter's cult classic *Halloween*. Nobody who ever stared into them forgot them. Of the hundreds of interviews I conducted for this book, everybody I spoke with remembered Wayne Chapman's eyes. There was nothing there. Chapman was always an empty vessel.

CHAPTER 4: BROCKTON 1974

The David Jon Louison Center is on Newbury Street in Brockton, Massachusetts, and every day around 2:45 p.m., children overrun the place. They run around like crazy inside, playing tag on the playgrounds that adjoin the center, happily guiding their parents in to enjoy the facilities. Every time I stop by the center, I cannot help but wonder if the kids, or the adults for that matter, even know why the center bears the name of a five-year-old boy. The community raised funds to help find the missing child, but when the boy didn't return home safely, the family opened the center in their son's honor in 1982. The Center caters mostly to disadvantaged families who are unhoused. I spent a few long months living in a car when I was younger. In July 2006, the Center merged with the national YMCA and still stands as a beacon of hope to disadvantaged families in a tough city.

Little David Louison showed no fear of strangers and was a little wanderer.

He would often wander the woods behind his home on West Elm Street in Brockton. Young David was always careful to spray paint trees to mark his path as he explored the woods. He would often brag to all the other kids in the neighborhood that he was already an ace explorer, and that there was no chance he could ever get lost in the woods. In June 1974, David was playing in his backyard. He wore blue shorts and a white sports jersey with the number sixteen in bold letters on the back. He had buckets and was moving sand all over his yard. His mother, Naomi, was inside doing some odds and ends, talking on the phone, and considering starting dinner. Around 3:30 p.m., she realized David was no longer in the backyard. Initially, she thought he'd gone into the woods like he always did. He didn't always let his mom know where he was going; just the previous year, David walked a mile down to the local mall without telling his mom.

Someone found him in the mall parking lot.

Naomi yelled out for little David, receiving no response. She began to panic like only a parent can when they can't locate their child. David had been playing with Victor Martelli, the boy next door. Naomi went over and asked Victor if he had seen anything. Victor told her the story that he always stuck to. He told Naomi, and then the police, that a man named "Africa" had come and taken David by the hand and taken him out to the woods behind West Elm Street. Just the day before, Victor had run into his house in a huff because Africa had taken his toy gun. Mrs. Martelli heard Victor talking about somebody named Africa once or twice in the weeks leading up to David's disappearance. Joanne Connor, a West Elm Street neighbor of theirs, also supported Victor's story.

Joanne had mentioned to the police that when David was visiting her son, just the day before his disappearance, he mentioned he was planning to get Victor's toy gun back from Africa. Forty-seven years later, I still cannot find any person, known to the police, who had an alias or a nickname that even remotely resembled Africa. The few files I have read about the Africa lead were completely fruitless.

At the height of the search, which began on June 18, 1974, there were more than five thousand volunteers. Locals from Brockton joined with Massachusetts National Guard members from the local armory. They searched everywhere, including Avon Reservoir and Field Park. Brockton Police Detective Frank Gentile was assigned to David's case. Frank was close to retirement, only three years away from taking over security at Brockton High School, and he was known for being an extremely sharp, old-school police officer. He was an excellent communicator and tended to throw himself headlong into his cases, sometimes to the detriment of his own mental and physical health. Frank knew that statistically, the first twenty-four-to-forty-eight hours after a child goes missing are the most important. The likelihood of children getting home safely plunges after that window. Frank immediately got to work chasing down a report that David had been abducted in a car with California plates, which turned out to be bogus. Frank began by combing the woods behind West Elm Street and looking at David's father, attorney Melvin Louison.

Melvin was a powerful, prominent attorney and a well-known man in Brockton. He was once the front-runner for a mayoral campaign that eventually came up short. Frank immediately focused on Melvin's criminal defense practice. Had Melvin made enemies who may have wanted to hurt him? Frank scoured through the practice's records but came up with nothing.

Then something happened. Two men came forward claiming they abducted David. Frank thought he had gotten the break he sorely needed, but sometimes in an investigation, patience is a virtue. Someone out there knows something, and people always talk. As it turned out, the men were trying to extort the Louison family. They had no connection to David and could not have been near his house at the time. They called the Louison home with demanded money in return for information they didn't have. It got to the point where Naomi and Melvin stopped answering their phone. They opted for a recording service that answered and went to a prerecorded message. Frank returned to Melvin's law practice for any leads.

Melvin had been front-page news in the lead-up to his son's disappearance. He was fighting hard to keep a woman who shot and killed her boyfriend out of prison.

Roberta Scheffler had a daughter who was terminally ill, and Melvin argued that Roberta needed to be in home confinement. He posited that the justice system should rethink its position on special cases, like Roberta's. Everyone in Brockton had an opinion on her case. Some thought Melvin was a hero for fighting for a woman who was in an abusive relationship and exacted revenge on her abuser. Some thought he was just a typical scummy lawyer who was defending a cold-blooded killer. Frank thought it was too much of a coincidence that Melvin was a public figure in a controversial case when his son went missing.

Frank felt he needed to run Roberta's case angle to the ground. Some thought he had too much tunnel vision in the beginning. He was fixated on Melvin's law firm and the Schaffler case. Frank investigated everybody involved in the shooting. He interviewed the victim's family repeatedly, hoping someone would give him something he could work with. Their story was always the same: the family was mourning their loss, but they would never hurt a small child in retaliation. Frank ruled out the victim's family systematically, one by one, and his angle died before it got any traction.

Frank then turned his attention to the idea that a stranger might have abducted little David. He was convinced it was a local from Brockton. Nobody could have gotten a boy out of those woods in broad daylight without having extensive knowledge of the wooded area behind the Louison property. Frank began investigating local sex offenders, but in 1974, there was no national registry for sex offenders. Law enforcement could not run to Google and see who was registered in the area, or who may be of interest. Frank had to keep his ear to the ground and grabbed every offender police knew in the area. He told patrolmen to keep an eye out for any bizarre behavior concerning children. Frank's thought was there was a predator in their community and they would strike again. The detective thought the stranger might even be in Louison's neighborhood on West Elm. He told the patrol to keep an eye on the Louison home. Extra Brockton patrolman on overtime made regular rounds past the Louison's residence. Frank's antennae were constantly up. He would drive the streets of Brockton in his grey Ford and scan the streets. He thought if he saw the kidnapper, he would instantly recognize them. Frank gave some credence to Vincent's "Africa" story. He also had to remind himself that a four-year-old told the story. He understood the vivid imagination small children can have, but he was struck, however, by how many times Vincent stuck to the story. Vincent never wavered or stated a fact out of order, and he had passion in his eyes when he told it. Even at four, he sounded like a kid who was pleading with police to believe him and go find his friend's abductor.

Detective Gentile started finding known gang members and wise guys on the street.

He knew that Raymond Patriarca, the Providence Mob boss, had people in Brockton. Perhaps one of his guys knew about a man nicknamed "Africa." Maybe a low-level drug dealer they shook down went by that moniker? Frank never found anyone who could say with certainty that they had ever heard of a person who went by that nickname. As time went on, the searches ended. Frank was continually baffled by David's case. He knew the chances the little boy would be found alive were slim. Eventually, the FBI got involved and researched the wooded area behind the Louison home. How the FBI got involved in a missing person's case is somewhat of a mystery. Had they been asked by Brockton police to help? I could never get a straight answer from Brockton officials. Brockton is a town with a large police force and many tactical units. It is not a small city with little resources. It was always odd to me that the feds came in.

Not until years later, it was learned that Wayne Chapman was known to the federal government. Chapman was assigned a federal identification number in his file, sort of a unique identifier showing that this man, woman, or group has been investigated. What the feds turned up about Chapman is a mystery. I have always been stonewalled in my requests to get a look at Chapman's FBI files. Multiple Freedom of Information requests have always been flatly denied.

Nevertheless, the FBI couldn't turn up anything in their search for Louison. There was no trace of David —not a shred of clothing, not a shoe. Nothing. It was as if he'd vanished off the face of the Earth. Frank Gentile remained obsessed with David's disappearance throughout the rest of 1974 and all of 1975. He stayed in touch with the Louison family, talking to Naomi and Melvin at least every other week. Sometimes Melvin would call randomly at three in the afternoon or seven in the morning, and Frank was there. He looked at other cases throughout the state and nationwide, searching for any similarity between his case and missing children's cases throughout the world.

On May 18, 1975, Jason Foreman, a five-year-old boy from South Kingstown, Rhode Island, went missing. Jason had been out playing with his older brother and three friends. When he announced he was going home, Jason was last seen running down a hill to a volunteer fire station that was in Peacedale, Rhode Island. Foreman lived no more than thirty yards from the fire station and disappeared on his mother's twenty-fifth birthday. She last heard him laughing outside their home at around 3:30 that afternoon. Frank Gentile watched his case closely. Even as the searches unfolded and turned up nothing for the Foreman family, the news in New England covered the case incessantly. Frank had a close eye on the situation some thirty miles down Route 95, it reminded him a lot of what he was facing with his case.

On September 5, 1976, Frank Gentile got the break he'd been praying for for two years. It was the break he told himself to be patient about. It turned out to be unsatisfying and incredibly frustrating. Sergeant Tony Vatter of the New York State Police made it a habit to check the logs for missing people, or even stolen vehicles that may have been reported. Tony wanted to know what BOLOs (be on the lookout) had been reported. He was a distinguished member of the New York State Troopers. He made it all the way up from a patrol trooper to sergeant.

Tony was responsible for all the troopers who patrolled the highways in his sector, was no-nonsense, and was well respected. Tony patrolled New York State's nearly six-hundred-mile-long thruway. Its south end starts in the Bronx and its western ends in Ripley, Pennsylvania. Around Waterloo, Tony began following a 1965 blue and white Dodge van. The van had a terrible paint job and was a converted bread truck. It bore a Rhode Island license plate that started with the number 4145. Tony trailed the van for a bit. The driver changed lanes from the far-left fast lane to the slow lane on the far right of the Thruway. Tony was driving while checking the day's BOLO notes and became frustrated because he couldn't find the note about a Rhode Island tag.

The system police used in the 1970s for BOLO was rudimentary compared to today's. They often had to rely on handwritten notes from the prior day's patrols or teletypes from other agencies. Tony remembered hearing something about a stolen bread truck with those exact tags. He followed a little longer and initiated a 10-28 (code for vehicle stop) which came back with a hit. This tidbit gave Sergeant Vatter adequate legal authority to initiate a stop. Just to be clear, another minor mystery in this story is why Chapman's vehicle ended up being on any BOLO list. Chapman had not stolen that truck, and his Rhode Island license plate was valid at the time. I have long wondered if someone was ready to make a move on Chapman. Someone from federal law enforcement, potentially. His vehicle was clean so it's just another odd mystery in a story full of them.

After exiting his patrol vehicle, Tony visually scanned the vehicle's exterior. He looked through the van's window and observed small-caliber shells consistent with a firearm. Tony also saw what he believed were developed pictures strewn about the van. Upon closer inspection, he observed young boys in sexually suggestive poses in the pictures. Tony was struck by the sheer amount of Polaroid pictures out in the open. Some of them were even spread out on the dashboard, almost strategically; obviously, the driver made no effort to hide the photos. It was almost like he needed them. Upon contacting the driver, who identified himself as Wayne Chapman, of Providence, Tony asked Chapman if he had a firearm. Chapman replied yes, but that he had the firearm legally.

At this point, another trooper arrived, and they ordered Chapman to retrieve the gun, which was not legal in New York. It was a starter pistol, which violated the New York State fireworks statute. The troopers followed Chapman into the van and could see rolls of movies and pictures of children in various stages of undress. They also saw adult pornographic magazines with young children on the covers. The movies had handwritten tape on them with descriptions of young boys. Horrifically, Chapman had maps of various towns in New England where he had committed crimes. After Chapman produced the weapon, he was arrested on charges of illegally possessing the starter pistol. After arriving at the police station, the troopers reviewed and documented the van's strange contents. Troopers booked in numerous slides and photos of boys, some of which were fully nude, two 8mm movie films, and various pornographic magazines with nude male children performing sexual acts. Law enforcement was now aware that they had far more on their hands than just a starter pistol and a stolen license plate.

On September 8, 1976, while still in police custody, Waterloo Police interviewed Wayne Chapman. The police were extremely interested in the pictures and videos he had in his stolen converted bread truck. It was during those interviews Chapman began talking about his crime spree across the United States. In those interviews, Chapman would identify at least twelve victims between seven and twelve years old. He went into detail about how he would lure boys into the woods or a secluded area, even sometimes into his apartment on Linwood Avenue in Providence. Chapman admitted to touching the boys and raping them.

He told the police he would often photograph his victims. This was also when Chapman exposed his methods for luring children. Sometimes he would dress as a police officer and tell boys they needed to come with him right away. One can only imagine the betrayal those young boys felt when the man in uniform broke their trust and turned on them. He talked about the story of his lost dog, Scott, who of course didn't exist. The ploy was an easy way for him to prey on the emotions of a child. Chapman said he would tell that story over and over to children. He would find children and plead with them to help him find his lost puppy.

After entering the wood line, he would turn on his victims. He would take pictures after the assault and then ask the victim for his name and address. He would tell them he worked for *Playboy* or owned an adult bookstore and needed their contact information to send them money for their pictures. Surely, money exchanged hands for these photos, but the victims were just pawns in a big scheme. It was during those New York interrogations in September 1976 that Chapman admitted to just how well-traveled he was. He admitted to picking boys up in Connecticut, Virginia, New York, Pennsylvania, Rhode Island, and Massachusetts. New York authorities knew they had a serial predator on their hands, and they had to notify authorities in all the states he had visited or in which he had lived. A teletype went out on the night of September 8 with some of the photos recovered from the van attached. New York officials wanted to identify these boys quickly and noted that it might be smart to investigate some cases that the other agencies might have.

Al Mintz had been working sex crimes for the Providence Police Department for nearly three years at that point. He originally hailed from Jacksonville, Florida. He loved the beaches and the weather in Florida and never planned on leaving. A four-year term in the US Navy changed his plans. Al was posted at the naval station in Newport, Rhode Island. Newport is known for its scenic views and amazing beaches. Celebrities like Taylor Swift now make permanent residences in Newport. It's a haven for the young and beautiful.

One day towards the end of his enlistment in late 1967, Al was enjoying a day out in Providence and noticed a sign outside the Providence Police Department's headquarters encouraging people to apply to become officers. Al had grown to like Rhode Island. He had a girlfriend and the state was located close enough so he could fly home to Florida and be there for a nightcap. He had known plenty of snowbirds who escaped to Florida for a few weeks during the brutal New England winters. He figured he could do the same. Al decided to apply for a job. He figured his military status would at least score him some points with the recruiters. By 1968, Al transitioned from navy sailor to Providence police patrolman.

Al got to work during turbulent times in the United States. The late sixties presented law enforcement with a lot of unique problems. The hippie revolution had already started on Haight-Ashbury in San Francisco. The overwhelming sentiment in the country was that the United States was involved in an illegal and immoral war in Vietnam. An anti-authoritarian movement was brewing. Providence was no different. It was corrupt and was run by guys like Raymond Patriarca. Al worked hard in the early years and kept his nose clean. He made detective rather quickly and by 1974, he was investigating corruption and sex crimes.

Al received that teletype from New York. They had a man in custody with had an address less than two miles from Providence police headquarters. Al immediately scanned the pictures. He noticed a young, fully clothed boy posing in front of a statue of a Labrador retriever and quickly recognized the background. The photo was taken at Roger Williams Park located just eleven miles from where he was sitting. The nearly five-acre park, just east of the Rhode Island State House, was eleven minutes from Chapman's third-floor apartment on dingy Linwood Avenue.

As Al scanned the photos and read the reports, he became increasingly tense. This man haunted the children of Providence right under his nose. Al immediately took a drive over to 129 Linwood Avenue; he needed to see where this monster emerged from every morning. Al noted the apartment's downtrodden condition and saw nearby trash bins flapping open and closed in the late summer wind. The paper blew around the streets and the driveway was clear. Al decided to do some snooping around, opening the trash barrels and looking for anything of interest. He found milk cartons, eggs, and empty cigarette cartons.

Eventually, Al found gas station receipts from all over. Brockton, New York, Rhode Island, and Ohio. He knew these receipts were Chapman's after he had read the reports from New York, and he knew that Wayne was a serial predator who struck at home and in other communities he visited. Chapman lived right off the I95 Expressway; it was easy to get in and out.

It did not take the seasoned detective long to start piecing together Wayne Chapman's life. Al knew he moved to Providence from New York and soon found out Chapman was employed as a janitor at nearby Miriam Hospital in Providence. Al talked to officials at Miriam and Chapman's supervisor; the man knew nothing about his activities and thought of him as a model employee. Chapman was never late and rarely had issues with the staff. Al also intended to connect with law enforcement from the communities in which Chapman could be placed through his receipts.

Al was curious if there were any cases involving child molestation or child pornography in those communities. When he contacted Brockton Police, they mentioned some of their cases that involved child sexual abuse. None seemed to fit. The big case they had was that of David Louison, who went missing just the year prior in June 1974. Al asked for photos of the missing boy. He thought David looked strikingly like some other boys he saw in Chapman's massive photo inventory. Al also heard about another missing boy in Maine, and there was also another case developing north of Boston in Lawrence.

Al was starting to see a pattern. He decided to appeal to his boss for clearance to go see Chapman in New York. Al had some questions and wanted to gauge Chapman's reactions to pictures of the missing boys. He needed to know the full breadth of crimes Wayne Chapman was committing against children in Providence.

On September 16, 1976, Al sat across from Wayne Chapman in Waterloo. This was the second of his two interview sessions. Al had gotten him to open up about his childhood in Jamestown and his alcoholic father.

Chapman began to trust the detective, which is why I believe every confession he made in these two interrogations. He was not capable enough to deny his crimes and stick to a fabricated story. After he was cornered, the floodgates opened. Another dynamic unfolded during the first interview as well: the realization that he was in for some hard prison time.

For most offenders, prison is just part of the deal. It comes with the territory. Like mobsters, the eventuality of prison is something some offenders seemingly make peace with. Al could see that reality setting in for Chapman, who had begun to ask more questions about what prison life would be like for him; even he understood prisons have hierarchies. Al decided to use that concern to his advantage. They made a deal: if Chapman were completely honest, Al would report that he was completely cooperative. Chapman believed that his cooperation could land him in a psychiatric hospital where he could be around his kind, and most importantly, protected.

Al had brought a picture along with him. It was a picture of five-year-old David Louison.

The detective knew Chapman had been in Brockton. Al had the receipts. By this point, he knew wherever Chapman went, a trail of destroyed lives would lie in his path.

Al made small talk first. Like most good interviewers, Al wanted him to get his bearings. Chapman's Southern twang and dead eyes struck him anew. Then Al got to it.

"Have you ever been in Brockton?" Al asked.

Chapman admitted he had been to Brockton a couple of times since settling in the New England area and stated that the prior year, he raped two boys he saw on their bikes. Al thanked him for being so forthright and produced David's picture.

Had Chapman recognized this boy? He had. He told Al that the picture looked like the boy he had taken behind the Melrose Cemetery in Brockton. Al responded that he did a good thing by being honest and asked him to describe the day he met David. Chapman walked Al through that day.

He left his house in the mid-afternoon and decided to head to Brockton "to look for a boy to have sex with." Did Chapman wake up that morning, look at a map of Massachusetts, and throw a dart to hit Brockton? Not likely. He had connections in Brockton and whomever his connections were in the city, they gave this serial offender a lay of the land. Chapman had tapped into his ever-growing network of predators and decided Brockton was prime territory for finding victims. Maybe one of those connections had seen David in the past.

Chapman could have easily lured David from his front yard, maybe with the lost dog story. The Melrose Cemetery sits just 2.8 miles from West Elm Street. It's a short ride. He went on to describe in incredibly graphic detail how he raped the little Brockton boy in the cemetery woods. At one point, David started crying that he was hurt. After Chapman realized David was bleeding, he noticed he wasn't moving. He thought David was probably unconscious, maybe even dead. He started to get nervous. Chapman grabbed the boy's t-shirt and wiped himself off. He left David, who was unconscious, lying alone in the woods. Wayne Chapman exited the wood line believing he probably killed David.

After being notified of Chapman's admission, Massachusetts State Police and Brockton Police searched the area just north of Pearl Street behind Melrose Cemetery. They used metal detectors to locate zippers from David's pants or jacket. They never found a thing. There was no evidence David had been left there for dead. Frank Gentile decided he was going to get a warrant for murder even though there was no physical evidence or a body. Frank saw Chapman's confession—Chapman recognized the boy in the picture and told the Melrose Cemetery story.

That was enough for Frank. *The man made a goddamn confession*, he thought. Frank was close to retirement and had been obsessed with finding David or his abductor for two years. Frank would lie awake at night running through the neighbor's story about David's disappearance in his head. He needed to end this investigation as much for himself as for David's family. He had Chapman within his grasp. The first time Frank saw his face, he knew he had his guy. The old cop did a lot on feel and gut instinct. Chapman raised all his red flags.

He eventually got his murder warrant and started the extradition process in mid-October 1976. Chapman's head was already in the gallows over another boy who went missing that August. Frank thought he could make a compelling case off Chapman's confessions and the circumstantial evidence, even without a body. He just hoped like hell they would find David's.

Eventually, in 1980, police found David's body in a steamer trunk in a basement on Highland Street in Brockton. David was wearing the same number 16 jersey as he was last seen on April 8, 1974. In 1978, a Plymouth County grand jury dropped Chapman's murder charges citing lack of evidence. He recanted his 1976 Melrose Cemetery story. Lawyers had gotten to Chapman and advised him not to talk so freely to law enforcement. He was suddenly not so forthright about his crimes.

As I previously noted, there is zero evidence linking Chapman to David. No eyewitness testimony. Nothing. I have walked Brockton's streets for years asking anyone who may have been in the area that June day if they recalled anything. I petitioned Brockton Police to allow me to view the records. The investigation is considered ongoing and open, so records are sealed. The most baffling thing about David's case is just how his body got to the Highland Street basement. 47 Highland Street is 1.8 miles away from Melrose Cemetery. If you believe Wayne Chapman's confession, which I do, you have figured out just how David's body got from the graveyard to the basement.

One thing I am certain about is that Wayne Chapman was not a criminal mastermind. If he killed David that day, he would have needed guidance on how to get rid of the body. I believe he got that guidance. He never worked alone. He was a cog in a multimillion-dollar machine that produced child pornography. He had a series of handlers wherever he was. When Chapman realized what he had done, he would have needed help.

My first theory is that Wayne immediately moved David's body. There had to be someone else in the shadows. Chapman likely took things too far with David, never setting out to hurt anyone in his crimes. His deal was a lot about his sexual urges and supplying his master with photos. He also could get overzealous. These were just kids. They could be fragile and he could get too rough with them. Chapman couldn't care if the kids cried out in pain, he just kept going; children were simply objects. Chapman had to have known someone in the area who had ties to that Highland Street basement. Whoever this accomplice was, they were probably a local Brockton resident.

I investigated the property history at Highland Street. My thought was the answer might lie in who lived in the seventeen-bedroom, four-story multi-unit dwelling. I wish I could report that an offender was living there during the time that I could tie directly to Chapman. Of all the families that lived on Highland Street, I could not find one person of interest. The property changed hands in 1984 and sold for ninety-two thousand dollars. I must believe someone who lived there was connected to Chapman. Perhaps someone asked to store the steamer there and unbeknownst to the resident, David's body was in it. I must imagine the smell would have overtaken the house in six years, if in fact, it landed there in April 1974.

That likelihood brings me to another theory: perhaps Wayne Chapman *did* leave David in the woods behind Melrose Cemetery.

The police weren't tipped off to the cemetery story for nearly two years. They didn't immediately focus their search there. Law enforcement was entirely focused on the woods behind David's residence in the early searches. If Chapman left the body there, he would have had ample time to go home to Providence and make a phone call. Police found an extensive address book at his residence after he was incarcerated. It contained the names and numbers of many predators from around the country. He had an extensive database on call. Just whom he would have called on is impossible to know, unfortunately. There is one man I have long suspected may have helped him with body disposal.

That man is a serial predator and necrophiliac Charles Pierce. Pierce was a drifter and a carnival worker. Weeks before he died in prison in 1999, he shockingly confessed to murders in Lawrence, Massachusetts, and Connecticut. Charles traveled the United States as a carnival worker and had major access to children, often working the concession stands and conducting the rides. In late November 1969, he was convicted of murdering thirteen-year-old Michelle Wilson, who was abducted in Boxford, Massachusetts. Her family had just moved to town six weeks earlier. Pierce dragged her off her bicycle and shoved her into his van. He strangled her, kicked her in the head, and bit her. He eventually engaged in intercourse with her lifeless body and dumped her body, weighing it down with a one-hundred-pound rock and covering it with leaves.

Of all the sordid, despicable characters in this story, Pierce may be the worst of the worst. He was arrested ten years later for Michelle's killing while serving a prison sentence for raping three young boys in a suburb in Hillsborough County, Florida. He ran his mouth in the Florida prison about murdering Michelle, which came back to haunt him. Perhaps he did it on purpose—Florida prisons were notoriously tough, especially for rapists who pick on young children. He knew that in Massachusetts he could be designated as a sexually dangerous person and get his time commuted to a state hospital. Florida officials agreed to extradite him to Massachusetts where he pleaded to second-degree murder and was given a twenty-year sentence.

By then, Pierce had been diagnosed with cancer, which gave him a sort of plea deal. When he summoned the police to his deathbed at MCI Shirley in Massachusetts, the seventy-nine-year-old made incredible admissions about his life murdering children. He told State Police Sergeant Jack Garvin he picked up a young boy at the Strand Theater in Lawrence, drove the boy up near George's Diner, then murdered and buried the boy in a field near West Street, which is now Massachusetts Electric Company property. The murder, Pierce believed, happened sometime in the 1950s or '60s. Sergeant Garvin was flummoxed about what to do with the information. He knew the Strand Theater had been renamed in 1956, so it had to be before then, but no officer or detective could remember a missing child from that time. The sergeant thought it was probably the ramblings of a demented old man who was near death.

Pierce continued to talk about his crimes. He stated that he killed another little girl in Connecticut and buried her in that very same field. He also confessed in late 1979 to the murder of a missing Tolland, Connecticut, girl, Janice Pockett. In 1981, while serving his sentence at Bridgewater Treatment Center, Pierce once told investigators he was responsible for killing around fifteen to twenty children. He also admitted to killing a Chicago boy, Billy DeSousa, and Mary Catherine Oleschuk, who disappeared on August 9, 1970, in Ogunquit, Maine. Eventually, police took cadaver dogs to the Lawrence field in which he claimed to have buried the bodies. The dogs found no sign of human bodies anywhere.

Probably the spookiest story about Pierce was when state police brought him back to the Boxford murder in 1979; they told him he should probably confess to all the murders he committed in Massachusetts. Police implored him to give the families some closure if he was involved in the disappearances. Pierce sighed; he couldn't give a direct answer. He said he had no idea where to start: "There's just so many," After his response, his face contorted like a man possessed by a demon. He began spitting at the troopers interviewing him. Charles Pierce was diseased, likely with tuberculosis, and was trying to spread it to the troopers questioning him.

So, could Charles Pierce have been in the area the day of David Louison's disappearance in June 1974? Much like Wayne Chapman, Pierce was a prolific traveler, for the same reasons Chapman traveled so much. He was not behind prison walls in 1974, and we know he frequented the New England area and traveled a bit in Florida. Pierce was a pedophile and a total deviant. A truly vicious killer, he was raised in Haverhill, Massachusetts, and became a dishwasher at a seafood joint on Boston's North Shore in the 1970s. He also had some wits about him and was a smart criminal.

Pierce would confess to crimes to get moved to better facilities and remain safe. He would later coach Chapman and Nathaniel Bar-Jonah on the powers of denial while in Bridgewater. He also implored his understudies to get rid of bodies. He was livid that he did not bury Michelle Wilson's body. In his mind, if there was a body, there was a crime. "No body, no crime" was his mantra, and he preached it to Chapman and Bar-Jonah. Pierce saw them as two simpletons who were driven by their sexual desires. They were liabilities, but they took all that stewardship to heart. Zachary Ramsay's and Andy Puglisi's bodies were never recovered. No body. No crime.

I think Chapman could have sought Pierce's counsel on the situation he found himself in at the cemetery. He may have sped down the expressway to Providence and grabbed Pierce's number out of his address book. Things had gone too far and he had a dead boy on his hands. Pierce would be more than willing to do the dirty work and recover the body. What would be his motivation for helping? Perhaps Pierce thought that if Chapman got jammed up for David Louison's murder, he would give up some of the secrets he knew about Pierce. Maybe Pierce assumed a dead boy would bring unwanted heat to their operation. Maybe he had made it known in his circles that if something needed to be done, like disposing of a body, he was the guy to do it. Just a few years later, still at Bridgewater, Pierce and Chapman were close. They ate together. They huddled up together instead of seeking treatment or attending groups. They acted like they had known each other in another life because they had.

Pierce could very well have stuffed David's body into the steamer trunk and deposited it over at Highland Street. Maybe he broke into the basement there. Maybe he had a connection. I have a hard time seeing Chapman doing it by himself. He simply was not mentally capable of handling that scenario. How they met on the outside is hard to nail down. What I know about predators is that they flock to one another. Chapman and Pierce were operating in the same area at the same time. They functioned in the same ecosystem. They were all in it and they all knew one another. One may have been a producer, the other the consumer, or vice versa. Either way, it was the machine that killed David and later Andy. Their killers were likely just cogs in the wheel.

The second enduring mystery of David's disappearance is just how the police became aware of the steamer trunk. The official story from Brockton Police is that they came to Highland Street on a source's tip. The real story has never really come out. There are scant details available as to who tipped off law enforcement. By 1980, Chapman was already serving a lengthy prison sentence. I believe, in a move that no doubt Pierce would have approved of, Chapman led police to the body.

Chapman had designs on moving from the prison where he was serving time into the Massachusetts Treatment Center for the sexually dangerous in Bridgewater. He would be protected there. He would be among friends there, like Nathaniel Bar-Jonah.

Chapman and Bar-Jonah had been best friends on the outside. Things were good at Bridgewater. Chapman could get back to his tribe and would have done anything to get the hell out of prison. He was an incredibly weak man and he felt like his time was coming. The other inmates had it out for him. They called him things like "baby fucker." It was only a matter of time before they killed him.

He cut a deal—he would lead Brockton Police to the body and the police would get him transferred to Bridgewater. The police would never charge Chapman with the murder nor would they ever charge anyone else. At the time, officials probably believed, and rightly so, that Chapman would never see the light of day anyway. So why not cut a deal? Bringing the Louison family some closure was the utmost thing on law enforcement's mind. The case will never be solved because the man who committed the crime has already confessed and led officials to the body. Officials have never come forward with that information and never will. To this day, if you try to do a check on Wayne Chapman in the Brockton Police database, you need a sergeant or above's approval to log in.

Chapman's name, in the eyes of the Brockton Police Department, is red-flagged and blacklisted. Only a supervisor and above can see the results. I have no idea what that means, but it's all very curious. The more questions that are answered, the more questions arise. Melvin Louison died in 1984. He had his son's body but went to his grave with no answers. Later in her life, Naomi could not even speak David's name. She was overcome with grief for her little boy. Years after I wrote this chapter, more reports have come to light about David Louison's disappearance and the murky details about his body being found.

Police had found a shoe that closely matched Louison's foot and the other shoe that was found with his body. The shoe was found near a rest area at a ball field close to where the young boy's body was found. The found shoe was never public record; it was another situation where the police held back information that only the killer would know. Just who found David Louison's body has also been a matter of suspicion and fodder in some circles. The police were alerted to the body by a twenty-year-old man named David O'Meara.

O'Meara was allegedly in the basement of the old rooming house looking for items to steal when he fell upon the steamer trunk with David Louison's remains. O'Meara had come from a rough background and was found dead in a cemetery in Randolph in 1985. I investigated the O'Meara angle for two years in the lead up to the update of this book. What I found was a lot of rumors and innuendo and very little evidence. O'Meara was indeed an abused and vulnerable child who had grown up in the Brockton area in the 1970s and '80s. At the time, he was a very suitable victim for Chapman, but I cannot substantiate any rumors that O'Meara was a Chapman protégé who was groomed by the predator in the 70s, only to go on to tip police off to the body years later. Other reports that O'Meara was removed from Louison's funeral may be true, but I can only print what I can back up. The mystery of Louison's murder is one of the most sordid and sadly forgotten stories in New England history. All I can hope for is people will read this and think of David.

Chapman had a few more secrets to tell, however. We will go back in time, just days before the traffic stop in New York, to August 10, 1976, to Higgins Memorial Pool in Lawrence.

Chapter 5: Lawrence 1975

To fully grasp the entire story here, you must go back to the summer of 1975. Wayne Chapman was not spooked by his experience with the little boy in Brockton. By June 1975, he was right back at it in Seekonk, Massachusetts, which is just about seven miles from where he lived, and I imagine he made connections there.

Chapman had started driving around Seekonk that summer, which was and still is a quiet town. Much like Jamestown, nothing happened there. I was interested in the Seekonk assaults due to their proximity to my house. Chapman was very active in the neighborhoods in which my kids go to school. That strange connection has always unnerved me, even if decades later. Chapman assaulted two boys near Seekonk Memorial Veterans Park, which is located on the main road that leads back from the last sliver of Massachusetts into Providence's East Side. It was easy for him to get in, commit assaults, take his pictures, and get home. I visited Seekonk around 2015. Having worked in the area, it was easy for me to ask lifelong residents questions about the 1970s.

My mission was to get to some middle-aged residents and get a feel for whom Chapman could have related to in the area. That was always the key to my investigation—connecting Wayne Chapman to other predators and building out his network of vile, child abusers. Residents who lived through that era told me that they felt like they lived in a surveillance state. They felt like they were always being watched, maybe even filmed, as they played in parks and rode their bikes. They couldn't quite put their finger on it. Residents told me that a parade of creepy guys would come in and out of the city. I heard stories about a guy who would pay kids to jump up and down on him, even hug him. Kids would get tickets to a show, beer, or money for a little work. Few people remembered June nearly six decades prior. Police files were even harder to come across. I was able to acquire thousands of files for this book, but I could not get anything on the Seekonk case. It was lost to time and history. Chapman had a vast network on the South Coast of Massachusetts. He brutally raped two boys in 1974 in the waterfront town of Fall River located just eighteen miles from Providence.

I found it curious that when he was petitioning for release decades later, he would cite a friend he had living in Fall River as someone who would take him in. What kind of person would take in a man who had just spent decades behind bars for the serial abuse of scores of children? What kind of person would be able to hold their nose as a man who was a major suspect in the death of two young boys walked through their door? A man whom Chapman had known for years was ready to take him in, no problem. They weren't pen pals. They did not meet through some prison website guaranteeing a life of love outside. They were friends for years.

This man is still alive, so I will call him "Matthew" here. Matthew lived in the South Coast area for years and is a sex offender who is on the registry in multiple states. Matthew left a trail of victims across the country in the late 1960s and '70s.

Chapman and his associate eventually did time together at Bridgewater. They were known to socialize often in the treatment center. Matthew told Chapman that if he ever got out from behind the walls, he was welcome to stay with him. Chapman was careful to never tip off treatment center staff that he had a relationship with anyone he socialized with before being there. In this case, he did. I believe Matthew supported Chapman in his crimes in Fall River and Seekonk. They met in the underground child pornography trade. Matthew told Chapman that he was likely to find easy prey in Matthew's neighborhood. Chapman never struck anywhere he didn't have connections. After Chapman was committed for life, Matthew faced charges of rape and abuse of a child and that's how they eventually reconnected at Bridgewater. Matthew's bid was a lot shorter than Chapman's. He told Chapman to give him a ring if he saw the light of day again. It never materialized. Someone thought it was probably a bad idea to shack up with another sex offender after decades in prison. Even after all the years behind bars, Chapman was trying to integrate right back into his tribe. I may sound repetitive, but the point of this book is to tie together the vast network of predators.

What forces brought Wayne Chapman sixty-one miles away from home to the town of Lawrence? It was his crimes in Lawrence in 1975 and 1976 that finally took him down. There is nothing more central or important to unlocking this story than his connections to the city that sits on the Merrimack River. In the 1970s, Lawrence was a tough town; its median population was around sixty-six thousand.

Higgins Memorial Pool stands in the shadows of the Stadium Housing Projects. The pool bears the name of Lieutenant Colonel Edward J. Higgins and was constructed in 1973. It was a welcome addition to the neighborhood for project parents. In the summer of 1975, Wayne Chapman was already stalking the kids at Higgins Pool. Someone familiar with the pool had tipped him off to the easy access to children. It was probably Charles Pierce. If you believe Pierce's confessions, he killed a boy in Lawrence years prior worked at a Woolworth's department store near the pool and was intimately familiar with the Lawrence spot. Chapman could go into the dressing rooms and sneak pictures of kids in various forms of undress. This exact scenario of snagging pictures of undressed children played out repeatedly in various cases against men who I believe were part of Chapman's criminal ring. I believe that is one of the key reasons why he frequents the pool so often. He needed material for the ring and dressing areas were an easy place to get it.

That summer, Chapman lured two boys away from the swimming pool. He took a route only a local would know—from Crawford Street over to Den Rock Park on Winthrop Avenue. Den Rock Park is one hundred and twenty acres of trails, beautiful views, and sheer rock faces. He sexually assaulted the two Lawrence boys there. One boy later reported that he could hear the distinctive sound of an older-generation camera going off during the assaults. That was why he was there. The '75 rapes are a study of both courage and evil.

At one point, Chapman tried to isolate one of the children, his preferred victim. He did have a type, or maybe a customer had a type. Chapman lured the boys with the lost dog routine and suggested the three of them split up to cover the ground. One of the boys immediately sensed something was wrong. He refused to leave his friend's side, for fear Chapman would kill him. Of all the heroes in this book, like Detective Al Mintz or Melanie Perkins-McLaughlin, this young man is right there with them. He remained in harm's way because of his love and concern for his friend. He very well may have saved his friend's life. The boy thought that Chapman might kill him because of the size of the large knife he was carrying.

In all that I uncovered, I could never find a documented instance of Chapman carrying a weapon in the commission of his crimes. Why on that day? I am not sure. Perhaps he had a more sinister plan or thought he might need protection. Lawrence was a tough town, and these were tough project kids—I know, I am one. They were liable to spit in your face if you tried to abduct them. Perhaps he was forewarned about the kids in Lawrence being a bit different than Seekonk, which is a much more affluent community. Later, the victims stated that the only thing that prevented Chapman from using the knife was that he dropped it and couldn't locate it during the assaults in the dense brush of Den Rock Park.

The bravery of that young man has always stuck with me. The undying need to protect a friend from a monster like Wayne Chapman was a major motivation to tell this story. There are heroes and villains in every story. This young man was presented with a choice, and he chose to do the difficult right over the easy wrong. How many of us could say the same? I am sure in his darkest hours, alone at night, he has seen Wayne Chapman's face. I know that feeling. It is completely inescapable, like your DNA. It is always there when you wake up in the morning, an unwanted companion that never leaves.

Chapman stayed off the radar for a bit after the Lawrence assaults in the summer of 1975. He was not immediately suspected of raping the two boys and it would be nearly a year before he was caught. August 1975 to August 1976 would be his last year outside prison or mental health facility walls; he wouldn't see the light of day for decades. Chapman kept associates all over the state, especially in a downtown Boston neighborhood called the Combat Zone. The Combat Zone is centered at Washington Street, between Boylston and Kneeland Streets in the end of Boston. It was just a few miles away from where the Irish Mob was waging a turf war over in South Boston. The Combat Zone was a haven for adult entertainment—filthy adult bookstores lined Washington Street. *The Boston Record* first exposed the Combat Zone in 1960 in a series of articles describing the area's high rates of violence and the presence of navy sailors who would frequent many local haunts while on leave from the Charlestown Navy Yard. Strip clubs and peep show booths popped up everywhere on Kneeland Street. Whatever you were into sexually, there was a place to consume it in the Combat Zone.

Some of the famous establishments included the Naked I Cabaret (outfitted with an actual eye on the signage), Club 66, and the 2 O'clock Club. There were even popular gay clubs like the Playground Café and the Stuart Theater, which was particularly notorious. It was a dingy two-screen theater that the *Boston Globe* once coined "Satan's playground." The Zone was not without corruption either. Police knew the Combat Zone was a haven for illegal gun sales, racketeering, and gambling operations. One Boston Police supervisor told me that you could never arrest anyone in town who might have contact with the Mob for fear of retribution from your supervisors. The Mob ran every racket in town, including prostitution. Officers working area A-1, where the Combat Zone was located, were stuck to arresting low-level pushers and pimps. In 1975, police arrested ninety-seven underage sex workers in the Combat Zone. Their customers were rarely ever charged, however. The relationship between law enforcement leadership and the mafia in Boston was so cozy that nobody batted an eye when a ranking member of the police department from area A-1 showed up at a Gennaro Angiulo associate's funeral.

What did this all mean to a pornography producer like Wayne Chapman? He was essentially working for the Mob. The mobsters from Providence to Boston had their thumbs all in the Combat Zone's adult entertainment. The smut theaters and peep shows paid up at the end of the week the same way the construction guys shook down. The money was due on Friday. How it got there and how it was made was irrelevant. I am certainly not going to say that Chapman showed up to Federal Hill in Providence and broke the bread with organized crime. Chapman would never have gotten close to those guys. The mafia had the run of all the porn theaters in the city, which featured videos of underage performers on certain days. The demand was high for those performances. I talked to at least a dozen sources who begged for anonymity, many of whom I connected with during my years of working in the Combat Zone, who had extensive knowledge of the bookstore and theater scenes in the 1970s.

It was almost an open secret that you could easily access pictures and movies featuring underage performers, and some were self-produced pictures and videos. The men who had this predilection would meet at Combat Zone theaters or in adult bookstore booths and trade photos. They would ask each other for certain types of boys with certain characteristics and body types. Some men were enlisted to be producers by profiting off these evil deeds. It was a major multimillion-dollar business even in the 1970s, which was pre-internet; the industry prospered purely on word-of-mouth.

Chapman stated in later interviews with examiners and police that children were just objects to him in the 1960s and 1970s. He wasn't lying then. Many police officers that pursued these crimes against children were often told by their bosses that they weren't even sure producing child porn was a crime. It's a small wonder these men were able to operate in the shadows for so long. Detective Al Mintz, who got Chapman to confess to many of his crimes, was often told by his superiors to focus on other things besides this weird Wayne Chapman character. He and men of his ilk weren't found mostly because absolutely nobody was looking. When Chapman's apartment at Linwood Avenue was finally cleaned out after he was incarcerated in 1976, police found address books in his home. There were folks in that address book from all over the country. If someone was paying attention, that address book may have exposed so much more.

One more bizarre twist I found during my investigation of the Combat Zone in 1975 was that sources often said there was another man who loved to frequent the theaters. The longhaired man would come by late after the theaters and bars closed and the pimps and pushers hit the streets. He would preach outside the different theaters and make connections with the pornography producers. He would give sermons in the streets about how boys who want to love older men should be allowed to practice that freely. Hell, if they wanted it, why would it be a crime? The man was flamboyant and charismatic, and he referred to himself as a street priest. He had a way of making you believe. I will never forget being in front of the State Transportation Building in Boston on a Saturday when someone first recounted this story to me. The bars and clubs had just emptied, and the Boston Police Gang Unit had the streets blocked off as they often do during a Saturday night in the summer, with an unruly and, no doubt, inebriated crowd. It was during that conversation that I started to put some things together.

The man that the source mentioned was a man named Paul Shanley. In 1975, Shanley lived on Beacon Street in Boston, just 1.7 miles away from the Combat Zone. These early outspoken views that he shared with other predators are the same ones he would espouse a few years later at a conference on sexuality in 1978.

Thirty-two other men and teenagers saw the speech Shanley had given many times in the streets of Boston. The men in attendance were so moved by Shanley's charismatic delivery that they immediately convened after the speech. It was right there that it was decided they would create an advocacy group for "boy lovers," or "BLs" as they called themselves. It was then after a sermon from Shanley that the North American Man/Boy Love Association (NAMBLA) was born. Shanley didn't bother to join the conference after the speech, but it was his ideas that spurned the "original 32" into action. He graduated to abusing children for decades working as a Catholic priest across Massachusetts and in California.

He once even owned a bed and breakfast that catered to gay customers in San Bernadino. Eventually, Shanley spent twelve years behind bars for his crimes against children while in the clergy and died in 2020. NAMBLA still lives in some form today. Many former members have been arrested and gone to prison for crimes against children.

Chapman loved to haunt neighborhoods. He would follow behind school buses and talk about the children he would stalk into his tape recorder. He would drone into his recorder in a semi-Southern twang about how he could hardly wait for the seasons to change in New England. The audiotape from sometime around 1974 to 1976 was introduced into evidence. If you are reading this, you might have heard it. If you haven't, it is a truly dark glimpse into a deranged human being. He is breathing heavily; a school bus is driving in the background. At one point, Chapman lets out a yelp when talking about "getting into some of the stuff that's in those buses." He continues to discuss the feeling he gets when he commits an assault. It's a sickening look into the mind of a predator who's alone with his thoughts.

The singular incident that would propel Chapman into national news was ten-year-old Andy Puglisi's disappearance from the Higgins Memorial Pool in Lawrence. Unlike some of his earlier crimes, Andy's disappearance has been the subject of many news stories, including an Emmy-Award-winning documentary, *Have You Seen Andy?* produced by Melanie Perkins-McLaughlin. Melanie was a childhood friend of Andy's. She was present the day he disappeared. She had gone home to grab a bite to eat while Andy stayed back at the pool. When Andy disappeared, she made a promise that when she grew up, she would find him.

This book and the research are a tribute to that promise. Melanie has worked for decades to get to the truth about her friend's disappearance.

On August 22, 1976, Chapman was back at the pool in Lawrence. Just the year prior, he had taken the two boys from the pool over to Den Rock Park. He heard nothing about the assaults the summer prior when he watched the news. He thought he was in the clear. Now, you may think that a predator like Wayne Chapman might think it's not such a good idea to go back to the place where he committed two brutal attacks. Was he concerned someone may recognize him? What if he saw the kids again? Would they report him? None of these things crossed his mind. He was singularly focused. Chapman had a somewhat pronounced limp, from a childhood bout with polio. He spoke with an accent that was recognizable and was tall and slender with greasy long hair. He was hard to mistake. He found the pool in Lawrence to be fertile hunting grounds and there was no chance he was going to abandon it.

The kids got to the pool in the morning, ready for a long day of swimming.

The temperature in Lawrence in the dead of August was in the mid-nineties. Parents were more than happy to hand over a towel and sunscreen and send their kids to the pool in the project shadows. The kids would never have known they were being watched. There were multiple offenders present that day at the pool—at least five that I have heard. Knowing what I know about predators, I am sure there were more in the shadows. Melanie went home to eat sometime in the mid-afternoon, while Andy stayed at the pool. Around 3:30 p.m., Andy made a phone call home; his brother stated that nothing seemed off about the phone call. Andy was 4'5" and fifty-five pounds with a medium complexion. He was Chapman's preferred victim, which were little boys with brown hair and olive complexions.

Somewhere between 5:30 and 6 p.m., a lifeguard last saw Andy. He was wearing his green bathing suit and sneakers with white stars on the sides. When Andy's mother,

Faith, realized her son didn't come home with his siblings, she began to panic.

She reported to police that her ten-year-old son hadn't arrived home from the pool across the street from the housing projects. A search party was organized and nearly two hundred volunteers showed up. National Guardsmen and a company of Green Berets from the now defunct 10th Special Forces Group out of Fort Devens, under the command of Lieutenant Colonel George Maracheck, mobilized to join in. Andy was last seen one hundred yards east of the housing projects in an area next door to the Naval Reserve Training Center. Faith spent that night wracked with nerves over her missing son.

In the morning, the search commenced. Massachusetts State Police brought in bloodhounds to search the area and Faith watched on as Green Berets like Captain Richard Mika searched an area known as the Pit where witnesses last saw her son. She had a moment of anxiety when one Green Beret unearthed a bundle from the thick brush. The soldier brought the bundle up to his superior and they sifted through the contents. Faith scurried towards the soldiers, but there was nothing of interest to the searchers, just a small calculator and a cassette that Faith didn't recognize as Andy's.

Tips began flooding in from all over the country. A psychic called the Lawrence Police and stated that she had a vision that the ten-year-old was in a diabetic coma and was close to a body of water. Young Andy did have a mild case of epilepsy but he was never diabetic. She said that if he weren't found by that Friday, it would be too late. Police took every tip seriously and ruled them out systematically. Police started their investigation inward, with those closest to Andy, and worked it out. Lawrence officials learned that Andy's mother was divorced from his father, Angelo Senior. Police immediately questioned both parents. Lawrence Lieutenant Joe Fitzpatrick oversaw the case. When he spoke to Faith, she readily admitted her life was a "revolving door" of boyfriends. Like any case involving a missing child, the lieutenant began with the parents. Faith was even given a lie-detector test about Andy, one she promptly passed. Officials also polygraphed Faith's fiancé, Andy's father, and even Andy's paternal grandmother. Even though Andy's mother passed her polygraph, the police were concerned about some conflicting stories the Puglisi family told them. There was a good faction of law enforcement officials in Lawrence who believed someone in the family was hiding Andy early in the investigation.

This hunch was just the beginning of police missteps. Faith recounted a story where an off-duty officer confronted her and interrogated her over Andy's disappearance, cornering her for nearly three hours and berating her. The officer tried to get Faith to call the police department anonymously to report his body's location. He told her she would get the glory for finding him and Andy would receive a proper burial. You can only imagine the hell Faith must have been living in those early weeks of the investigation. Her son is missing and officers who believe she is the real culprit are pursuing her. Faith had no idea about the dark forces her son encountered. She couldn't have. Lawrence Police Captain Carl Schiavone fielded some calls that the boy had been seen right after the disappearance, he ran those threads to the ground, but they proved fruitless.

Schiavone called the disappearance a "puzzle, a big puzzle" in the August 26, 1976, edition of the *Boston Globe*.

The search was called off after an exhausting six days. The 10th Group, which had been so active in Vietnam just a few years prior, was redeployed back to Fort Devens. Scuba divers thoroughly searched the Shawsheen River which is in the nearby town of North Andover. There was no sign of the little boy from Dalton Street. The volunteers, who had a makeshift command post setup and would communicate through CB radios, were told to clear out. Many have argued against the search having ended so swiftly. Perhaps, if they had stuck it out a little longer maybe they could have found Andy's remains.

Faith was so frustrated with the police that she even went to a private investigator. Who could blame her? If your child were missing, what ends wouldn't you go to find answers? I find it very difficult to criticize law enforcement, but there's one thing I do know: the minute an investigator leaves their office in the evening, by the next morning, something more important might be waiting for him or her.

There is never enough funding or staffing to adequately investigate crimes as complex as Andy's. Another case hits your desk the next morning with another set of grieving parents and questions. It's a battle of human nature. The gears of law enforcement investigations grind slowly. In retrospect, this case is a stranger abduction, hence the importance of private investigators who can focus on one case at a time, with little politics or red tape. Faith hired an investigator from the local Independent Investigation Bureau. There was some controversy in the media over Lawrence Police Chief Charles F. Hart denying he ever met with an independent investigator, then returning a day later and confirming he did. It was all unnecessary distractions and pain the family did not deserve or need. Lawrence Police had no solid leads on the disappearance after the search ended on August 28. Andy's disappearance would soon have a suspect, but the mystery would play out for decades.

It was not until the police stopped Chapman in Waterloo that the picture started to become clearer. Chapman had a mountain of pornography in the van that day. He also had rope, fake police badges, state-of-the-art camera equipment, and a pair of socks. Bloody socks. Knee-length socks with wool fabric, made perfectly for cold, New England winters. Detective Al Mintz interviewed Chapman up in New York State for the first time on September 13, 1976, he knew that

Chapman had been in Lawrence. He had the receipts from his trash barrel. Al had some other statements as well.

He had hung around the neighborhood on Linwood Avenue after receiving that teletype from New York. Al noted the number of children who lived in Chapman's neighborhood and decided to ask around a little bit about the man who lived on the third floor. Al was blown away by the stories about the "weirdo" who lived upstairs. Chapman had victims in the neighborhood who were waiting to talk to someone like Al. As soon as the local boys admitted to Al that Chapman had assaulted them, he immediately brought the boys back to his unit located at Providence Police headquarters. Al enlisted Lieutenant Phillip Bathgate, who headed up the juvenile division, to help him interview the victims. After interviewing the kids for more than two hours, Al knew he had a predator on his hands. The detective headed back to his office and wondered out loud how the hell Chapman had been off his radar for so long. Al worked all the sex crimes in Providence. He had arrested the city council president for having sex with an underage boy. He thought he had his ear to the ground. He wanted to nail Chapman's ass to the wall. He was genuinely concerned he might lose his temper and haul off and whack Chapman when they finally met. Al gathered pictures of the victims he had spoken to in Providence. He also took photos of the Louison boy from Brockton and the missing Lawrence boy, Andy Puglisi.

In that first meeting, Al sat down for his interview with Wayne Chapman in Waterloo. Al laid down the gauntlet quickly. He told Chapman that he had talked to some Italian kids in Providence near his home who fingered him as a serial child abuser. They told Al that Chapman had lured them up to his apartment where the dark room was. Al kept going. He said Chapman would need to go into a photo lineup in front of the boys. "How well would that work out?" he asked him.

Chapman knew that this was it for him, so Al seized on that opportunity. He knew that Chapman lived and operated in Mob-controlled cities. In those days, the mafia was more feared than the police. "How would they feel when they find out you're abusing Italian kids?"

Al reminded Chapman that many of their associates were behind bars right now and they would eagerly await his arrival. Al built rapport with Chapman as well. He had already found Chapman's old Sunday school certificates citing his perfect attendance and his recognition from the national 4-H leadership as an outstanding volunteer. The fact that Al knew all this impressed Chapman and seemed to ease him. The detective told Chapman he'd better be honest about everything; it was his only hope. Al told him he didn't belong in prison; he belonged in a hospital—he had problems.

Chapman did have some issues he needed to work out and he agreed. He said he did what he did because he needed love. Al showed Chapman Andy's photo and said he knew Chapman had been in Lawrence; did he know the boy? Chapman went on to describe the area around the pool. The dense woods. The gravel pits. Al was struck, when he viewed the scene for himself sometime later, just how accurately Chapman had described the area around Higgins Memorial Pool. When he asked Chapman to describe what happened to the boy, he described in excruciating detail what happened to Andy. Much like his Louison confession, he was graphic. I will spare you the details, but at a certain point, things got out of hand. Andy was bleeding from his backside and wasn't moving.

Chapman panicked.

This goes along with my theory. I believe the killings of the two boys were not necessarily planned; they were just a by-product of his cruelty when he was out stalking. Al asked him if the boy had been ill, perhaps things went too far. Wayne agreed. After he made his confession, he stopped talking for a bit. He said that Al had him "believing his lies," but Al was unconvinced. He knew what Chapman had in him—a cold-blooded, rotten-to-the-core predator.

After Lawrence's officials got wind of the arrest and subsequent interviews, they immediately got his booking photo and went to re-interview witnesses. The first person re-interviewed was the lifeguard who had last seen Andy at the pool around 5:45 that afternoon. She immediately recognized Chapman's "vacant eyes" as the man she had seen that day with Andy. He was following the young man into the locker room after he exited the pool. The lifeguard also recognized the man from the very next day. While the searches were raging on for the missing boy, the lifeguard said that Chapman arrived at the pool to ask questions about why search parties were scouring the area. The two boys from the previous summer were also re-interviewed. Had they recognized this man as their assailant? Yes, they did. Chapman had already struck at that pool once and he came back. Another child came forward and said that Chapman had been asking kids all around the pool that day for help finding his lost dog. This young boy had refused, thankfully, but the evidence was starting to mount for Lawrence Police. Chapman might be their guy.

Another boy came forward years later claiming that he and Andy were abducted together. The boy was just four years old in 1976. He said that he and Andy agreed to help Chapman find his lost dog. Andy immediately became suspicious when they arrived in the woods and saw two other men hiding in the bushes. Andy sensed an ambush and immediately screamed for his friend to run away. He even ran behind this young boy to push him further down the trail and out of the woods. When the little boy crested the top of the hill he was on, he turned around to locate Andy. When he saw Andy, he saw two men leaning over him. Andy was pinned under a large boulder with the weight of two grown men on top of it.

I realize, dear reader, that you might be teleporting to this moment, and you're stomping Chapman's guts out and bringing Andy to safety. It's a healthy reaction. I would never advocate for violence, but we are all human.

The last thing the four-year-old boy heard was his friend Andy screaming at the top of his lungs for help. The little boy was so stricken by this visual and this attempted assault that he could not speak of this incident for years. It took the young man nearly six years before he could recount this story to police. The last act of Andy's life was saving his friend from monsters like Wayne Chapman. Incredibly, this young man's report is nowhere in Lawrence Police files. Unfortunately, during the subsequent years after Andy's disappearance many pieces of evidence would just simply go missing. It would call into question Lawrence's Police tactics and overshadow some of the great work Lawrence officials would do in the ensuing years.

Al had convinced New York officials to extradite Chapman to Rhode Island.

He had twelve days to serve on a weapons charge for the possession of the starter pistol in his van. Al immediately had Chapman moved to the state hospital in Cranston. The Cranston psychiatric wing was an offshoot of the Adult Correctional Institution, which housed the toughest inmates in Rhode Island. Al was ready to get to work on Chapman and get him to once and for all admit to his crimes in Providence, Brockton, and of course, Lawrence. Al thought Chapman had turned on him a bit, however. Chapman confessed and then recanted, all in the same interview, the last time they met on September 15. He had pissed Al off. The detective had started to think about him in his off hours. He needed to nail Chapman down on what they both knew he was guilty of. Al had something in his figurative toolbox he thought might get Chapman to talk: sodium pentothal.

The drug was highly controversial. Al didn't care; it was a fair practice at the time. The Central Intelligence Agency

(CIA) made a habit in those days of using sodium pentothal on guerillas they captured in the Killing Fields of Southeast Asia. The precursor to the CIA, the Office of Strategic Services, often wrote in their cables from the Pacific Theater about the effects of sodium pentothal on war criminals. OSS officers would write about the effects, noting that it was like alcohol and that a subject's inhibitions would drop under the drug's influence. It's hard to imagine this not being a violation of the Fifth Amendment (the right to remain silent), but it was often used at the time. Law enforcement, which had to deal with a tidal wave of professional liars, saw it as an equalizer. Chapman became a professional during that time. He had been running with a circle of people who schooled him to shut his mouth.

Al was preparing for another round of interviews with Chapman at the state hospital in Cranston. He brought the sodium pentothal and Chapman agreed to take it. It was here, during these interviews, that the picture would begin to clear—or get more muddied, depending on how you look at it. Al was fielding calls from all over the country on Wayne Chapman. The teletype sent from New York after his traffic stop landed in police departments as far as Nebraska. Everyone wanted to talk to him about cases they had been investigating in their jurisdiction. Al had another missing boy he had wanted to talk about: Jason Foreman, the child from South Kingstown, Rhode Island, was still missing. Al knew no amount of distance was out of Chapman's reach and he strongly suspected him in that case. Chapman flatly denied ever meeting Jason.

***

It wasn't until April 1982 when another boy was apprehended for another crime that details emerged. Michael Woodmansee lured a fourteen-year-old paperboy into his home, giving him alcohol and then trying to strangle him. The paperboy struggled and got away from Michael. The teen ran home and told his father about the attempted strangulation. The boy's father marched over to Michael's home and punched him square in the jaw and when the father exited Michael's home, he flagged down a police officer. The officer immediately took Michael to the police station. The officers had a strong hunch during the interview that Michael might have some information on Jason's seven-year-old cold case.

After hours of interrogation, Michael told police that they would find a journal in his home about the Foreman murder, but he stressed everything he wrote in there was pure fiction. When police finally searched the home, they found the journal as well as five-year-old Jason's skull. Presumably, Michael kept Jason's skull hidden for seven years before it was discovered. Michael was a sixteen-year-old junior in high school when he killed Jason. Wayne Chapman was telling the truth back in 1976; he did not know about Jason Foreman's disappearance. Incredibly, Michael was released from prison on September 28, 2011. Citing the controversial "Good Time" law that is on the books in Rhode Island, Michael served just shy of thirty years for the murder of a five-year-old boy. True to form, Jason's father was very clear in the media about Michael's release, stating that he planned to murder Michael as soon as he was released. As of 2021, Michael Woodmansee was still alive and living somewhere in Southern Rhode Island.

**

Al knew he had Wayne Chapman nailed. The two boys who made the complaint about the summer 1975 rape had already positively identified Chapman as their assailant. They planned to testify against him at trial. Some people were certain these two young boys were going to take this man off the streets for a long time. David Louison and

Andy Puglisi's disappearances were the main topics of conversation. Al recounted this story to me on multiple occasions for my research. At some point during the interviews, Al was pushing hard on Andy's disappearance. Weak-minded Chapman began to crack.

Eventually, he blurted out, "I killed the kid. Okay?"

The detective was ecstatic; it was all coming out. At that crucial moment, Al's interrogation partner pounced and asked Chapman to tell him about how he murdered Andy. Al knew that was the wrong approach. He knew Chapman saw himself as some sort of sympathetic figure. Even Chapman knew that the crimes he committed were so reprehensible he had to shield himself from them by making himself the victim. It was merely a defense mechanism. Al Mintz, who looked like a mobster himself, always in a suit and slicked-back black hair, learned you had to massage the information out of Chapman with a sympathetic tone. Even decades later, Al would recount that that moment was the one where he lost the confession.

On September 17, Wayne Chapman accompanied Detective Frank Gentile and state police in a search behind Melrose Cemetery in Brockton. Chapman knew all of this was for naught, but Frank was able to secure the murder warrant. All of this was just a charade of course Chapman knew he wasn't there and that there would be no trace of David Louison found in any of the searches the twenty state troopers and a hoard of Brockton police detectives made. It's interesting to note the misdirection Chapman ran with police at the time.

Officials spent a ton of time searching areas based on Chapman's confessions in those interviews with Al Mintz.

Chapman made some other interesting admissions while under the sodium pentothal. During the interview, Al threw down a picture of Andy Puglisi. Chapman said that the boy looked very much like the boy that he lured away from a pool with another much younger friend. Chapman described what Andy was wearing, right down to his green bathing suit. Search parties went out again behind the pool and the areas surrounding it but turned up absolutely nothing. It was not until October 1976 that Wayne Chapman was publicly named as a suspect in Andy's case. The media took right to it. Things were starting to move fast for the cases against him. Governor Michael Dukakis signed an extradition warrant. He was to stand trial for the rape cases in 1975 against the two Lawrence boys. Before he could be extradited, Bristol County got in on it as well. He was also indicted on the three rapes in Seekonk and Fall River.

Al Mintz was also concerned about one thing that was found in Chapman's van. The bloody knee-high wool socks. Al thought that they looked like something a little girl would wear with a Catholic school uniform. Al thought he better ask anyway. Perhaps Faith Puglisi would recognize the socks? Al knew that Andy came from a big family and had sisters. Maybe the socks belonged to one of them? Al let Lawrence officials know that there was a pair of bloody socks in the evidence room in Providence. Faith rode south down Interstate 95 to look at the socks. The thing was, the morning of the disappearance, Faith had been ribbing her ten-year-old son over the fact he had put his sister's knee-highs on.

Like most kids his age, Andy had either misplaced his socks or needed some clean laundry. He woke up the morning of the disappearance unable to locate a fresh pair of socks and solved his problem by throwing on a pair of his sister's wool knee-highs. Faith admonished her son that morning, saying it probably wasn't a good idea to wear those thick, heavy socks on an early August day that was promising to be in the mid-nineties. Andy headed out in them anyway; he wasn't going to let a silly thing like socks get in the way of a day at the pool with friends.

Al recounted how Faith just about fell over when she saw the wool socks. They belonged to her daughter. They were the socks Andy had left the house wearing that morning. She recalled the conversation with her son with incredible clarity. Al thought he had Wayne dead-to-rights even though the Lawrence case wasn't his. Chapman had a pair of bloodied socks in his van that the mother of the missing boy positively identified. *It was a slam dunk*, he thought, and he planned on handing the evidence over to Lawrence.

The complaints were issued on October 6, 1976, for the two sexual assaults in 1975. At that time, Chapman was under a thirty-day observation period at the Rhode Island State Psychiatric Hospital. He knew he currently existed in purgatory before prison's hell. It wouldn't be long before the extradition came through and he would be in front of a jury on at least the rape charges. Fortunately for him, DNA testing did not exist yet to test the blood on the wool socks found in his van.

Chapman still recanted all statements he made about Andy and denied involvement—even with eyewitness statements placing him at the pool that day. The police were not confident a jury would look at that evidence and vote guilty without a reasonable doubt. They bid their time and continued to search for Andy and Hammer Chapman when they could. He would sit in purgatory until the 1977 New Year. In January, Chapman was extradited to Massachusetts to face charges. In May 1977, the two young victims told their story to a grand jury.

About a year after Andy's disappearance, Chapman was found guilty of two counts of sexual assault. A jury in Essex County needed little time to convict him of the capital offenses. Lawrence Police Captain Joseph Fitzpatrick and Detective Thomas Carroll, along with other witnesses, all testified. The entire trial was closed off to the media and the public under Massachusetts General Law Part IV, Title II, Chapter 278, Section 16, which allows a judge to close a trial that involves sex offenses against minors. The judge presiding over the speedy trial sentenced Wayne Chapman to two concurrent fifteen- to thirty-year sentences, which meant he had no less than fifteen and no more than thirty years to serve.

Chapman was sentenced to serve his term at MCI-Cedar Junction, better known to locals as Walpole Prison. The prison sits just off a main road in the shadows of where the six-time Super Bowl champion New England Patriots play their home games at Gillette Stadium. Walpole is a maximum-security diagnostic center that contains some medium-security components. The prison was well known for violent uprisings and even murder. An inmate murdered Albert DeSalvo, the self-confessed Boston Strangler at Walpole in 1973, just a few years before Chapman's arrival. When he heard his assignment to Walpole, he thought he was given a death sentence. He knew about prison hierarchy and was sure he was a dead man. You might think this sentence would have a neat and tidy ending to the story. The bad guy gets his comeuppance and is sentenced to decades in prison. It's really kind of the beginning.

There are so many questions to answer. Who were the other sex offenders at the pool with Wayne Chapman on the day of Andy's disappearance? Was Chapman or anyone else ever charged with Andy's murder? Who was the other man Andy's four-year-old friend saw? How did Chapman stay alive in prison? Whatever came of Nathaniel Bar-Jonah and Charles Pierce?

What was uncovered from the ensuing years after 1977 is shocking. One thing that Wayne Chapman never figured out is that Andy's friend, Melanie Perkins, would do anything to make good on her promise. She would haunt Wayne Chapman for decades. Also, something was going on in a nearby Massachusetts city just forty-two minutes away from Lawrence, 31.6 miles to be exact. What was happening would send police across the country scurrying out to make arrests and destroy a generation of youth.

The apparatus was becoming exposed.

CHAPTER 6: REVERE 1977

It was a neighborhood rumor. Some of the neighbors had seen it and found it curious. Some neighbors thought he was a weird guy. He would come out of his house in the morning, and they would say hello, but he would just look down. He was always looking down, always in his head.

Nobody saw the inside of his apartment. He didn't do neighborhood dinners or invite people over for the bridge. He kept to himself. The neighbors had begun to talk about the little boys and young teenagers coming in and out of his place, sometimes shirtless. They would reek of marijuana. Sometimes you could see them on the back porch with unmistakable red, white, and blue Budweiser cans, especially in the summer months. There was also a parade of men who came in and out of the apartment. Maybe these boys were their children? It was a party house. Everyone knew it. Maybe the neighbors thought they were mistaken about the boys' ages. *They just* looked *young*; they thought. Either way, in those days, people mostly minded their business. They mostly gossiped at the coffee shop or the bus stop. There was no social media to share stories about the weird neighbors.

Then it happened.

The police raided the apartment at 242 Mountain Avenue in Revere and the rumor mill started churning. A child sex ring? The weird, quiet neighbor was pimping out boys?

On March 2, 1978, a young Boston city employee sat silently in a courtroom as his fiancé watched on. She would dry her eyes now and again. They were wet and heavy from crying. Thirty-one-year-old Pasquale Intraversato was facing two eight- to twelve-year terms. He was being sentenced that day and he was headed to MCI-Cedar Junction at Walpole. Intraversato pleaded guilty. He *was* guilty and there was no point in dragging his fiancée through a trial. Assistant District Attorney Leonard J. Henson had done a great job prosecuting the case.

He laid out in graphic detail just what Intraversato had done to the two young boys. Intraversato lived on Salem Street in the North End of Boston. The jury considered that Intraversato had volunteered as a youth coach. He coached Little League Baseball and Softball as well as hockey.

Police discovered Intraversato through the address book of a long-time offender, a true menace to society: city bus driver and fellow North End resident Frank Damiano.

By 1978, Damiano was serving twenty-three life sentences for decades of crimes against children. Few details are available about his upbringing, but we know his offending history began at age twenty-one. In 1950, Damiano was serving time at California's Mendocino State Hospital for a sodomy charge. He was then transferred to Boston State Hospital, which was originally called the Boston Lunatic Asylum, in 1951. Later that same year, Damiano was released in Boston instead of being sent back to California, where he stayed and continued to wreak havoc. In 1953, he was arrested again for open and gross lewdness and suspicion of rape and was released with a suspended sentence of three months.

Just three months later, he was again charged with sexually assaulting a young female child. Again, he received a three-month suspended sentence. In November 1953, just a month after his last arrest, Damiano was again arrested and charged with sexually assaulting a young female. This time, he received a nine-month sentence. Damiano was released from jail in the spring of 1954. During the next year and a half, he would accumulate three more arrests for lewdness, contributing to the delinquency of a minor and violating parole. Again, he was not given more significant prison time and was only given a suspended sentence. This time, the judge sternly warned Damiano that if he saw him again, he would get the three- to five-year sentence he had "hanging over his head." The judge ran into him again in September 1956 and was promptly awarded the sentence the judge had promised.

Frank Damiano was also convicted on other sodomy charges he had pending in the state and sent back to Walpole for at least three years. Only twenty-three months later, though, he was paroled and a free man again. Of course, he had zero ability to stop offending. He managed to keep his nose clean until 1959 when he was arrested on sodomy charges and thirteen counts of open and gross lewdness. This time he knew his sentence wouldn't be suspended; he thought maybe he was going away forever. Surely, the system was sick and tired of him offending repeatedly. He received a nine- to twelve-year prison sentence and was bused back to Walpole.

There were no sex offender treatment programs I could find that existed in Walpole prison in the late 1950s or early 1960s. Most people had no handle on what exactly a sex offender was. Frank Damiano received no treatment while in Walpole, and as far as I can find, he received no psychological assessment. He was allowed to sit in his cell and rot. His first parole review came up in 1966 and he was promptly released again. He hit the Boston streets in late 1966. From 1966 to 1972, he was caught driving without a license in the North End and he was arrested in possession of a stolen motor vehicle. He had three new sex crimes charges: indecent exposure, corrupting the morals of a minor, and sexual assault. He was back in court. Incredibly, through the appeals processes and myriad suspended sentences, Damiano was not sent to Bridgewater until 1972.

The Bridgewater Correctional Facility houses a few separate units and operations. There is the Old Colony Correctional Center, which is a minimum and medium prison; the Bridgewater State Hospital, which is a medium-security psychiatric treatment center that treats a variety of psychiatric patients with varying ailments; and then there is the Massachusetts Treatment Center. To tell a coherent story, I will refer to the treatment center as simply Bridgewater here.

One activity my father and I always bonded over was fishing. Growing up as a child, we would often find the blue spots on Massachusetts maps and head that way. We loved the adventure of finding out-of-the-way fishing holes. The best freshwater fishing hole I have ever found in Massachusetts is in the wooded area directly behind Bridgewater's facilities. I still remember being young, probably about eight years old, driving past the barbed-wire fences around the back through an incredibly thick wooded area to get to the small ponds out back. I would often wonder just what the hell we would do if the car got stuck. *Would the inmates eat us? Would we have to walk home? Arrested?* It was all quite jarring. There were signs everywhere that read, "NO INMATES PAST THIS POINT." It was incredibly eerie, but what did I know? As I got older, I often fantasized about stealing the sign closest to the water. Who would know? It would make interesting décor. My conscience wouldn't let me, though. The bass were always biting at that fishing hole. I realize now that the fishing was so good because either nobody knew about the spot or simply did not dare to ever go back there. Sometimes we would go at night when bass fishing is best, and we could hear the bells ringing inside the facilities. Almost like a school lunchtime bell.

Sometimes, the guards would admonish inmates over the loudspeaker. I was fascinated by these facilities that seemed to sprout out of nowhere in a random Massachusetts town. Bridgewater is also known for its deep roots in the paranormal. The Bridgewater Triangle is an area that encompasses the towns of Bridgewater, East Bridgewater, Abington, Raynham, Taunton, and Brockton.

There have been reports that date back seven decades of UFO sightings in the Triangle. Giant killer snakes and even Bigfoot have made appearances in the Triangle's wooded areas. The folklore about the ghosts and monsters that inhabit the surrounding Hockomock Swamp just adds to the unnerving atmosphere around the treatment center. The real ghouls, of course, are behind the treatment center walls. As time went on and I got older, I became fascinated with what went on behind those walls. I realized the worst the state had to offer usually landed there in one form or another. My childhood fishing spot, where I used to watch older men fly model planes in the woodlands, is a major part of this story.

In 1895, Massachusetts established the Treatment Center as the "asylum for insane criminals at Bridgewater." The renowned Dr. Arthur Harrington was its first medical director. Through the late 1800s and early 1900s, Bridgewater was an insane asylum for both men and women. The first major incident at Bridgewater happened during the height of World War II in 1942. Two young patients attempted an escape and stabbed three guards, but the guards only suffered superficial wounds, and the would-be escapees were sent to solitary confinement. They served decades afterward. 1967 was the year the Bridgewater Treatment Center would ascend into national consciousness.

Producer Frederick Wiseman and director John Marshall were allowed access to Bridgewater. Their movie, *Titicut Follies,* was filmed over twenty-nine days at the campus. Wiseman became fascinated with Bridgewater while attending law school at Boston College and began calling its superintendent the year prior, asking for permission to make a film about the asylum. More than eighty thousand feet of film was shot during the shoot. The unusual name was a homage to the annual talent show the staff would perform for the patients. The name *Titicut* was a reference to a Wampanoag tribe that ran the nearby Taunton River. Wiseman's original agreement with the superintendent was called into question as soon as people started attending the movie. Originally, the superintendent agreed that staff would follow Wiseman during the entire shoot. Also, filming would only take place when staff approved of it. The patients being filmed would also have to agree to the filming and be deemed mentally competent. Later, the film was shown at the 1967 New York Film Festival. In 1968, a Massachusetts judge ordered that all film copies be recalled. The Commonwealth of Massachusetts filed an injunction on the film's release, citing a "breach of oral contract" and a violation of patients' privacy rights. A judge ultimately agreed with the State and all copies of the film were ordered to be destroyed in late 1968.

Wiseman believed that the real reason for the injunction was that the film portrayed the State in a bad light. The shocking scenes of patients being force-fed and guards taunting naked patients were galling. Nearly twenty years later, an inmate who was restrained for two and a half months was given a cocktail of psychiatric drugs and died by suffocation. The inmate could not even swallow food. The death shined a new spotlight on Bridgewater.

The dead patient's lawyer, Steven Schwartz, openly cited Wiseman's film in statements. He stated, "There is a direct connection between the decision not to show the film publicly, and my client dying twenty years later," which pressured the media to rerelease the film.

In 1991, a judge cited that with thirty-four years passing patients' dignity was less of an issue. Most of the patients portrayed in the film had died. The judge ordered that a scroll be placed at the bottom of the film's showing, stating essentially that officials at Bridgewater had since cleaned up their act and conditions were better. The film was shown for the first time on September 4, 1992, on PBS. Charlie Rose introduced the film with warnings about the graphic content. The film is now widely distributed and can be viewed on channels like Turner Classic Movies.

Just five years after Wiseman and Marshall's documentary, Frank Damiano arrived at Bridgewater. The staff took inventory of Damiano's convictions and noted he had been offending since his teens. His first stint at the asylum in California was for sex offenses. Every year that he was not behind prison walls, he was hurting children; he was a true menace to society. So, what did the staff at Bridgewater recommend? Did they condemn him as a dangerous predator who should never see the light of day? Not exactly.

Damiano was back out on the streets of Boston by late 1974. All he needed to do was check in with the probation department. By the spring of 1977, he was working in Boston as a city bus driver for Management Transportation Corporation, which was based on Columbus Avenue downtown. His employer had no idea that their new bus driver had spent eleven out of the last twenty-six years in prison or state mental hospitals for a multitude of crimes. Damiano's employer could not have known. In 1972, the Privacy Act was passed in Massachusetts, which guaranteed people with criminal records their right to privacy so they could gain employment. Employers were prohibited from obtaining prospective employees' critical background information.

You can see where this law might help a certain segment of the population. Damiano is in many respects an outlier. The Privacy Act prohibited law enforcement from disseminating any information to private businesses about people's criminal history. The transportation company's manager went on record about his company's hiring processes. John Ferrer, Damiano's direct boss, stated that all that was expected of Damiano was a certificate of good health from a doctor, a valid driver's license, and a letter from his probation department. Ferrer asked for his probation letter, but Damiano immediately exploited a system loophole. In the days before we lived in an instantaneous world, you had to rely on getting physical documents. Damiano lied to his boss about his probation records and said the probation department was eight to nine months behind in issuing paperwork to probationers. His boss accepted the excuse. He had experienced longer-than-normal wait times with other employees in the past, but eight to nine months? Ferrer was feeling pressure from his bosses to get bus drivers on the road and decided to wait it out and hire Damiano anyway. Of course, Damiano was lying. He knew all he had to do was go to the court and fill out a one-page request for his probation records. He also knew that his records would arrive through the mail, at his home of record in about ten days. He had no plans on ever giving those records to Ferrer. Damiano was doing what all predators do—positioning himself close to prey.

I often hear pundits and people on the street say that it's no surprise Catholic priests get caught up in sex abuse scandals. "They have to remain celibate." "They can't get married." "They are so deprived!" This opinion seems to excuse the behavior, even letting them off the hook. That line of thinking is utterly absurd. Pedophile priests don't just become pedophiles due to their job constraints; those priests go into the priesthood *because* of their pedophilia.

When you are that depraved, your sexual appetite fuels everything you do in life. Those priests who abused boys were always pedophiles. They joined the priesthood to gain positions of power so that they could better manipulate children to abuse them. The cloth is just a front. That was exactly what Frank Damiano was doing in his school bus driver position. It wasn't long before he was asking the boys he met on the bus to meet up with him at his apartment on Margaret Street in the North End. He would encourage the boys to engage in sexual activity.

Often, he would snap pictures of them and even record movies. He even brought some boys he met on the bus to an apartment on Mountain Avenue in Revere, just minutes away from where young Leigh Savoie disappeared in 1974.

The apartment's owner would pay Damiano to bring him fresh kids and he would give a few bucks here and there to the kids. All these kids were in elementary school. A few bucks could buy some candy or maybe some baseball cards. Damiano made a good bit of money selling the kids to the guy on Mountain Avenue. Eventually, one of the kids who rode the bus spoke up to the police with a story to tell. His bus driver had been taking him to a third-floor apartment in Revere and was given drugs and alcohol. He was encouraged to engage in sexual acts with men and other children; his bus driver was Frank Damiano.

Police quickly descended on that North End apartment on Margaret Street. Police questioned him about his activities with the children, and he was initially very tight-lipped about his lifestyle. Damiano knew if exposed he was done forever. He planned on denying it all until the end. Police searched his apartment and found pictures of children and a few movies. They also found his address book. In the days before you could plug a person's contact information into a minicomputer that fits in your pocket, you had to write down the names and information about your contacts. Damiano had a vast list of associates. One name that interested police was a man named Richard Peluso.

Peluso had sex crimes charges from 1962 and 1963 on his record. He was living in Revere on Mountain Avenue. The boys who went to the police had complained about the apartment. They stated that the place was often overrun with children and adults, where payments were made and alcohol flowed. Some men who came in had funny accents. Not Boston accents, but almost Southern drawls. They weren't from around here, the boys concluded. The police started to think they had a brothel, or maybe a prostitution ring on their hands.

In the winter of early 1977, police applied for search warrants for Peluso's apartment. They needed to thoroughly search the premises. Plainclothes officers had already begun surveilling the residence in December 1976. They took note of the men coming in and out and gathered intelligence on Peluso, whom they observed as the ringleader. He was a self-employed advertising salesman who made his hours. This point was important to the police. If he was at work nine to five, then who ran the operation? He, as they initially suspected, ran the operation right out of his apartment.

That same month, a grand jury convened. Evidence and testimony were presented from the victims in Damiano's case. By that time, he was in Dedham, Massachusetts, at the Norfolk County House of Corrections. He was undergoing psychological evaluations and was also beginning to talk. He suggested they check out the house and gave them some names associated with the Revere apartment. Men from as far as Atlanta were alleged to have participated. All these statements were presented to the grand jury, which issued secret indictments for Richard Peluso and several others. On June 3, 1977, police raided the home on Mountain Avenue in the predawn hours and everything was about to be exposed.

Richard Peluso was home when the police knocked on the door. Officers from the Revere Police Department, Massachusetts State Police, and at least one federal official served Peluso, who was clad in a t-shirt and boxer shorts, the search warrant. No boys were present at the time of the raid. Peluso was immediately cuffed and told to sit on the couch in the living room. The search warrant was handed to him. The premises were to be thoroughly searched by the police and Peluso could do nothing about it. The police went to work and hit pay dirt immediately. Officers uncovered more than one hundred pictures of boys in various stages of undress and engaging in sexual activities. Videos were also uncovered involving young children in the same acts. Peluso was immediately booked into the Charles Street Jail in downtown Boston and the interrogation began.

Officials were hoping he would give up who else was involved in the apparent sex ring. Peluso was far more interested in catching a break in his sentence. He knew the police had a mountain of evidence against him. All he could focus on now was his accommodation during his inevitable prison stay. Police had already seized his address books. They knew who he associated with and were in the process of rounding them all up and taking them into custody. Peluso gave police some names but had also made some bizarre statements.

When police questioned him on the list of names, he stated that he couldn't reveal all of them.

"Why not?" the detectives asked.

Peluso said that there were certain big shots involved in the sex ring. At one point, he stated that he "didn't want any contracts out on" him and that "there are names I will not give you." He insinuated that organized crime figures might have been involved, maybe even public officials. Detectives continued to quiz him on who exactly his customers were.

"Were there any police officers?" the detectives asked.

Peluso said he didn't know of any.

"There aren't any?" the police asked.

"There *weren't* any," he stated.

Peluso rolled over on many of his customers. Police were not entirely convinced they had even scratched the surface of how many men were involved. Sure, they had the names of the major players, the men who had patronized his apartment often. The men who conspired with him to pimp boys out, but the police wanted everyone. Officials had a hard time letting go of the customers who visited once or twice a month. Officials scoured Peluso's vast, handwritten address books. Massachusetts officials also wanted to understand the inner workings of his diabolical operation.

Peluso, whose father founded a very prominent advertising agency in town said that he met the boys everywhere—sometimes at donut shops in Revere. Other men brought some to his apartment. When word got out in the gay community surrounding Revere gay bars in Boston, especially in the Combat Zone, were abuzz. One source told me he started hearing about the pay-to-play ring as early as late 1974. The man had been working as a bouncer in the Combat Zone. He was not gay, but he was very connected to the gay crowd, which was allegedly very loose with information.

This source was astounded with the openness in which the rumor mill churned. Folks just started to show up on Peluso's doorstep. The men who got rolled up in the sex ring came from a vast background. The arrests would shake communities, prestigious schools, and even major hospitals. Some of the men had no prior arrests and were looked at as trusted community members, but some had very sordid backgrounds.

I waded deeper into the waters of the 1970s gay bar scene than I ever expected I would. I was very active on message boards filled with nostalgic older gay men who lived in or frequented Boston during that time. The scene was a subculture all to itself in those days. I was fortunate to interview many men who were part of that scene. Most were gracious and patiently answered all my emails and text messages about the culture. What I was trying to accomplish was simple: I wanted to understand the scene where Chapman and his cohorts circled in the periphery. Chapman's story cannot be told without mentioning this scene. While I am positive that nobody told them to go out and kill. His crimes were committed to feed a much more vile monster.

The Regency Health Center in Boston's Winthrop Square is where the news of the ring started to catch fire. The Regency was a well-known gay bar and was just one of a few of Roger Spear's major haunts. Spear was very active in the underground gay community. Outside of the Regency, he would mostly frequent the seedy Playland Café on Essex Street downtown. Playland was known for its edgy clientele and year-round Christmas light display. It was also known for the sheer number of hustlers and pimps who would congregate outside after the club let out for the night.

Spear had disposable income to spend on account of being the president of an investment firm in affluent Wellesley. Spear would often open his Wellesley home to gay hustlers from all over the country. Men like Eddie Kopacz would often sleep at his house. Eddie would later make national headlines when he was charged with shooting another gay hustler from Baltimore named Curtis Dale Barbre. Curtis' mutilated body was found under a bridge. Eddie testified under oath that he was in California on February 2, 1978, the day of the shooting. He also testified that when he was in Massachusetts, he mostly socialized with Spear and a man named Mark Davis. Mark was a social worker at the Massachusetts Department of Youth Services. He would often counsel youth who came from disadvantaged families and was later indicted for his role as a customer in the Revere sex ring.

As years passed, rumors persisted that Spear and Davis were involved in Curtis' murder, which included everything from Spear supplying the shotgun used to kill Curtis to helping move his body and dump it under the Lowell Connector. Eddie even made statements to police implicating Spear and Davis. He later recanted those statements, saying the police "beat the names out of me." Spear and Davis would often complain to the press that the police were trying to frame them. Even prominent gay rights activist and investigative journalist David Brill took up their cause. Brill was a correspondent for *Boston Magazine* and the main investigative reporter for the *Gay Community News*. He would often write about law enforcement's unfair treatment of Boston's gay community. He also contended that law enforcement was framing Spear and Davis.

While I disagree with most of his opinions about their cases, he was an important voice in the '70s gay community. A few years later, Brill was found in his parents' Winthrop home dead of an apparent suicide in 1980. Officials tried to indict both Spear and Davis for Curtis' murder three times, but each time, a grand jury declined. Eddie was also acquitted and was arrested again in the early 1980s for sex crimes. Eddie is now a registered sex offender who still lives in Massachusetts as of 2022. Curtis' murder was never solved. The Spear-Barbre-Davis connection is just another bizarre layer to an incredibly dense story.

As police were identifying victims and interviewing them, they began to grasp the full breadth of Richard Peluso's recruiting tactics. Police interviewed one seventeen-year-old victim who told them that Peluso courted him for two years and constantly reminded the boy that if he wanted to make some money, he should stop by the triple-decker on Mountain Avenue. Another sixteen-year-old told police in incredibly graphic detail how two prominent sex-ring members, Arthur Clarridge and Dr. Donald Allen, abused him.

Dr. Allen's involvement shocked the community. He was a clinical professor of pediatrics at Tufts University School of Medicine in Boston and a trusted community member whom parents adored. He was very active in the underground gay scene in the 1970s. Some of the older boys testified that they often saw Allen downtown in the Combat Zone gay bars. Peluso stated to police that he met Allen through Clarridge. Clarridge was also a trusted community member who was employed as an assistant to the headmaster at the prestigious Fessenden School for boys in the high-income town of Newton. When I reached out to alumni of the Fessenden School, most seemed to focus on Clarridge and another man, the headmaster's brother, Hart Fessenden.

I was told on numerous occasions over the years that Hart was way too "loose with his thoughts" around young boys.

Teachers and administrators at the prestigious school often offered to take the students on car rides. Students were offered "extra special attention," and former students recounted decades later that gym teachers often made them exercise in tightly fitted shorts while commenting on their physiques. The sex rings in Revere and the Fessenden School are completely interwoven. James Dallman, who taught fifth-grade English at the school, was also a customer of Peluso's. Dallman's students explained to me later that he was a vicious man. He would often physically confront students and berate them. He seemed to take perverse pleasure in terrifying children. Some former students mentioned a janitor who worked at the school and showed them homemade pornography in the school's basement. The boys noticed that the pictures looked like Polaroids. I could never corroborate these claims, but former students mentioned them repeatedly.

Clarridge and Dallman were quite "touchy-feely" with students. When I found a message board for alumni, I immediately contacted men who posted that they had stories to tell. The stories about Clarridge are horrifying. Some students were drugged and raped, some students were "boarders" at the school who were taken off-campus. The sheer number of institutions that were intertwined with the child sex ring is overwhelming. Men shared stories of joy upon learning that law enforcement arrived at the school in 1977. They had no idea what was going on. Was there a shooting? A fire? No. Arthur Clarridge and James Dallman were being arrested.

The school's headmaster was shaken by the arrests and the allegations so much that he died by suicide a few years later. Some thought maybe the former headmaster's suicide was less about his guilt and more about protecting what he knew. Unfortunately, he took whatever he knew to the grave. Years later, I took a trip down to Fort Lauderdale, Florida, to ask Arthur Clarridge some questions. I had been communicating with many Fessenden alumni and getting firsthand stories about what an evil, despicable man Clarridge was. He had tortured a generation of youth at Fessenden by drugging them, raping, and threatening them after the crimes took place. I had been tracking Clarridge for a long time and knew that he was living in an apartment building on Gault Island Drive in Fort Lauderdale.

I arrived in the dead of winter and was immediately struck with heavy heat and humidity. I was at my worst then, battling severe mental health problems and making sense of my years of sexual abuse. Young people were running around Fort Lauderdale without a care in the world. I walked by smiling faces, holding beers, and playing volleyball. It was like we lived in two different worlds. Very few people were still alive from the Fessenden staff, so it was imperative that I find Clarridge. I had multiple questions to ask him and I was not taking no for an answer. I arrived at Clarridge's swanky building with palm trees leading up to the plate glass windows that doubled as an entrance. I found the name on the listing and walked to apartment 104. I don't recommend taking this approach. In retrospect, it was incredibly dumb to show up at an old man's house unannounced and expect them to give you answers about decades-old behavior. I was not in my right mind. I banged on the door and a young, dark-skinned nurse cracked it and asked me if I needed help. I asked her if I could speak to a man named Arthur Clarridge.

Immediately, I could hear the whirring sounds of a fan which I found out later was medical equipment. Arthur Clarridge was on dialysis and was close to death. I immediately began shouting that Clarridge was a pedophile who had abused a generation of kids. The nurse protested but remained calm. I was out of control and was asked to leave multiple times and I did not. I just kept ranting and raving about Clarridge. I didn't even see the man. He was out of my view, but I hoped within earshot. Eventually, I was confronted by two sheriff's deputies and asked to walk outside. We went out into the blazing sun, and they asked for my identification and what I wanted to accomplish.

I Googled Clarridge's name and showed the law what I was dealing with and what I was there for. I was told in no uncertain terms that I would be booked into jail nine hundred miles from home if I didn't leave immediately. The deputies gave me a break. I was creating a disorderly scene. I deserved to be arrested. I think the only thing that saved me was the deputies had my wallet and saw my military ID in my wallet. At the time, I thought I was doing something heroic. Both journalistically and for the victims. In retrospect, flying down to Florida to question a near-dead pedophile who could barely speak was a hare-brained idea. Arthur Clarridge was an evil monster but there is a time and place for everything. The time and place are here in this publication and future writing to expose Clarridge. I am in a much better headspace now than I was in 2018.

Edward Mede was the next domino to fall. Mede was another predator who based his life on getting close to children. Mede owned a karate studio in Revere, which was quite popular with parents who were looking to get their kids an extra shot of discipline. Mede was found in Richard Peluso's address book and was arrested in full view of parents and staff at his martial arts studio. He later became a member of the Boston Boise Committee, which gay-rights activist John Mitzel created in response to his belief that police were entrapping gay men. Mitzel believed that the Revere ring was nothing more than a media creation and police had entrapped the gay men because they were homophobic, which he wrote about in the *Fag Rag Collective*, a newspaper that operated from 1971 to 1980 in Boston.

The collective often published sympathetic interviews with NAMBLA members and articles about their criminal cases. The FBI agents assigned to NAMBLA often read the *Collective* to keep tabs on its operations. They noted the names of guest columnists. Mitzel owned an adult bookstore in Boston decades afterward that focused mainly on gay pornography. It was a well-known hustler and pimp hangout. The bookstore was like a nostalgic gathering spot for the men who lived through the 1970s.

Edward Mede pleaded out on four counts of rape and received no time for his involvement. He was pictured as a free man as early as 1978 and was a guest speaker at the Boston Pride Rally in Boston Commons. Clad in a grey polyester suit with thick glasses and a wavy clump of hair, he reportedly gave a fiery speech. No one bothered to mention or ask about his sex charges against the young boys. Other names came out, like Jack Spellman, an auto mechanic from Braintree, and Louis White of Mattapan. The local neighborhood was shocked about hearing what was going on right under their noses. The guy was weird, but the sex ring stuff was hard to fathom.

In December 1978, Richard Peluso testified at Dr. Donald Allen's trial. Peluso admitted under oath that he had been programming boys for nearly twelve years. The admission shocked the jury and the community. Had he been operating since 1965? This admission doesn't shock me at all. Men like Peluso and Wayne Chapman were completely fixated. Every move they made was based on their peculiar predilections. Richard was thirty-eight by 1978; I suspect he started these activities as soon as he moved out on his own and started earning some money. It all made perfect sense. He admitted that he had approximately two hundred victims and referred to himself as a "master pimp;" he knew he was sunk anyway. Maybe his honesty would earn him some points behind bars. Peluso pleaded guilty at his trial and received a fifteen- to twenty-five-year sentence earlier that year and ended up at Bridgewater.

Allen's defense team argued that he was simply doing research on gay hustlers at Peluso's residence, claiming in court that he would show up and interview the boys about their lifestyles and upbringing. He said he paid the boys to divulge personal information about their sexuality. It was a misunderstanding, nothing more than a research project. Peluso painted a different picture under oath and testified that Allen would visit his home weekly. The second time Allen visited, he brought a bag of what he called "stag films." When prosecutors asked Richard what the so-called stag films contained, Richard stated it was softcore and hardcore pornography involving young boys. Peluso then shared that the fourth time Allen visited his apartment, he went into the bedroom with a fifteen-year-old boy and shut the door. They stayed in the bedroom for an hour and a half, and when he exited the room, he left fifty dollars for Peluso.

Prosecutors were particularly interested in the boys depicted in the films. Peluso stated he recognized the boys from surrounding neighborhoods and that the videos were all self-produced pornography. He also told the Court that Allen admitted he produced the films himself with kids he picked up around Boston. Allen, who looked young for his age and was tall and slender, sat quietly listening to Peluso's statements intently. Sometimes, he wrote notes about the testimony. Allen's lawyer, Lawrence F. O'Donnell, asked Peluso how he came to meet Allen. Peluso stated that they met through Arthur Clarridge whom he met at a swanky apartment on Beacon Street in Boston during a party involving young boys. Kenneth Huntoon, another major child pornography pusher introduced them. Later, Huntoon would also be indicted in the sex ring; he was let off with a slap on the wrist and died in Florida in the early 1990s.

After their introduction, Clarridge immediately asked Peluso about some boys he knew and whether he could fix him up with them. Initially, Peluso said the pornography was not about money, but he began complaining to clientele that it cost money to bring the boys in. They ate a lot and gas was expensive. The money part just grew organically. Clarridge said he didn't mind paying, and Peluso testified he paid the boys anywhere from three to ten dollars.

In the end, Clarridge testified against Dr. Allen as well. He admitted he met Allen at dinner at Café Vendome in Boston's Back Bay. Clarridge, a big, pale balding man whose shape resembled a pear, immediately started chatting about his sexual urges. Eventually, they both admitted they liked little boys. They met again on March 8, 1977. He told Allen he knew a place in Revere where you paid a few bucks you could have your choice of young boys.

Allen said he would like to visit, but Clarridge admitted that he hadn't been over to Revere in a while. He had been spooked about men being arrested around the country who had sex with boys. He was scared. He estimated it had been about a month since he'd last been to Revere. Clarridge admitted he had been to the apartment for sex with boys about forty times. He ultimately received five years' probation for his crimes. He was a lifelong offender and serial pedophile.

The stories that have come out about Clarridge in the ensuing decades are spine-chilling. As one man told me, "He murdered my soul."

Dr. Donald Allen's trial lasted a little more than two weeks. He continued his "research" defense in front of a jury of fourteen women and two men. He dressed perfectly for his testimony, mostly with tweed jackets. He had bright black hair with an almost perfect mix of grey. He looked young for fifty-one. Often, his children and his estranged wife would watch from the spectator's box. The jury didn't buy his defense. Two days before Christmas in 1978, the jury returned a guilty verdict on four counts of rape of a child. Allen sat completely still and serene as jury forewoman Susanna Finamore read the verdict. Assistant District Attorney Thomas E. Peisch recommended Allen serve a sentence of no less than five years and no more than seven years in Walpole.

Superior Court Judge Joseph Ford sentenced Allen to five years' probation. Judge Ford also ordered that a copy of Allen's conviction be immediately sent to the Board of Registration in Medicine. A "fit for duty" hearing was set for January 15, 1979. Scant details about him exist after he fell out of the news in late 1978. Allen's medical license was eventually revoked in 1981, just two years into his probation period. I made significant efforts to find Donald Allen. First, I wanted to ask for an interview, and second, I wanted to see if he had continued to offend. I came up with nothing. Dr. Donald Allen seemingly disappeared off the face of the planet.

In all, twenty-four men from the sex ring were indicted. Only two, Frank Damiano and Richard Peluso, had a hard time. Roger Spear, the wealthy executive from Wellesley who was once implicated in the murder of a gay hustler, got off as well. He lived quietly in the nice suburb of Ipswich, Massachusetts, until his death in February 2017. Louis White, Jack Spellman, and Mark Davis all were released with relatively light punishments as well. Many names were never recorded in public record and some simply were never implicated. Many LGBT+ community activists and journalists weighed in when the sex ring trials wrapped up. David Brill often wrote in 1979 that the sex ring was way overblown and that the men didn't know one another—it was just a police witch hunt against the gay community. Art Cohen, a very influential Boston media personality, often blamed District Attorney Garrett Byrne, who was running his re-election campaign midway through the sex ring indictments. Cohen saw it as a cheap bid at the gay community's expense. He openly accused the district attorney and law enforcement of fabricating the case's details. Byrne had commented at the beginning of the indictment that this ring was just the "tip of the iceberg."

John Mitzel even wrote a book on the Revere ring and described it as the biggest gay "witch hunt in the history of the United States." While I respect Mitzel and Cohen's abilities as writers and personalities, they are wrong. Richard Peluso had been abusing Revere's youth for well over a decade and had already been arrested for child molestation six months before the sex ring broke. He was a known predator. Revere Police found sixty-four pictures of local youths in Peluso's apartment. The court documents are black and white. Some of the victims were foster kids in the system, living on the fringes of society, and these predators preyed on that. Cohen stated in one of his long-form works on the sex ring that nobody involved got significant time in prison. This was incredibly dangerous misinformation. While most did get off way too lightly, Frank Damiano never saw the light of day again, and it would be a few decades before Peluso got out of prison.

Most of the gay underground in Boston was aghast by the Revere ring bust and subsequent trials. Paul Shanley was keeping a close eye on the situation as well. He had never been over to Revere, but Shanley had heard of what was happening a little north from his Beacon Street apartment. David Thorstad, president of the Gay Activist Alliance based out of New York, was also paying attention. David saw the sex ring bust as a blatant political attack on gay men and had no issue with consenting boys loving men. Thorstad once referred to child sexual abuse as "hysteria." Frankly, Thorstad was a virulent pedophile advocate and pederast. He was also one of the "Original 32" NAMBLA members. He may have even been the founder. NAMBLA traces its roots to that Mountain Avenue apartment in Revere. John Mitzel, David Brill, and Art Cohen's coverage of the Revere bust in the underground gay media galvanized the men to stick together and create the advocacy group. The group's formation would repulse most Americans. *Rolling Stone* once called NAMBLA the "most hated men in America."

Nobody outside of the FBI had a look into NAMBLA until the 1993 film *Chicken Hawk* was released. Adi Sideman, the film's director, had been molested as a child and wanted to explore NAMBLA from the victim's perspective. The film has little narration and allows these monsters to talk and reveal their true selves. The men depicted in the film were more than forthright about their "boy-loving" activities. Allen Ginsberg, who came into prominence in the 1940s as a Columbia University student, is featured in the film. He was a pro-Communist, anti-capitalist writer and poet who was a popular thinker with the American Communist Left. He said he joined NAMBLA in defense of free speech. Others who knew Allen thought differently.

Feminist Andrea Dworkin once said of him, "He did not belong to the North American Man/Boy Love Association out of some mad, abstract conviction that its voice had to be heard. He meant it. I take this from what Allen said directly to me, not from some inference I made. He was exceptionally aggressive about his right to fuck children and his constant pursuit of underage boys."

Leyland Stevenson, the main character in the film, talks freely on screen about sexually abusing children but frames himself as a child lover who is an older brother-type who likes to horse around with kids. He also talks about owning homes in Sri Lanka, a hub for underground sexual exploitation, and being a frequent traveler. Leyland was eventually arrested on multiple sex offenses, including having homemade child pornography in Fort McCoy, Florida. He died in Sri Lanka in the late 2000s.

So, were Rick Peluso and his band of men connected to Wayne Chapman?

Of course.

Whether directly or indirectly, Chapman and the Revere sex ring are inextricably linked. Peluso would have needed a vast army of men on the streets to recruit boys and report back. That's why the friendships with Donald Allen, Arthur Clarridge, and James Dallman were so important. Their jobs put them in front of children every day. They had the access Peluso never could have had. These men could report back to Peluso on different kids and their situations, which ones were vulnerable. I believe these men met on the underground child pornography scene, not how they testified they met. Clarridge and Allen talked about how they met at a random luncheon and immediately struck up a conversation about boys. It makes little sense to me. The level of comfort it would have taken to broach that conversation hardly takes place over one lunch. They were part of a subculture, and they protected it until the end. Chapman was a member of the ground army, just a low-level guy who was told to get out on the street, lure kids, and get pictures. If the victims were open to more, great; Peluso could employ them. The fact that Chapman could get violent and sadistic was irrelevant to his handlers. If these crimes happened decades later, these men would have congregated on Facebook or Kik Messenger. They would have operated behind their laptops anonymously trading pictures and stories. The timeframe dictated their tactics.

As far as I'm concerned, anything is on the table as far as how deep the network went. I hate the term conspiracy theorist; I believe that term was created to discredit people who think critically. On certain topics, thinking for yourself is not allowed and you must be discredited if you do. Donald Allen, Arthur Clarridge, James Dallman, and others skated on their crimes. Most of the men disappeared from public view forever.

Frank Damiano and Richard Peluso had to be imprisoned for a long period, or the public outcry would have been far too large. I think many more powerful people were probably involved and it was never reported. Also, the mafia aspect must be considered here. No commerce in the Boston area happened without the Irish mafia having a hand in it. The underground porn trade surely was their territory, regardless of the subject matter. The Massachusetts police had an incredibly cozy relationship with Irish mobsters.

It's been well documented that James "Whitey" Bulger, the ruthless head of the Boston Irish Mob, had handlers both in the Massachusetts State Police and the FBI. Past associates accused Whitey of having an interest in younger women. Most honest people in Boston, who lived through the time would tell you it was common knowledge he had pedophiliac tendencies. Regardless of how many old ladies he helped across the street, the fact remains Whitey killed women and had no problem peddling questionable pornographic material if it lined his pockets. If Whitey's name came up about the pornography underground, it certainly would have been pushed under the rug.

Mobsters from Providence like Patriarca associate Ken Guarino saw so much money in the pornography trade in the 1970s that he jumped headlong into the industry. Guarino created Capital Video in the late 1970s and now owns all the Amazing Intimate Essentials stores, which are profitable and can be found all over Rhode Island. Some of the stores have private viewing booths where gay men are most of the customer base. All have vast libraries of pornographic magazines and videos for sale. Guarino's entrance into the pornography industry is well-known in Providence Mob circles. In FBI files regarding New York mobster Roy DeMeo, I found an interesting tidbit about the New York pornography empire—at a certain point in the early 1970s, DeMeo was told to push the business towards Rhode Island and the Patriarca crime syndicate that ran the state.

I suspect it was that decision that pushed Chapman towards Rhode Island. It was a career move. Guarino was a pusher and a packager for the family. He packaged pornography and housed it in a warehouse in Providence. The warehouse was eventually raided and Guarino did prison time. I was warned more than a few times about including Ken Guarino in this book. He is still an organized crime figure who has a bit of a hold on Providence from his headquarters in California. In the future, I plan to visit him outside and ask a few questions about his involvement in the early days.

It is impossible to understand Wayne Chapman's story without understanding the period in which he lived. I hope this chapter sheds a little light for you. Everybody had a stake in the production of child pornography. It lined up a lot of pockets and ultimately that is all that mattered. Andy Puglisi, David Louison, and others were abused and ultimately killed feeding the monster.

Wayne Chapman, Richard Peluso, Frank Damiano, and others were about to be reunited. In the nondescript building surrounded by the Hockomock Swamp, they would stew, plot, and discuss what they would do differently if they ever got out again.

Ultimately, some would.

CHAPTER 7:
BRIDGEWATER 1978

In late March 1978, Wayne Chapman was civilly committed to Bridgewater for one day to life. Massachusetts is one of twenty states that have civil commitments for sex offenders. The legal jargon for civil commitments is as follows: *the Massachusetts SDP statute, G.L. c. 123A allows for an individual to be civilly committed for a day to life if that person has been found to meet the criteria for sexual dangerousness beyond a reasonable doubt.* The criteria are lengthy and I won't bore you with all the jargon here. Chapman, with his lengthy history of sexual offenses against children, was an obvious choice for civil commitment. In lay terms, theoretically, he could finish all his prison sentences and still be civilly committed. It was a way to keep sexually dangerous people behind bars even if they had no more prison time to serve.

Chapman had concurrent fifteen- to thirty-year terms on the books for the sexual assaults in Lawrence in 1975. In August 1978, he was found guilty of the sodomy charges in Seekonk and the Bristol County judge gave him six to ten years on those charges. Thirty-one-year-old Wayne Chapman had at the very least thirty-six years to serve before his sentence ran out—sixty-six years at the very worst. In the best-case scenario, Chapman would be in his mid-sixties when he was released, or his mid-nineties. His outlook was grim. He could annually petition the State on his civil commitment; a yearly opportunity to prove that he was not a sexually dangerous person. It would take decades before he found doctors who would sign off that he was no longer a threat to the community.

In July 1978, Chapman received a bit of good news. A jury in Plymouth County declined to indict him in the murder of six-year-old David Louison. Plymouth County cited "no bills" because there was no hard evidence to present that linked David to him. Chapman had already recanted the Melrose Cemetery story and as we discussed earlier, David's body had not yet been found in 1978. Plymouth County could never convict Chapman in a court of law thereafter. There was no way forward for indictment, so he was cleared. Bridgewater officials began looking at Chapman's files. The Institute of Mental Health watched him intently when Detective Al Mintz brought him back to Rhode Island. The Institute's clinical director interviewed Chapman in October 1976 and noted that the genesis of his condition was difficult to pinpoint exactly but was "quite insidious" at an early age.

Chapman told the doctors that he first engaged in sex at age seven with another little boy, and his activities continually increased until his arrest in Waterloo. He was very open with the doctors at the Institute for Mental Health about his problems. He thought he needed help because he couldn't stop sexually abusing children. The doctor noted that Chapman was not a management problem, that he seemed mentally competent, and subsequently diagnosed him with a personality disorder. It was also noted that Chapman was "inadequate, immature, with sadomasochistic tendencies, and depressed tones."

Chapman had his first competency evaluation at Bridgewater in February 1977. He was found competent to stand trial. Doctors thought he had a personality disorder and not so much a mental illness. Later that May, acclaimed author and psychologist Nicholas Groth, a Webster, Massachusetts, native and a graduate of Wheelock College, interviewed Chapman. The psychologist's book, *Men Who Rape*, published in 1979, is an incredible read and a great study of the criminal minds of men like Wayne Chapman.

Dr. Groth was a leader and pioneer in the field of identifying the psychology behind sex offenders. Chapman opened to Groth a good bit and bemoaned that his attraction to boys was intense; he had tried to curb his attraction by watching straight hardcore pornography and even getting married, but nothing could thrill him like young boys.

Dr. Groth noted four issues with Chapman that worried him. He admitted to Dr. Groth that he purchased a professional pair of handcuffs and a gun that shot mace. He told the story he had told many times about tying a boy to a tree and leaving him there. Chapman also made one last chilling admission by confessing he had often thought if he didn't get help soon, his activities may turn to murder. Chapman said he whipped himself into such a state when he committed these disgusting acts that he was bound to hurt someone. Chapman was nothing if not self-aware. Dr. Groth couldn't help but note that at the time of the interview, this man was a major suspect in two missing boys' cases.

It was from that interview that Dr. Groth recommended Chapman be committed to Bridgewater and designated a sexually dangerous person and noted at the end of the spring 1977 report that his prognosis was "not favorable." Dr. Groth was spot on.

Chapman had friends at Bridgewater. The unit he was housed in was a "Who's Who" of predators. George Lopriore, who had a history of rape convictions and sexual assaults against children dating back to 1968, had grown close to Chapman during his time at Bridgewater. Thomas Tripp, a serial rapist and pedophile with a lifelong history of offending, was housed in the unit. In the research for this book, I realized Thomas is now a free man, living blocks from my home.

Keith Donaldson, a serial child abuser, became a close friend, and, of course, Frank Damiano and Richard Peluso were there as well. Chapman was about to get a shot in the arm soon. A man from Webster, where he found victims in the past, who often used the same modus operandi, was about to land in the unit. That man's birth name was David Brown but he would soon christen himself Nathaniel Bar-Jonah.

Nathaniel Bar-Jonah arrived in prison in 1978 after being sentenced to eighteen to twenty years in prison for abducting two boys at a Shrewsbury cinema in 1977. He was far more sadistic than Chapman and seemed to enjoy psychologically torturing his victims. Psychiatrists who interviewed Bar-Jonah at the prison's intake center noted that he seemed to be completely driven by his violent sexual fantasies. His designation as a sexually dangerous person was borne out of those interviews.

Bar-Jonah was immediately shipped to Bridgewater to serve most of his sentence and he was ecstatic to get away from the Massachusetts prison system and into a hospital setting. Much like Chapman, Bar-Jonah would not have lasted unless he was in protective custody inside the prison, but prison officials were not inclined to give him protective custody. Now, prisons almost always place prisoners convicted of crimes against children into special management units. Coincidentally, someone else was looking for a lifeline—Charles Pierce, Chapman's old buddy.

He had been convicted of sexually assaulting two youngsters in Broward County, Florida. Pierce was given a prison sentence of no more than five years and found the notoriously tough Florida prison system lived up to its reputation. I can speak directly to how tough the Department of Corrections in Florida can be. I worked at a facility for a year in Central Florida to begin my law enforcement career. In the blazing, stuffy summers, the inmates had no air conditioning system. The industrial fans at either end of the old-style barracks the inmates lived in were the only relief from the oppressive heat. It was hell on Earth. The other inmates were not kind to him and he almost immediately feared for his life. He knew he had to get the hell out of Florida. He began talking about the 1969 murder of Michelle Wilson to anyone who would listen. Other inmates. Guards. In March 1979, he confessed to the murder to the police and got his wish. He was extradited to Massachusetts and evaluated. Pierce hit all the right talking points with the psychologists. By winter, he was in court and astoundingly pleaded not guilty. In the meantime, he landed in Bridgewater for observation, which was exactly what he wanted. It was around that time that Connecticut police departments, including the Connecticut State Police, started looking into him for some missing children's cases. Janice Pockett, Dawn Cave, Debra Sprinkler, and Lisa Joy White were all missing from Connecticut. Police had no solid leads and were hitting major dead ends. They formed a special task force.

Charles Pierce, Bar-Jonah, and Chapman immediately allied behind Bridgewater's walls. Pierce would constantly scold the two idiots for their sloppiness. *Chapman was way too open with the police*, Pierce thought. Bar-Jonah? Way too brazen. He didn't even bother to hide his crimes. Just leave a body at the site. *You always get rid of the body*, he said. *No body. No crime.* Bar-Jonah would take this discussion to heart. After all, he only had eighteen to twenty years to serve, and he was in his early twenties. He was going to have a long life outside the treatment center walls after this. Bar-Jonah was earning a PhD in how to get away with murder. Decades later, he would remember Pierce's words.

***

The Lawrence Police Department was still grasping at straws in Andy Puglisi's case. Investigators even turned their attention to a developing story out of Illinois. A man who once made his living dressing as a clown at children's hospitals had made a drunken, rambling confession to his lawyer. John Wayne Gacy had been killing young men and burying their bodies in his basement crawl space. Gacy allegedly strangled thirty-three young boys using what he called the "rope trick." Most of the boys were teenage runaways or male sex workers living on society's fringes. Illinois officials had the unenviable task of digging the victims' bodies up and trying to positively identify the remains. The story played out like a weekly melodrama on the daily news and the media went crazy. Lawrence officials paid particular attention to the news out of the Midwest.

Had Gacy been to Massachusetts? Is it possible Andy Puglisi was abducted and taken to Illinois? He was arrested in December 1978 and the next month, Lawrence officials sent Andy's dental records to Illinois. Maybe they would get a hit there. But none of Andy's records matched any of the bodies exhumed from Gacy's crawlspace. It was another dead end in an incredibly frustrating case for Lawrence detectives.

As of 2021, multiple bodies were exhumed from Gacy's crawlspace and were still unidentified. The bodies have been recovered but officials have no idea who they are. John Wayne Gacy was given the death penalty and was executed at the Statesville Correctional Center in Illinois on May 10, 1994. In the end, police believe he may have killed far more than the thirty-three victims to which he admitted.

***

Wayne Chapman continued to be evaluated in his first full year behind the walls of Bridgewater. Examiners noted no real change in his condition. Doctors noted Chapman's fantasy world continued, which was triggered by watching commercials on community television that included young children and persisted as strong as ever. Chapman was a sullen, rigid character outside of his small circle of friends. He worked as a maintenance man on the unit, replacing trash bags in different patient rooms and community areas. Patients and staff constantly complained about his job performance. Chapman did not put much effort into sweeping and mopping the ward's floors. He would mostly stare at the pictures of children he kept in his Bible that he faithfully carried when he was on lawn duty. Just like years prior at Miriam Hospital, he was far more interested in his pictures than his job. Chapman claimed to turn to religion behind prison walls. Religion is often the last refuge of a desperate soul.

Bar-Jonah had done the same. He fancied himself some sort of persecuted soul and it was the catalyst to changing his name to Nathaniel Levi Bar-Jonah. The former David Paul Brown wanted to know what it was like to feel persecuted as a Jew. He would later state he just wanted to get closer to his Jewish heritage. It is more likely that it would be easier to get out of that place early if he appeared to have committed himself to religion. Chapman and Bar-Jonah played the religious angle to the end. Charles Pierce didn't bother, though. He was rotten to the core and did not try to hide it. He was often nasty to Bridgewater staff and inmates alike. He would hold court with whomever wanted to listen in the common areas about how dumb other patients were for getting caught, and what they could have done differently. Pierce would pick on Bar-Jonah, often calling him a "fat boy," and Chapman a "dummy." He had good reason to pick on Chapman.

His stupidity put Pierce in some sticky situations on the outside. By 1980, Pierce was the main suspect in Janice Pockett's disappearance from Tolland, Connecticut. Janice disappeared on July 26, 1973, shortly after returning home from shopping with her parents. She was fascinated with insects and had tucked a dead butterfly behind a rock while out on a walk just two days before disappearing. Janice begged her mother to let her ride her bike to the trail where the dead insect lay. She was hoping to retrieve it and bring it home.

Around 3 p.m., Janice's mother relented and told her to go but to hurry back. When she didn't return quickly, her mother ran up the road to the trail and found Janice's bike abandoned close to the Pockett residence. Seven-year-old Janice was nowhere to be found so a massive search was organized. Janice was last seen wearing navy blue shorts with an American flag printed on them, a blue-and-white striped pullover, and blue sneakers. She carried an envelope with her to the rock and had planned to put the butterfly in it. Neither was ever found.

In 1980, Pierce confessed to murdering Janice. Connecticut Police had feverishly searched for her body on his word but nothing came of them. He often confessed to crimes it wasn't clear he committed. He was Wayne Chapman's exact opposite, a cunning psychopath who would often toy with the police. I believe he did all of this to keep his living accommodation intact because he needed to stay in Bridgewater with its lax rules and safe living quarters. Nobody was killing pedophiles in Bridgewater— many of their charge sheets were almost identical.

Janice Pockett was just one of five young girls and women from seven to twenty years old who went missing from the Tolland area from 1969 to 1978. None of the cases have been solved. I am not sure who did it nor the motive. One thing is for sure, however; there was something sinister going on in Tolland during that decade. It's interesting to note that Tolland is only a thirty-one-mile ride from Webster, where Nathaniel Bar-Jonah grew up and Wayne Chapman was active. Young girls were not their preferred victims. Both ardently fixated on boys and had zero interest in girls.

Charles Pierce, however, was a brutal, equal-opportunity child killer who would strike out at any target, male or female, who was weaker than he was. If Bar-Jonah or Chapman introduced him to the area, then I think he may be responsible for some of these disappearances. He must be at the top of any suspect list if he was even remotely close to Tolland. I took a long detour into Janice Pockett's disappearance while researching this book. Her disappearance and Andy Puglisi's case are inexplicably linked. I have grilled Connecticut police officers who were on the job when Janice disappeared. The consensus is that Charles Pierce murdered Janice and kept her body in his van. Eventually, he likely buried Janice in some unknown location. Some in Connecticut also have a theory about Andy's disappearance, speculating that Pierce also kept Andy's body in the back of his van. Maybe that's true. I am not here to spread unsubstantiated rumors, but instead simply offer different theories I've heard. Charles Pierce admitted to police that he would watch kids at the pool in Lawrence and admitted in prison that he knew Wayne Chapman and had discussed his sexual activities with Chapman.

In the years after the first version of this book was published, a Connecticut detective reached out to me, and we discussed the Janice Pockett case in depth. I no longer believe Pierce was responsible for Pockett's disappearance. There is more compelling evidence that it was someone local and not some deranged outsider like Pierce. This begs the question: why did Pierce make false confessions? Did he like screwing with the police? Was it a game he played to throw people off the trail? The false confessions of Charles Pierce will never stop mystifying me.

Charles Pierce did the work for me. Throughout the entirety of my research on these men, I looked for a smoking gun, like a picture of them together outside the walls. Or witness statements that could be substantiated. Pierce verified what I long thought—they were partners in crime. They passed Intel both ways. Maybe he told Chapman the pool in Lawrence was a great spot for finding victims or vice versa. Either way, both admitted to stalking children there. Pierce continued mentoring Chapman at Bridgewater for most of the 1980s until he became ill and then made even more claims about his life of crime.

During the long years of researching this book, I found myself dropping my son off at school in the morning and hanging around. I would stare at the wooded area that directly faces my oldest son's elementary school. I allowed my mind to wander and think about Wayne Chapman luring young boys into woods exactly like that, just miles away from where I live. I would wonder what my son would do if a disheveled man asked for help looking for his daughter's lost puppy. My oldest son's default setting is to help anyone who is in need. Chapman would prey on that compunction. I would warn my son not to help anyone looking for anything.

"If someone approaches you, scream!" I would say.

I was losing my grip. I shelved the book at the time. The subject matter was taking me to a dark place and I was seeing Wayne Chapman and his ilk at my kid's baseball games and the local YMCA. I would drop my son off to school at eight in the morning and sometimes stay there all day. My mind would race back to my abuse. I would feel the shame all over again. I would lie awake at night tortured and considered suicide many times. The selfishness of that act was incomprehensible to me but the feeling was hard to shake. I would see what happened to these boys through a victim's eyes. I know it all too well. Ultimately, that's why I continued. I am all these boys' kindred spirit.

They are my tribe and I feel that you always go back to your tribe.

***

In 1982, Lawrence Police began reinvestigating Andy Puglisi's disappearance. By then, his case had been closed and reopened three times. Lawrence Police had four suspects: Andy's parents; Faith Puglisi's former fiancé, a man named Gary Thibedeau, from Lawrence; and Wayne Chapman.

Gary had been accused of some acts with little boys at the pool that were mostly unsubstantiated. Police interrogated him but the interviews were mostly fruitless. He might have been an odd character, but he wasn't connected to Chapman and the other predators. Gary seems to be just one of many red herrings that can easily sidetrack an investigation.

The police, of course, continued to focus on Wayne Chapman. They assumed he was involved but had zero physical evidence. The socks Faith Puglisi positively identified in Providence as the same socks Andy was wearing the day he disappeared were seemingly lost during their transfer to Lawrence. It is inexcusable that the police would lose such a crucial piece of evidence. With the advent of modern-day DNA analysis, it's not too far-fetched to think that losing the socks ultimately cost police the case. If the socks still existed today, I imagine the DNA evidence on them would be abundant and the hard evidence law enforcement needed would be there.

Sometime in the spring of 1982, Lawrence Police Department Officer Mike Carelli arrived at the Texas A&M University campus to attend a seminar on forensic and investigative hypnosis. The featured speaker at the seminar was a psychic named Andrew Barnhart. Mike began working on Andy's case of his own accord, and like me, he was sucked into the ten-year-old boy's disappearance. He was impressed by Barnhart's presentation to the law enforcement professionals. After the presentation, Mike made a beeline right to Andrew with one thing in mind: ask the psychic about Andy's disappearance. The Puglisi case was so cold. He was open to anything and was struck by there being no answers in Andy's case. *If Andy were murdered,* Mike thought, *his family would not even have a grave to lay flowers.* Mike cornered the psychic and told him they had a missing person's case back home in Massachusetts. He was wondering if Andrew could tell him anything using his psychic abilities.

"The boy is dead," he replied flatly. Mike was jarred. He hadn't told him the missing person was a boy. "But the body is still there," he added. Andrew also stated that Andy is probably buried somewhere like a tidal flat, where the ground is sometimes wet.

Mike was floored by their conversation. He thought about it the entire way home. When the patrolman returned to duty, he asked his superiors if he could continue his dialogue with Andrew, whose contact information he'd grabbed at the conference. Mike continued his correspondence with the psychic after receiving clearance. Andrew shared incredibly detailed visions of Andy's burial site. He told Mike that the body was buried three feet down, with three feet more on top. He was certain the site was near pipes and two white towers. Mike was astounded by this detail. The psychic had not visited Lawrence before these conversations.

Andrew continued by saying that a middle-aged person was stepping on the burial site right now. The man had salt-and-pepper hair, a paunch, and screwed-up front teeth. He was sure the burial site had been covered with sticks and brush and kept mentioning there were alphanumeric denominations near the site like the area was numbered for some reason.

Mike thought he needed to visit the site downhill from the pool near where Andy was last seen and was shocked when he arrived and realized that construction crews were building a new soccer field there. He was also taken aback by the contractor he encountered who looked exactly like the man the psychic had described walking on Andy's grave. Engineers had come out and made a grid of the area, which they dotted with numbers. Everything Andrew told Mike seemed to fit.

Mike returned to Andrew and pressed him for more details. "Was Andy murdered?" he asked.

No, not exactly. The child died because of a rape; his mouth had been stuffed full of something to quiet his screams, and maybe, Andrew thought, Andy had a seizure. Andy had a mild case of epilepsy. Maybe the stress of the event had caused him to seize. Mike pressed Andrew hard on what monster might have stuffed a young child's mouth to keep him quiet.

Andrew described what he saw: a mustached man, tall and thin with greasy hair, and he walked with a limp on his left side. Mike quickly followed up with the lead investigator in Andy's case, Captain Joseph Fitzpatrick. Mike knew Wayne Chapman had terrible hygiene and unwashed hair. He hadn't seen this purported limp reported anywhere, however. The captain confessed to Mike that Chapman had battled polio as a child and confirmed he walked with a slight limp. Mike was astounded and blown away by Andrew's abilities. He needed to get him to Lawrence.

Mike raised fifteen hundred dollars to fly Andrew and his wife to Lawrence because officials did not have a budget to fly psychics in. He left jars in local businesses to raise money to help solve Andy's case and bring the family some peace. Like the two boys in 1975, Melanie Perkins, and Albert Mintz, Mike is one of the many heroes of this story. He was not skeptical of Andrew because he hadn't given him any background on the disappearance before collaring with him at the presentation. There is no way Andrew could have known the details he gave Mike, and when he arrived in Lawrence in 1982, the police began to dig the area around where he felt the burial site might be. Puglisi family members showed up to view the digging and curious bystanders joined as well. Andrew referred to the scene as a "circus without the vendors." He wanted the area to be completely serene and free of people. He said anyone hanging around could disrupt his psychic "energy." The site was not fully excavated that day and Andrew left Lawrence directly after.

Police hatched a new plan: Andrew could come back to Lawrence and confront Wayne Chapman in Bridgewater. The idea was Andrew could at least rattle weak-minded Chapman with his abilities; perhaps he would leak some previously undisclosed information or confess altogether.

Unfortunately, Andrew never got to meet Wayne Chapman face to face. They did have one phone conversation, which upset Chapman to the point his lawyer stepped in and told him that under no circumstances should he talk to anyone about Andy Puglisi's disappearance. Right before Andrew left for the last time in 1983, Andy's family gave him some of Andy's items, including some poems he had written. Andrew planned to meditate over Andy's belongings. The Puglisi family would do anything to help him find their son or recover his body. His final visit would be the last time for decades that police would excavate the site near the Higgins Pool. Mike thought that Andrew's visions would galvanize Lawrence Police to double down on their efforts to dig around as much as they could. *Hell, he* thought, *there was a missing child in their books for six years now. Wouldn't you throw every available resource at it?* He got the sense that other officers who outranked him thought he was overstepping his bounds by voluntarily working on Andy's case. There were other detectives officially assigned to the case, so maybe Mike should stay in his lane. Nobody is beyond jealousy, especially police officers. It was beginning to get in the way of the investigation. He thought maybe he should step back. Frankly, he was getting sick of the interoffice politics and the bullshit.

Mike encountered one more bizarre twist in this story. He had tried to contact Andrew for months after Andrew returned to Texas. He wanted to see if Andrew had come up with any more information about Andy's disappearance. Had Andy's items helped him at all? He lost contact with Andrew. He couldn't get him on the phone and his voicemails went unanswered. Mike even contacted the police in Texas to conduct a wellness check. He felt that if Andrew did not want to help with the case any longer, the least he could do was return young Andy's personal belongings to his family, but he could not reach him. Andrew eventually was found dead. The psychic had died by suicide in his home. To this date, the Puglisi family never got Andy's personal effects back.

It was also in 1982 that ten-year-old Ray Clarke came forward with a story to tell. Young Ray had been the other child who was with Andy Puglisi the day he was abducted. It had taken Ray years to come to grips with what happened on that August day at Higgins Memorial Pool. I know that feeling. Ray told police in detail about the abduction. He recounted to the police about walking past the gravel pits with Wayne Chapman and Andy. Andy talked about the newest CB radio he had received during the walk, which was a minor detail that Chapman also recounted to Albert Mintz in a recorded interview. Andy had received a new CB radio just before he disappeared. Ray recounted important information as it related to Chapman's involvement with Andy on that day. Incredibly, no official records of Ray's interview seemingly ever existed. It is hard to tell if Lawrence Police discounted Ray's story due to his age or for another reason I simply cannot explain. No records indicate that police ever confronted Wayne Chapman in 1982 with the information Ray provided. Like Andy, David Louison, and the psychic, the interview seemed to disappear into thin air.

***

Wayne Chapman's prognosis remained very much the same at Bridgewater in the 1980s. His doctors wrote in reports that their patient was quite "rigid" in his thinking. He had no interest in talking about his past crimes and was only interested in his future. This defense mechanism is very common. The repugnant nature of his life of crime was such that *even he* needed to shield himself from it. He attended group therapy very sporadically. He never spoke about his crimes in a group setting, even when other patients openly shared their offenses and discussed their victims. Chapman remained tight-lipped. He saw himself as a victim. The Puglisi and Louison cases were just media creations. He was a persecuted man. Sure, he abused children. He needed love. His father was a distant alcoholic. Sure, his mom was good—when she was coherent.

Wayne Chapman blamed anyone and everyone he could for his behavior.

His biggest issue with group therapy was that it was not centered on Christianity. He found Christianity to be a helpful tool to gain the trust of examiners and staff. He fully used it. Of course, Chapman had no real interest in religion. If he were truly interested in being saved, he would have repented well before the 1980s for his crimes instead of simply ignoring them. While it is unknown if anyone ever pointed out this hypocrisy directly to him, I see the Christian angle for what it is: a front. His goal with this was to convince some qualified examiner he had turned his life over to Jesus.

Wayne Chapman's life never stopped being dedicated to loving little boys. Examiners continued to record how little they knew about his offenses. Sure, they could look at court records but they wanted to hear about them from him. Chapman speaking freely about his crimes was a sign to the staff that he was coming to terms with the pain he caused so many people. It never came. Psychologists wrote in February 1985 that Chapman never spoke of his crimes. He was completely closed off.

In 1983, a group of twenty protesters showed up at Bridgewater Treatment Center to protest the treatment of the patients. They held signs condemning the State of Massachusetts for admonishing boy lovers. It was a

NAMBLA protest. A lot of early members were behind those walls, including Richard Peluso. NAMBLA had taken up his case. In NAMBLA *Bulletin #5*, which was sort of one of the group's early press releases, they mentioned his case in the editorial section.

Peluso's name shows up more than once according to the FBI files kept on NAMBLA from March 1979 to August 1986. Agents all over the country, from Boston to San Francisco, infiltrated the group. Federal officials knew that the bulletins originated from a PO box that was located less than a mile from Fenway Park in Boston: PO Box 331 in Kenmore Station. Richard Peluso, Nathaniel Bar-Jonah, and Wayne Chapman watched the whole demonstration from the ward's common areas. The protesters looked through the thick chain-linked fence covered in barbed wire.

The bricks that layered the center could play tricks on your eyes. It was disorienting and almost maze-like. The predators behind the walls were no doubt filled with joy. Their tribe was still out there taking up their cause. It is just another illustration that NAMBLA and these men behind Bridgewater's barbed-wire fence were inexplicably linked. Present at the protest that day was David Thorstad. A very prominent gay rights activist whose papers still sit in the archive at the University of Minnesota. Thorstad rose to prominence authoring papers on the Socialist Workers Party and pedophilia. Thorstad was a founding NAMBLA member and even doubled as a communications director for the group until late 1996.

In the late 1980s, Nathaniel Bar-Jonah's mother, Tyra Brown, was given an edict from her son: a psychologist who can see the real me; a good Christian psychologist would be preferable. Tyra had no money, but her son, Bar-Jonah's brother, Bob Brown, did. They looked around for good Christian psychologists who could look past all of their relative's past crimes and see them for what they were—total injustices. Bar-Jonah was hunting for a qualified examiner who would be willing to sign off that he was fully rehabilitated. Sure, he was a compulsive liar and a total psychopath. He had also taken to carrying pictures of children in his hollowed-out Bible. When staff asked him who the kids were, he often answered that the pictures were of his nephews. The cops never fussed much if the pictures were of family. Bar-Jonah's last evaluation by Dr. Robert Levy on Halloween 1983 did not paint a pretty picture of the three-hundred-and-seventy-five-pound bearded man.

The doctor noted that Nathaniel Bar-Jonah began offending around 1963 when he strangled a female playmate. The report continued that Bar-Jonah had never had any heterosexual adult relationships. His sexual fantasies surrounded murder and even instruments of torture. Dr. Levy concluded that Bar-Jonah needed many more years of treatment to deal with his inner rage and he was still a sexually dangerous person. Bar-Jonah was enraged by the doctor's opinion. The cunning sociopath would control whom he spoke with the next time he came up for examination. He was hellbent on shedding his sexually dangerous label.

Bar-Jonah was a prolific writer in prison. He schmoozed ladies across the country during his stay at Bridgewater. He would respond to dating ads in *Sweetheart Magazine,* describing himself in eloquent letters. Reading his writings from that time, he strikes you as someone who is in total control of his faculties. He always included that the woman he wanted to marry must have kids in specific age ranges. He wanted to be a doting stepfather and prove to the world he was a reformed man. Of course, Nathaniel Bar-Jonah was doing what many predators do—he was trying to rearrange everything in his orbit to feed his pedophilia. His sentence would be coming up in a few short years and he needed to shed his designation. If he had that scarlet letter, the cops could keep him in Bridgewater for as long as they wanted.

Wayne Chapman and Nathaniel Bar-Jonah's friendship only grew closer at Bridgewater. They would often read the Bible together and talk about how they were persecuted by the cops and by the "lying" little kids who put them there. Bridgewater officials often wondered about their relationship. Those who knew about their crimes were curious just how well these two really knew each other beforehand. For years after Bar-Jonah left Bridgewater, he kept in touch with Chapman through letters. Other authors, like John Espy, who wrote the definitive account of Bar-Jonah's crimes, suggested he and Chapman met on a park bench in Lawrence well before reuniting in Bridgewater. I would never say that's impossible. He had access to Bar-Jonah that I could never have. If it were true, it would be chilling. As I have mentioned before, they had the same modes of operation and committed crimes in the same town.

There is one single comment that strikes me about the Bar-Jonah/Chapman connection. Wayne Chapman often stated that the only time he had been to Lawrence was when he pulled off the road there after a long drive to rest. He repeatedly used that story in the 1975 rapes and the timeframe surrounding Andy Puglisi's disappearance. Nathaniel Bar-Jonah offered the same exact explanation when asked if he was anywhere near Andy's disappearance. He stated he was passing through and got off the road to eat, then got right back on the road. Two men who did not know each other (allegedly) had the same story of their whereabouts on the days around when Andy disappeared. There is no way Bar-Jonah was at Higgins Memorial Pool that day; he was just way too recognizable for someone not to remember him. He was extremely heavy in 1976 with a large beard. That does not mean he wasn't nearby. I believe he probably was. Wayne Chapman and Nathaniel Bar-Jonah were so close on the outside that Chapman was instrumental in Bar-Jonah being committed to Bridgewater.

When Chapman arrived at Bridgewater, he began writing to Bar-Jonah, who was serving his eighteen-to-twenty-year sentence in Walpole. He found his accommodation to be less than satisfactory. Bar-Jonah was not housed in special management; he was thrown directly into the general population. He feared for his life immediately. Inmates earmarked child molesters for death upon arriving at Walpole. Tyra, Bar-Jonah Nathaniel's mother, went to see Chapman in Bridgewater to get his advice on how the hell she could get her son out of that ungodly situation. She found him to be a "nice man," which was an odd way of describing someone who had admitted to molesting fifty children at the very least. Tyra wrote letters to anyone and everyone in the Massachusetts Department of Corrections to plead her son's case for placement at Bridgewater. Chapman had gone through his drama at MCI Cedar Junction when he was first sentenced. He knew how brutal the world was when you are a "baby fucker" in prison.

Eventually, as I have noted, Bar-Jonah said enough of the right things to examiners to be placed at Bridgewater. As it turned out, it was both a blessing and a curse. Both men fought hard to be labeled sexually dangerous and then fought just as hard to shed that moniker much later.

Nathaniel Bar-Jonah, Wayne Chapman, and Charles Pierce were inseparable at Bridgewater in the 1980s. Staff kept a close eye on the three of them. The staff often speculated whether they had sex together when the staff wasn't actively watching them. Pierce did not engage in any sort of rehabilitation behind walls. He was truly rotten and completely devoid of any kind of redeemable qualities. When the staff were in his presence, their blood went cold. He was well over six feet tall and weighed two hundred pounds. He was an intimidating presence.

Staff knew that Pierce confessed to murdering a young boy from Chicago named Billy DeSousa, who disappeared from a carnival on 87th Street and Cicero after getting separated from his parents. Some detectives in Chicago thought Billy was a John Wayne Gacy victim. He had so many victims who were never identified and Chicago officials believed Billy was one of them. The clown angle made sense to them too. Maybe he was present that day and lured Billy away from his family with his shtick. There was no evidence that he was ever anywhere near carnivals. There was plenty of evidence that Charles Pierce was. He admitted to working carnivals all over the country. He would help set up rides and run the games. I have no idea if the DeSousa confession is real. As previously noted, Charles Pierce would confess to things all the time to run cover for friends or throw police off his real scent.

The fact he knew enough about the DeSousa case to confess to it is curious to me. Eventually, he recanted his confession. To this day, there are no leads about Billy's disappearance. It is a truly cold case. Billy's old classmates I talked to remember his disappearance vividly. Their sense of security was shattered when the ten-year-old went missing. It was the first time they realized that bad things could happen to young children. Most were struck by just how little the disappearance was talked about after the fact. It was never mentioned in churches. There was no counseling available for students. Teachers never spoke about Billy. It was almost as if William DeSousa never existed.

Wayne Chapman and Nathaniel Bar-Jonah continued going to the group as much as it took to retain their privileges. In 1984, an examiner noted that Chapman had worked within his therapeutic framework "very minimally." At that point, he showed up for group every day but hardly ever participated. He never discussed his crimes. He had learned from Charles Pierce that discussing crimes is useless. You deny, deny, deny. Wayne Chapman had often stated he had never even been to Lawrence, even though he pleaded guilty to two rapes there. No matter what the evidence, he would never admit culpability in a single crime ever again. In 1987, he got to the maximum privilege level. Incredibly, the new designation made him eligible for the Massachusetts furlough program, which allowed inmates a pass of sorts to leave their respective facilities and integrate into their community. The program was the subject of much scrutiny and even sparked national outrage.

Massachusetts Governor Michael Dukakis had been running a presidential bid against Vice President George H.W. Bush.

On the night of April 3, 1987, a Massachusetts prisoner named William Horton, who was out on furlough, was in a Washington suburb. He broke into the home of Angela and Clifford Barnes. He brutally raped Angela bound Clifford and stabbed him repeatedly. Vice President Bush used the Barnes case on the debate stage many times in 1988 to illustrate that Dukakis was soft on crime and incompetent. William Horton was a convicted murderer, Bush said. How the hell was he out on a weekend pass? The furlough program began in 1972 under Republican Governor Frank Sargent. It wasn't Dukakis's law but politics is politics. By 1988, 10,835 inmates had participated in the furlough program in Massachusetts, 428 had escaped, and 219 had returned late.

Wayne Chapman was one of them. While there was no evidence that he was ever late on furlough, you must question the notion that a man like Chapman, who was fixated on his sexual appetite, should be granted any kind of furlough. He would have had to fill out an application and get it approved. There were certain parameters for furloughs to be approved. The offender needed to show valid reasons for the furlough and how getting on the outside would benefit their treatment. Chapman had to explain how he would be transported and how much money he would spend on the outside. A week out from the furlough commencing, Bridgewater authorities would have sent out written notification that Wayne Chapman was going into their community. There is no evidence that he had any issues with the law while on his furlough. I am always of the mind that if he was breathing, he was offending. Everything in these predators' lives is based on expressing their pedophilia. Every move they make. Every breath they take. Wayne Chapman was dominated by his sickness.

Nathaniel Bar-Jonah was beginning to make some headway with psychiatrists in the mid- to late 1980s. Tyra and his brother Bob hired two psychologists to examine the morbidly obese Bar-Jonah. He was already writing letters to prospective mates on the outside, spinning the tale that he was getting out soon and planned to move to Montana with family. Bob was quite successful and owned apartment buildings in Montana and Bar-Jonah was looking for a fresh start. Bob had been so unnerved by his brother's behavior that he often wondered if Bar-Jonah was even his brother. Bob would ask the police multiple times over the years if they could perform a blood test to see if they were related. Bob thought maybe Bar-Jonah was switched at birth. *Maybe my real brother was out there in the world*, Bob supposed. He fantasized about finding the truth and telling Bar-Jonah to hit the bricks forever. All that was just fantasy, however.

Bob had to fork over five thousand dollars to the new psychologists so that they could examine his brother. The State of Massachusetts sure as hell would not foot that bill. Bob hit pay dirt with two psychologists named Dr. Richard Ober and Dr. Eric Sweitzer. They were completely hired guns. Bob's money was what drove them. Bob would go behind them and stick his hand up their backs like they were ventriloquist dummies. They would say anything for money. Dr. Ober was deeply religious and a former marine. He taught English to Vietnamese students at a Danang School during his Southeast Asian deployment in 1970. The doctor was active in the Providence area and even taught psychology at Rhode Island College before going into private practice. His practice was mere blocks from where I reside in the suburb of Attleboro. I would often walk past the small brick building across from CVS with my oldest son during the spring and summer in New England. I cursed Dr. Ober every time I walked by and caught a glimpse of staff and patients walking in and out. I found it ironic that Dr. Ober's practice was located directly across from a complex that housed sex offenders. Denis Bourque, a friend of Wayne Chapman's from Bridgewater, resided right there on North Main Street. I wondered if he ever walked across the street and talked to Dr. Ober about his decades of offenses. Dr. Ober did what he was paid to do when he evaluated Nathaniel Bar-Jonah.

Bob contacted Dr. Sweitzer through First Congregational Church in the South Coast suburb of Middleboro, Massachusetts. Sweitzer had been very active in the church and even considered the priesthood at one point in his life. He earned his bachelor's degree from Wheaton College in Norton, Massachusetts, in biblical studies, eventually receiving his PhD in pastoral psychology from Boston University.

Bar-Jonah immediately went to work on them both. He told them a bullshit story about how he was gang raped by children when he was just ten years old. He told Drs. Ober and Sweitzer he saved his best friend's life during the brutal gang rape. It was that single incident, he would say, that was the source of his rage towards children. He told the Christian psychologists that he had forgiven the boys for what they did to him. The fact that Nathaniel Bar-Jonah was writing back and forth with women gave the psychologist confidence that his deviancy towards young children was well behind him. Dr. Ober stated in his final report, "It is in the opinion of the evaluator that Mr. Bar-Jonah is not likely to victimize others due to his uncontrolled desires."

Both ignored reports from other unpaid, unbiased evaluators and concluded Nathaniel Bar-Jonah no longer met the criteria to be deemed sexually dangerous. Of course, the Christian psychologists highlighted that above all his "religious faith" would help him control his impulses on the outside.

In February 1991, the psychologists pleaded their case before Judge Walter Steele. Judge Steele did not disagree with the two psychologists. Nathaniel Bar-Jonah was now a man of the Lord. He had put his past behind him. He forgave the boys who raped him and he was ready to start his new life outside. Judge Steele ordered Bar-Jonah's release. He hung around Bridgewater until June 1991. He told his friend Wayne Chapman that he better get himself evaluated by Drs. Sweitzer and Ober; a good Christian man like him did not belong in Bridgewater.

Wayne Chapman was more convinced than ever that he also should be released from his sexually dangerous status, even though evaluators had noted he was as detached as ever in the late 1980s and 1990s. He had become a major "source of resistance and dissonance," one evaluator wrote. Chapman had been incarcerated since 1977. Thirteen long years and he had grown nasty. Much like Nathaniel Bar-Jonah, nobody understood that Chapman had given himself to Jesus. "A true man of God did not need therapy" in the traditional sense. Staff knew and reported they didn't know the real Wayne Chapman. He was so full of rage under the surface. He would often invite confrontation with other group members and then use religion to project back their arguments. Chapman hid behind the cloth for the remainder of his life.

Nathaniel Bar-Jonah was released from Bridgewater on June 28, 1991, and was deemed not sexually dangerous. He had no strings attached to his release. He was a free man. Thanks to God with an assist from his psychologists. What they didn't know, or maybe just chose to ignore, was that his proclivity for violence was as strong as ever. Everything in his life was centered on his pedophilia. He was making plans to move to a state where the police didn't know him. He was going to meet a woman who had two young sons he could groom as victims. His mother, Tyra, picked him up from the treatment center that afternoon. It was brutally hot and stuffy that day. Tyra edged her Corolla along the slow lane of Route 24, the main route that leads to the treatment center.

She got to her son around 3 p.m. After loading the car up, Nathaniel Bar-Jonah performed his first act as a free man. As he was leaving, he dropped his pants and showed his ass to the Bridgewater staff in a last act of defiance. He had won—for now.

CHAPTER 8: GREAT FALLS 1990S

Wayne Chapman was galvanized and, frankly, jealous of his good friend Nathaniel Bar-Jonah. Bar-Jonah had pulled the wool over the State's eyes. Chapman figured he better jumpstart his case to shed his sexually dangerous designation. He continued to go to therapy to use "basic behavioral techniques." In the early 1990s, he still displayed no remorse for his victims. He even stated one time or two that the children he victimized may have even gotten some enjoyment out of his assaults. This, of course, is an insane assertion but a common one for offenders. They will do or say anything to shield themselves from the heinous nature of their crimes. As delusional as he may have sounded, his examiner thought Chapman was of sound mind. He would bizarrely and randomly mention his crimes and discuss the media narrative surrounding Andy Puglisi's case. He felt unfairly prosecuted because reports named him as the only suspect in Andy's disappearance. Former Bridgewater staffers later revealed to me how bone chilling it felt when he mentioned Andy's name. Most everyone who worked around Chapman believed he was a child murderer, maybe even a *double* child murderer who had somehow skated through the criminal justice system.

Nathaniel Bar-Jonah's years at Bridgewater didn't seem like nearly enough punishment. Bar-Jonah immediately reoffended after his release. Just a month and a half later, he was out for one of his many walks in Boxford, Massachusetts, and got caught in the rain at a post office parking lot. He saw a woman getting out of her vehicle, leaving her little boy behind in the backseat, and his predatory instincts activated. He ripped the door open and began to drop his nearly three-hundred-pound frame on top of the seven-year-old boy. Bar-Jonah was so full of rage that he planned to kill the boy manually with his body weight. By the grace of God, the boy's mother returned from the post office and tore him off her son just in time. Like the rat he was, Bar-Jonah scurried away, slipping through the rain.

By that point, he was so well known to local officers that when the victim's mother contacted police with a description of her son's attacker, an officer recognized his description from years earlier. Police picked him up at Tyra's house that afternoon. He had "only been trying to get out of the rain," he said in his defense. The local police were angered. This guy was a menace to society. He had been out only a month or so and the little boy was now traumatized for life. The police berated Bar-Jonah after they got him back to the station. He wrote a confession affirming he had planned to kill the young boy in the parking lot. He, like his best friend Wayne Chapman, had zero self-control around children but he was far more cunning. He got off on terrorizing his victims.

After his mother paid his bail, Bar-Jonah went to the local Yellow Pages and looked up the name of the victim from the post office. He got the family's address, called himself a cab, and headed over to the victim's home the night of the assault. The cabbie brought him halfway up the driveway and let him out. He told the driver to wait right there. All the lights went dark. The family saw the obese man get out of the cab and were immediately gripped with terror. Bar-Jonah stood outside for a moment then got back into the cab and returned to his mother's house. He loved to psychologically terrorize his victims. He needed you to remember him. He enjoyed one thing more than anything—being the boogeyman.

Drs. Ober and Sweitzer were very wrong about Nathaniel Bar-Jonah. They never intended to examine him anyway. Instead, they did what they were paid to do—get him out of the state hospital. They were now trying to do the same for Wayne Chapman. Dr. Sweitzer began to see Chapman in 1990 or 1991. He was impressed by how Chapman had dedicated his life to God behind bars instead of loving little boys. Chapman, in Dr. Sweitzer's estimation, realized the seriousness of his crimes and had shown genuine remorse. He still hung out on A1 with Frank Damiano and Richard Peluso but he expressed the fact that he missed his longtime pal, Nathaniel Bar-Jonah.

Bridgewater was a drag by then anyway. The early to mid-1990s saw a lot of facility changes. Furloughs were almost nonexistent and the family atmosphere in the 1980s had all but dried up. Chapman was now singularly focused on getting the hell out of there. His hard work with Drs. Sweitzer and Ober paid off in December 1991. The Christian doctors testified to Judge John A. Tierney that Wayne Chapman, a man who had admitted to a hundred victims and was the main suspect in two disappearances, was no longer sexually dangerous. Judge Tierney did not put up much of a fight. The judge agreed and Wayne Chapman's sexually dangerous status was stripped. The civil commitment of one day to life was gone. 2007 was the very latest Chapman would be released. It would be more than likely quicker with parole and early release programs. Chapman was returned to Walpole to finish out his sentence. That was the only drawback; Walpole was far less friendly than Bridgewater, but it was necessary. If he survived Walpole, he would see outside the prison walls again, like his buddy, Bar-Jonah, with whom he was in regular contact.

A Dudley District Court judge ordered Bar-Jonah to have a psychological evaluation after he assaulted the seven-year-old boy in a Boxford parking lot. He thought for sure that in the very best case, he was heading back to Bridgewater. At worst, he was going to Walpole or New Hampshire State Prison for Men.

Bar-Jonah knew he wouldn't survive in either of these places. The judge would be signing his death warrant. Through a series of missteps and miscommunications between two different judges, he was not ordered back to prison. Astoundingly, the two judges who saw his case hatched an agreement: he was to serve two years' probation and needed to leave Massachusetts. He offered this bargain himself. Besides, he had plans to leave anyway. The Boxford crime just accelerated his thought process. Nathaniel Bar-Jonah skated here; it's an astounding miscarriage of justice that he was allowed to simply leave the state.

Now Montana would have had to agree to take him per the agreement. Unfortunately, nobody in Montana was ever contacted until he arrived and started committing crimes. Nobody in Montana had any idea who he was until he showed up on their doorstep. It's interesting to note that he never attended that evaluation nor did he ever see his probation officer in Massachusetts again. He simply packed up and left with his mother. Massachusetts officials' incompetence would set the stage for a crime that would shake Montana and have officials in Big Sky country wondering just what the hell motivated the State of Massachusetts to dump Nathaniel Bar-Jonah in their laps.

What I found even more curious than Bar-Jonah's relocation to Montana was *whom* he contacted when he arrived. I always worked under the presumption these predators would find like minds wherever they went. Whether behind prison walls or in different states, predators like Nathaniel Bar-Jonah and Wayne Chapman immediately start networking. He arrived in Montana in September and immediately settled in an apartment on one of his brother's properties. He and Tyra lived on 11th Avenue and

4th Avenue in their time in tiny Great Falls. I tracked Bar-Jonah intensely while researching this book. I needed to find out exactly whom he associated with while living there. My thinking was that whomever he brought into his inner circle might hold answers to the questions that burned inside me about his and Chapman's partnership in crime.

Sometime in 2015, I found a man named Keith Forrest Donaldson, who settled in Great Falls two years after Bar-Jonah arrived. Donaldson also hailed from New England and was six years younger than Bar-Jonah. Police also charged him with child rape in 1987 in Greenfield, Massachusetts. He has a long history of crimes with varying degrees of seriousness—everything from petty theft to holding a knife to a coworker's throat in the 1970s in Vermont.

Had Donaldson and Bar-Jonah known one another? Maybe they met in the Massachusetts prison system. They were both sex offenders with the same sexual predilections. Consider this as well: when Donaldson arrived in Great Falls in early 1993, he never lived more than two miles from Bar-Jonah. Bar-Jonah moved twice and Keith Donaldson's address history confirms he moved closer to Bar-Jonah shortly afterward. One cannot ignore the coincidence of two offenders from Massachusetts moving into the same neighborhood in the same general timeframe—or at least I couldn't ignore it. I have contacted Donaldson on social media many times over the years. Like any source, I promised complete anonymity. I explained to him I had no interest in his prior crimes and I didn't judge him. I simply wanted to know if he knew Nathanael Bar-Jonah. He viewed my messages, but I never got any responses. I tracked him to a diner called Kroll's in Mandan, South Dakota. The '50's-style diner, made famous by its tagline, "SIT DOWN AND EAT," was slammed with customers every time I called requesting information about Donaldson, who had been a cook there for a good bit of time.

Sometimes, I would wait twenty-five minutes to talk to the manager on duty. After we got past the awkwardness about a random person calling to ask about an employee, he told me Keith Donaldson was no longer employed there and was back in prison in Montana. Most staff who knew Donaldson thought he was the oddest guy. He often talked about his time in Massachusetts and spoke with a heavy Boston-style accent. Keith Donaldson is currently assigned Inmate Number 31696 at the Montana Department of Corrections in Helena. I have written to him many times in the last few years, asking probing questions about how he came to live there. Pedophiles never do anything by accident. I think it's possible Nathaniel Bar-Jonah was communicating with Donaldson and told him how great Montana was to live with his family. He has never answered any of my letters. I admit Keith Donaldson might be a total rabbit hole in this case, but I am dedicated to following every thread to the ground, no matter what.

Nathaniel Bar-Jonah continued to write letters back and forth with his good friend, Wayne Chapman, who was jealous of his freedom. Chapman missed his old friends in Bridgewater. The likes of Frank Damiano and Richard Peluso had stayed behind at the treatment center. Damiano was condemned to life, but Peluso was looking forward to getting out. Bar-Jonah's memory was still "spotty" about his crimes, he would tell evaluators. Staff noted that Chapman was still in major denial about his crimes. He never showed a second of remorse like the other sex offenders in his unit at Walpole. Psychologists thought if he refused to even acknowledge his crimes, there would be no chance he could ever benefit from treatment.

On January 13, 1994, Wayne Chapman fell sick. He had vomited half the morning and decided to take a long nap in his bunk. He woke up a few hours later with a claw-like grip centered in the middle of his chest. He felt short of breath. He'd had a heart attack but survived. It was a wake-up call.

He didn't want to die in prison. He wanted to beat the cops and lying kids who put him behind bars. Lying kids. *Most of them liked it,* he thought. The media slandered his name with Andy Puglisi's disappearance. Chapman would show the world. He would show them the reformed man of God he had become. After his heart attack, he stopped going to sex offender treatment altogether. His lawyer advised him to never speak about his crimes. Just wait it out, the lawyer told him. The day was coming when his sentence would end. He focused on his religion and his monthly phone calls with Dr. Sweitzer. He kept his head down, wrote his letters, and bided his time.

Meanwhile, Nathaniel Bar-Jonah kept busy in Great Falls. He opened an unsuccessful antique business and began seeing his probation officer, a man named Michael Redpath. Redpath was flummoxed by how the morbidly obese, unkempt man ended up one of his probationers. *How the hell did we get lucky enough to get this guy?* he thought. *All the way from Massachusetts?* Massachusetts officials were useless when Redpath questioned them about Bar-Jonah. Nobody back East seemed to have any clue on how he'd gotten there. Massachusetts sent nothing to Montana about Bar-Jonah's crimes before the Boxford assault in 1991. They knew nothing about the 1975 or 1977 abductions. Montana knew nothing about his years in Bridgewater or his former sexually dangerous offender status.

These miscommunications are unconscionable and would end up having cataclysmic effects.

Nathaniel Bar-Jonah met a local boy at one of the antique strip malls he began haunting. He fancied himself an independent businessman there. He would blow all his money on worthless old toys and sell them beside other vendors at the Great Falls strip mall. I see this for what it was—an easy way to get in front of children. Bar-Jonah would hang out and show these toys off to kids. He would gain their trust and often their parents' trust while grooming potential victims. Everything in these monsters' lives is centered on expressing their paraphilia. Bar-Jonah immediately took a liking to a young boy who would often visit his booth at the strip mall. The boy's mother began to trust the obese, scraggly bearded man. She thought he was good with her son, who sorely needed a father figure.

This trait was a hallmark of his and Wayne Chapman's ideal victims. They preyed on children who were fatherless and came from broken homes. A man in the home would have been a complete nonstarter for these two. Bar-Jonah began spending a lot of time with this young boy and his mother. He was invited to their home for dinner and was even tapped as the young boy's babysitter. His mother had no idea what grave danger she was inviting into her son's life. Nathaniel Bar-Jonah was a patient predator. He was very organized, unlike Chapman, who was, for the most part, disorganized. Bar-Jonah would groom and wait for the perfect time to reveal his true self to a victim. He completely swindled the boy's mother, finding it easy to swindle people. He was extremely cunning and could even be charming when he targeted victims.

The boy had been hanging around with Bar-Jonah for months before the mother noticed the boy's behavior began changing.

Bar-Jonah often babysat, even staying overnight while the mother went out of town. Eventually, the mother cornered her son and asked him what was happening. Bar-Jonah had fondled the boy and he was afraid to go to his mother because he was heavily brainwashed. The young boy did not want Bar-Jonah to go to prison because of him. He made himself the victim all the while molesting the boy. Great Falls Police Detective William Bellusci took the boy's initial statement. He couldn't help but wonder how the hell this guy ended up in tiny Great Falls from Massachusetts, especially after he interviewed Bar-Jonah, who admitted to his prior crimes back East.

The detective was incensed about the damage Bar-Jonah had done to the little boy. He thought he might lose his cool and haul off and whack Nathaniel right where he sat. He was no longer anonymous in the eyes of the State of Montana. Incredibly, the little boy's mother was so taken with Bar-Jonah's hard-luck tales, like the gang rape when he was ten, that she agreed to write a letter to the Court on his behalf.

I know. Pause and take a breath. I cannot fathom what this woman was thinking when she sat down and penned this letter. It is just one more tribute to the influence Nathaniel Bar-Jonah could exert over some people.

Predictably, he denied ever touching the little boy, then promptly failed a polygraph. Bar-Jonah told the detective that he might have touched him, but he probably "blacked out" during the commission of his crimes. It was a fabrication; he knew exactly what he was doing. Every time. With help from the boy's mother's statement, his charges were dropped. He skated again in another complete miscarriage of justice.

Prisons were created for men like Nathaniel Bar-Jonah but he was again freed with nothing, not even probation. Probation officer Michael Redpath could do nothing about the charges being dropped; however, he put the word out to all the officers in Great Falls and the surrounding areas and made a point to mention to every member of law enforcement he interacted with on a day-to-day basis: *keep an eye on Nathaniel Bar-Jonah*. He knew Bar-Jonah was emboldened after avoiding the assault charges. It was just a matter of time before this guy struck again. He was a ticking time bomb.

***

Wayne Chapman took it easy for a while after his heart attack. He ended up in the prison infirmary for a short time. He wasn't such a young man anymore. Now in his mid-fifties, Chapman was on an array of medications just to make it through the day. Chapman was working with Dr. Sweitzer and was in group therapy dealing with his childhood issues. While he never admitted to being sexually abused as a child, I have always remained suspicious. He made progress. As noted, his father, Arthur, had been a very cold and distant alcoholic, and Chapman's brothers proved that the apple did not fall far from the tree. All his younger siblings battled alcoholism as they got older. Two of his youngest brothers, Bruce and Craig, both died of alcohol-related illnesses and neither made it much past fifty years old.

I have spent a considerable amount of time looking into the Chapman family tree. It seems like an eternal quest for answers on whether the oldest child was nurtured into becoming one of the worst serial pedophiles in American history. Presented with all the available evidence, I believe it was simply his nature. Wayne Chapman was born a pedophile, much like people are born straight or gay. Chapman was born attracted to male children. I am quite sure growing up in a cold, distant household with a father who could be cruel didn't help him develop normal sexual tendencies but it doesn't begin to explain his illness. He was exposed to child pornography early in Buffalo and when he crossed the border to Canada. After Chapman saw children as mere sexual objects, the snowball started rolling downhill.

In his twenties, Chapman fell in with other like-minded pedophiles who were involved in the selling and trading of child pornography. It just kept building. Eventually, he needed to be victimizing constantly to keep up with demand for the homemade smut. Chapman wasn't a sadist. Things just went too far and men like Charles Pierce and Nathaniel Bar-Jonah advised him that it's better to get rid of a body than to risk a child being left behind for cops to find. He agreed with that sentiment and cared more about his backside than hurting a child. A fixated pedophiliac disorder, coupled with low intelligence and a bad crowd, is what made Wayne Chapman who he was, I believe. There is no evidence I have ever seen to support the contrary. I think it's also crucial to point out there are no allegations of abuse from any of his immediate family.

None of the Chapman brothers ever accused Arthur or one of their brothers of anything. Surely that would have come out after his crimes came to light. In 2019, James Arthur Chapman, Bruce's son and Chapman's nephew, was arrested on sex charges in Jamestown. James had a nickname he used on social media sites (like Instagram and Facebook), going by the moniker "Perverted Doe." He was indicted on charges of enticing two minors to engage in sexual acts for commercial purposes. He found and contacted the young victims on Facebook. The FBI questioned James and he admitted to having child pornography on both his personal computer and cell phone. In July 2021, James Arthur Chapman was sentenced to thirty years in federal prison, almost the same amount of time his Uncle Wayne received for sex offenses decades earlier.

Perhaps, it was just a coincidence that Chapman's nephew also committed sex offenses against children, or maybe some deep family secrets are yet to be told. Perhaps we will never know.

***

Nathaniel Bar-Jonah struck up a friendship with a man when he passed through the local jail on his now-dismissed sexual assault charges against the little boy he used to babysit. The friend had decades of sexual assault charges against children as well; he was a true boy lover in every sense of the word.

Everything about this man's life, from the way he dressed to the way he decorated his apartment, was geared toward luring children. The man's name was Keith Corwin

Bauman. He went by the nickname "Doc," an ode to his old life when he was an army medic during the Korean War. Doc was a very well-educated man, graduating from the University of Houston in 1952 with a bachelor's degree. He also earned a PhD in Art Theory and Composition there. He ran a piano and organ studio in Colorado in the 1960s and would offer private lessons to "special students." Doc offered classes and discussions for the "very young" and chaperoned students of all ages to concerts all over the country and Canada.

Students who attended Doc's music class gave special monthly concerts to senior citizens in his studio on East Bijou Street in Colorado Springs. Doc would even take ads out in the local Colorado Springs newspaper *The Gazette,* offering inexpensive lessons to young students who wanted to learn the piano or organ. What the prospective students and their parents didn't know was the serial predator was using his position to get closer to children. Doc eventually had to flee, like most serial pedophiles do. The community had caught on to him. He was accused of numerous sexual assaults in Colorado during his time there as a music teacher. His offenses go much further back than that. I assumed I would find an assault charge in Doc's service record, maybe even a dishonorable discharge. Doc served in the army as a combat medic during the 1950s and even reached the rank of colonel after his army reserve time ended in the late 1960s. I have spent many years of my adult life in the United States Army. I know how tough it is to reach the rank of colonel. Doc had a completely clean military career with no blemishes on his record.

I investigated Doc Bauman as much as any person mentioned in this book. One simple fact got me on Doc's trail: he might have lived in Massachusetts in the 1970s. I could never verify this fact. Doc had no address history in the Commonwealth but he had often made statements about living in Massachusetts in the 1970s and being a founding member of NAMBLA. If that were the case, Doc would have been front and center during the Revere sex ring and may have run in the same circles as Wayne Chapman and Nathaniel Bar-Jonah. I found it curious that Doc was a complete ghost, on paper anyway, in the 1970s and 1980s. I can place him in Texas in the 1950s, Colorado in the 1960s, and then he seemingly disappears off the radar until 1993, living just 2.2 miles from Bar-Jonah. It's very possible, and even probable, that Doc ran off to Massachusetts in the 1970s. He had felt the heat in Colorado and Massachusetts was already well-established as a haven for pedophiles.

I mentioned previously that boy lovers from as far as Atlanta patronized the house in Revere. How and why Doc got to Montana is unknown. He showed up and immediately started sexually assaulting young boys. In 1993, he coaxed two little boys into his home on 7th Avenue in Great Falls. Doc had promised the boys alcohol and marijuana, which was always his MO. He filled his house with toys to attract younger children. He was an older man, sickly as well, and he needed a cane to get around, but his love of young boys burned inside as bright as ever. Allegedly, Nathaniel Bar-Jonah and Doc met while sitting in the local jailhouse.

Nathaniel Bar-Jonah was there on charges of fondling the young boy and Doc had been nabbed for luring boys into his home. Supposedly, they struck up a conversation and became fast friends. Perhaps it's true and was just a coincidence that they were thrown in the same cell, having been arrested on similar charges. I think it's also possible they might have known each other before each moving to Montana. Like Keith Donaldson, I think Doc might have gotten intelligence that Montana was a safe place and followed Bar-Jonah there. Remember, nothing in this story is a coincidence.

Doc and Bar-Jonah both beat the 1993 charges and remained in close contact, hanging out nearly every day. Like back East, Bar-Jonah found like-minded individuals and stayed close to them. They even operated as sort of a tag team. Much like Chapman and Bar-Jonah years prior, Doc would tag along with when Bar-Jonah visited department stores young children frequented as well as playgrounds. Bar-Jonah would often dress in a police uniform to gain children's confidence and Doc was always dressed in a suit and tie. Doc tried to project the image that he was a businessman, maybe even a wealthy guy in town on business.

Everything, from the way they dressed to how they walked together, was carefully coordinated to gain the public's confidence so that they could exercise their paraphilia. Their entire lives were built around this con. Great Falls Police kept a close eye on Nathaniel Bar-Jonah; he wasn't exactly hard to miss. A fat, chain-smoking man like him was hard to forget. Whittier Elementary School faculty had gotten used to Bar-Jonah's presence on 8th Street, however. He would often patrol the school grounds wearing garb that looked like actual police uniforms. He had bought police gear at local antique malls and overflow stores. Teachers at Whittier even began to believe he was an actual member of the Great Falls Police Department. *Maybe he was the school resource officer*, they thought, *or in some sort of undercover role*. Of course, Bar-Jonah was simply scouting potential victims during his daily walks of the school grounds. He would take pictures of potential prey while they were gliding down slides or playing tag. He would develop the film and put the pictures in large scrapbooks he kept in his room. Thousands upon thousands of pictures of children were all over his bedroom. Some were cutouts of ads and slipped into protective plastic usually used for rare playing cards. But he didn't collect Tom Brady rookie cards; Bar-Jonah collected pictures of children.

It wasn't long before Doc introduced his best friend to a boy whom he had been grooming for a long time. The boy fit Bar-Jonah's preferred victimology. He was olive-skinned with dark hair and eyes, a biracial child whose mother was White and father was Black. His name was Zachary Ramsay. Doc had fallen hard for the ten-year-old boy and was even planning to skip town with Zach, maybe even the country, if he had to. Doc had been grooming Zach with his usual tactics by doting on him with new toys and hot cocoa on cold Montana days. Zach's mother hardly paid attention to him, which made him their perfect victim. Doc introduced young Zach to alcohol and marijuana to get the boy chemically altered enough so he could molest him.

Bar-Jonah was also very smitten with the boy. He thought Doc wasn't good enough for Zach. Sure, Doc had a house full of toys, but he was old and in ill health. Doc was getting the sense that Bar-Jonah was trying to move in on Zach. Doc had been a good friend of his for a while but Doc also recognized what he was. Doc knew Bar-Jonah was a sadistic sexual predator. His size alone made it impossible for Doc to defend himself if it ever came to that. Doc thought Bar-Jonah was far too unhinged to ever last outside the prison's walls. Doc had avoided a serious sentence by biding his time and grooming children at a slow pace. He wasn't impulsive. He always discarded the boys when they aged out of his ideal age range. Zach was different, though. Doc was prepared to do whatever it took to keep him away from Nathaniel Bar-Jonah.

In early February 1996, Doc began planning his escape with ten-year-old Zach. He hatched a plan to take him and cross the Canadian border in Whitefish. He decided he would make up a story at the border about Zach being his grandson. Surely, none of the guards would question a frail old man traveling with his grandson. Doc thought Zach's mother didn't pay much attention to him anyway. She would be mad but hey, she had other kids. Doc planned to make the three-and-a-half-hour trip on February 6. It was his last chance at love.

Zach always took the same route to school in the morning. There was an alleyway right near the 400 block of 4th Street North. Zach always left his mother's apartment between 7:30 and 7:35 a.m. The alley he used as a shortcut to school ran through quite a few streets in Great Falls. Around 7 a.m., a neighbor spied a man in the alley smoking near 5th Street. He had seen the man before. The man was heavyset and always showed up when the kids got out of school and hung around. He would chain smoke and discard his cigarette butts all over the place around the kids. The neighbor thought the habit was in bad taste. *Why expose kids to toxic smoke at such a young age?* The neighbor didn't bother to confront the man that morning. He simply said, "Hello," and the man flicked another cigarette butt, nodded, and walked off.

Another neighbor noticed Zach in the alley that same morning. He also spied an obese man clad in black, stalking Zach. The neighbor estimated Nathaniel Bar-Jonah was just a few feet away, like a hyena stalking a fawn on the African plains. Another woman came forward stating she saw Zach standing between two garages. He seemed nervous and looked around as if he were waiting for somebody. Zach had been excited about school that day. The school was hosting a "Good Guy" breakfast. Students could bring their fathers to school and enjoy a hearty breakfast in the dining hall.

Zach never made it to the Good Guy breakfast. His teachers thought maybe he was too embarrassed to come. After all, Zach was from a broken home. His father was an active-duty master sergeant in the United States Air Force based out of Doc's old stomping grounds in Colorado. Teachers weren't incredibly alarmed by Zach being a no-show. It was when Zach didn't show up for the school day after breakfast ended that Mrs. Davis, Zach's teacher, became alarmed. She immediately got a note to Zach's mother that he had neither shown up for breakfast nor class. Zach's mother, Rachel Howard, found that curious and said

Zach was planning to attend the breakfast. He was excited for it, even. Rachel headed home to see if Zach fell ill and decided to lie down.

When Rachel realized Zach wasn't home, she retraced his steps through the alley to Whittier Elementary School. As any parent would, she screamed her son's name over and over again in the alley. Neighbors watched out their windows as she walked up and down the alley that led directly to his school. It was a freezing cold day in February in Montana. Rachel could hardly breathe through her screams as she sucked in the blistery Arctic air.

When Rachel finally arrived at Whittier, she thought *maybe* they had found Zach somewhere in the school. Perhaps he was in the gymnasium or the bathroom. Maybe he met a friend and decided to skip breakfast and walked in late.

Rachel was grasping at straws.

Nobody at Whittier had seen Zach yet. Even though it had only been a couple of hours, Rachel decided to call the police and report her ten-year-old son missing. Detective William Bellusci heard the calls about the missing boy and immediately saw Nathaniel Bar-Jonah's face in his mind's eye. The detective thought back to his last meeting with Bar-Jonah about the boy he allegedly fondled. Bellusci remembered him saying he must have blacked out during the encounter.

Bar-Jonah also added that if he had fondled the boy, he would have just killed him. The detective was chilled to the bone by that admission. He kept Bar-Jonah in front of his thoughts after that. It was only a matter of time, the detective estimated, before the fat man slipped up, and he would be there to put the screws to him. Bellusci immediately transmitted to dispatch that patrol units should head over to Bar-Jonah's apartment and knock on the door. Bellusci wanted to gauge what type of shape Bar-Jonah was in and how he would react to questioning. He had checked his creep list and Nathaniel Bar-Jonah was at the very top.

Of course, he was not home. The apartment was quiet. The opportunity to speak to him in the immediate aftermath of Zach's disappearance was lost.

It was just the latest misstep in a long chain of missteps that allowed Nathaniel Bar-Jonah to operate in Great Falls. By the afternoon, the Great Falls media had picked up the story of the disappearance. Zach's face was plastered all over local news stations. Neighborhood searches began in the bitter cold Montana twilight. Searchers swept the alley, seemingly a million times. The dumpsters that popped up every couple of feet were checked, rechecked, and checked again. There was no sign of Zach Ramsay.

Doc had seen the news reports. He was heartbroken. He *was supposed to take Zach away. It was* his *last chance at love.*

Detective Bellusci thought something sinister may have happened to Zach but kept that information to himself for the time being. He wanted to get in front of Bar-Jonah. He had no evidence linking him to Zach Ramsay; hell, he wasn't even sure Zach was technically missing. The detective just had a gut feeling that Bar-Jonah was involved. Later in the afternoon, he went back to Bar-Jonah's apartment and rapped on the door. No answer. He checked all the windows. He couldn't see inside. This time, Detective Bellusci left a handwritten note asking to speak with him and slipped it under the door. The note commanded Bar-Jonah to call immediately.

When he came home to the note, Bar-Jonah didn't think it was a pressing matter. He waited three days before deciding to call the detective back. They had a short conversation. Bellusci wanted to meet with Bar-Jonah immediately, face to face. Bellusci knew Bar-Jonah was a cunning liar but thought he could make the seat hot enough for Bar-Jonah to crack. Bellusci knew Bar-Jonah was nowhere near as smart as he thought he was. Bar-Jonah agreed to an interview, but it had to take place on February 26—eighteen days later. He gave no reason for this demand, other than that was the next available date when he had time. Bellusci didn't press but perhaps he should have. It was the early days of Zach's disappearance and getting a look at Bar-Jonah early on was imperative.

Nathaniel Bar-Jonah had good reason for delaying the meeting. He had physical issues, like a sprained left index finger. Two days prior, he had visited an urgent care facility for the finger and he didn't want the police to see the splint he now sported. Why the detective agreed to wait eighteen days, I will never know. He had no evidence, just a gut feeling. He knew Bar-Jonah was a sexual predator who had attacked young boys in Massachusetts. If he had done something to Zach, those early days would have been spent getting rid of evidence, maybe even the body. A seasoned law enforcement officer like Detective William Bellusci had to have known that. He had been an investigator for years. Well before Great Falls, he worked in the Office of Special Investigations in the Air Force.

Subsequently, Bar-Jonah never made it to that February 26 meeting. He instead visited his ultimate enabler, an enigmatic figure in this story, his brother, Bob. Bob thought it wasn't a good idea to see the police without consulting a lawyer. Bar-Jonah allegedly had no idea why the police wanted to meet with him. He played stupid to his brother about any crime he may have committed. He never mentioned Zach's disappearance, even though Bob had seen the media coverage and immediately suspected his brother of being involved. Bob knew Bar-Jonah had the use of their mother's white Toyota Corolla around the time Zach disappeared. Their mother, Tyra, had headed back to Western Massachusetts for a funeral in early February 1996 and he was completely unsupervised. Even though Bob often wondered if Bar-Jonah was his actual brother, he would often foot the bill for his lawyers and psychologists. Bob Brown's money was the entire reason Bar-Jonah was operating in Great Falls. I believe Bob has culpability for his brother's behavior. On Bob's advice, Bar-Jonah lawyered up.

Detective William Bellusci also had suspicions about Zach's mother, Rachel Howard. Rachel came home the night of Zach's disappearance and couldn't sleep. You can certainly understand the parents of a missing child having issues sleeping on the very day their child disappears. Rachel left that night and walked the streets of Great Falls, yelling her son's name and looking for any clues to her son's disappearance. As a father, I certainly understand this behavior. I would do the same thing. When Bellusci asked Rachel what she did during those couple of hours, she couldn't account for it. She told the truth. She simply walked the streets. Bellusci was highly suspicious of those unaccounted hours. He thought Rachel had done something on that night to dispose of her son's body.

He would focus on Rachel for the rest of his time at the Great Falls Police Department. Even when overwhelming evidence pointed towards Nathaniel Bar-Jonah, Bellusci remained steadfast. After hearing about those lost hours, Bellusci stopped contacting Bar-Jonah. He discounted the witness statements that put Bar-Jonah right behind Zach in the alley that very morning. He completely lost focus and developed tunnel vision. He was so focused on Rachel Howard that he would not consider any other suspects. He had the FBI polygraph Rachel; she passed. He had Rachel's phones tapped and a GPS tracking device attached to her vehicle. All this energy could have been focused on Bar-Jonah. If even half of it were, maybe Zach Ramsay's body would have been found.

Rachel was convinced that Zach was alive and well. A local team of psychics contacted her and they told her that her son was probably kidnapped. She was convinced that

Zach's father had taken him away from her. The psychics told Rachel that someone was brainwashing Zach and he wanted to go home. He was out there somewhere. Rachel would never let go of this possibility. In Andy Puglisi's case, the psychic was a major hit. It worked. His leads gave law enforcement more ammunition against the right suspect. In general, I am vehemently against psychics getting involved in criminal cases. The psychics did significant damage to Rachel's mental state. They convinced Rachel that Zach was alive and that she went to visit Nathaniel Bar-Jonah when he was finally locked up. She was convinced he was a man of God and would never hurt her son. He manipulated Rachel Howard and it seriously hindered the investigation into her son's disappearance.

Is Rachel in denial? Sure. Can you blame her? Not really.

Rachel ramped up her media appearances a year after Zach disappeared. She even flew to New York City and appeared on *The Montel Williams Show*. She became convinced that maybe federal authorities and the police in Great Falls had taken her son and covered it up. Perhaps he was part of a child porn ring. Years prior, Bar-Jonah had been involved in underground child pornography rings. This irony was not lost on me. Bar-Jonah continued to operate the way he always did but he now had a live-in fiancée, a woman named Pam, who he met while working at a Hardee's restaurant as a line cook. He had zero interest in adult heterosexual relationships but he figured having Pam around would give the public the notion that he was attempting a normal life.

The couple never had sex. Bar-Jonah told her he preferred his sex after marriage. He would never be able to perform with a woman. His relationship with his best friend, Doc Bauman, had cooled off significantly: Zach had gone away and Doc knew the fat man had something to do with it. Doc was cordial because he knew Bar-Jonah was dangerous and could fly off the handle, so he kept his distance as much as he could.

Pam found it strange that in the week leading up to Zach's disappearance, and in the following two weeks, he wouldn't take her calls. He had completely fallen off the face of the Earth. He had no contact with his then fiancée. He wouldn't be seen again until February 17. My thought is he took this time to plan Zach's abduction and have time with the body. The evidence that would later come out supports this speculation.

Bar-Jonah's brother, Bob, owned two garages near his apartment. Pam noticed that he spent a tremendous amount of time in one of those garages. She would repeatedly rap on the door, pleading with her fiancé to come out and spend time with her. He had turned the garage into a perfect space in which to lure children. There were toys and even a small theater set up for hand puppet shows. He was perfecting his craft as a child predator. Incredibly, neighborhood children would flock to this garage. Bar-Jonah's paradise for children was a major hit in the area. No parent bothered to question who this man was and sometimes, parents would even drop off their kids at the garage on Saturday afternoons. It adds to the point that children, most with no father in the home, are incredibly hungry for someone, anyone, to take an interest in them.

Bar-Jonah preyed on that fact with incredible ease—too much ease. He named his puppet Mr. Popcorn Head and the kids ate it up. Parents would even drop him a few bucks for keeping their kids busy for them. It's truly astounding and very disturbing in retrospect. Nathaniel Bar-Jonah, a sadistic serial pedophile, had seemingly become a pillar in the Great Falls community. It's unclear whether the police in Great Falls noticed his activities but I doubt it.

Detective William Bellusci investigated him for a bit in the aftermath of Zach Ramsay's disappearance, yet all of this took place in the immediate aftermath. As usual, Bar-Jonah confidently assumed he would beat the cops again.

In 1997, he met a woman named Sherri Dietrich when she stopped in Great Falls on her way to Washington State. She was browsing in the American Antique Mall where he had set up shop. Life had been rough for Sherri. She, like most of Bar-Jonah's victims, was looking for anyone to listen to her and he was there with an open ear. He listened intently to her hard-luck story and offered her a place to stay. By then, he was out of his mother's apartment and lived with Pam. Who knows what his motivation was but Sherri readily accepted the offer. She was desperate.

Sure, Bar-Jonah was incredibly unattractive and he had terrible hygiene, but he listened well and was nice. She needed a place to crash badly. The motivation behind his offer certainly wasn't sexual. I think his motivation was far more sinister. Nathaniel Bar-Jonah was dying to tell somebody about abducting Zachary Ramsay. He saw Sherri as crazy. She was also a transient he could send on her way at any time. Unlike his fiancée, she would be in his life for a short time. He had met the person with whom he would confide about Zach. Just hours into her stay, he commanded Sherri to take a seat at the kitchen table. Bar-Jonah chain-smoked and stared off into the abyss while spinning an incredible tale about a boy whom Sherri had never heard of. He no doubt got off on recounting the story. He relived every second of the story while telling it to Sherri.

He told Sherri the story in the third person and referred to himself as the "policeman." He no doubt dressed as a policeman while abducting Zach. He probably told Zach he worked undercover when they met. Zach was always under the impression his chubby friend was a local undercover cop, maybe even a US Marshal, as he had told other victims. Bar-Jonah confessed to Sherri that the policeman was involved in a love triangle of sorts with Zach and an old man (the old man he was referring to, of course, was Doc

Bauman). The policeman was upset Zach had been going to the old man's place a little too often; Zach wasn't paying enough attention to the policeman since the old man had gotten involved. The old man, he added, was a homosexual. This poor boy was caught in a lover's quarrel with two very sick men. The policeman's anger was beginning to bubble over, he told her. Zach had started to ignore him completely when the old man got involved. Zach had started making excuses to the policeman when he asked Zach to play. Zach had homework, he would tell him. The policeman knew he was lying and going to see the old man—he needed to punish both for their sins.

The policeman met Zach in between two dumpsters by the alley, Bar-Jonah told Sherri, and coaxed Zach into his vehicle. He was red with rage at this point. The policeman wasn't going to let Zach run away with the old man. The policeman owned Zach. If he couldn't have him, nobody could, and he would make sure of that. The policeman knocked the boy unconscious in the car. He tied a noose around the little boy's neck. Bar-Jonah began driving to a cabin he knew of near Holter Lake Campground located in Wolf Creek, Montana, and made the hour drive down I-15 South with the boy slipping in and out of consciousness. He broke into the cabin located near the lake. He took a piece of plywood out of the back seat of the car and planned to tie the boy to the board.

Bar-Jonah got Zach into the cabin but then the boy woke for one terror-inducing second and grabbed the policeman's coat and possibly tore the zipper right off. It was a momentary problem, however; Bar-Jonah put him down right away and made a note to have the zipper repaired. He loved the coat; he needed to wear it to lure children. Bar-Jonah strangled the boy on the floor of the cabin and administered a brutal beating to the head and face, furiously kicking and punching. A stolen trick from one of his old friends. He removed the boy's clothes and stuffed them in the boy's mouth.

He hung the boy on the board but Zach didn't scream. He didn't have much breath left. His eyes were swollen shut from the brutal beating Bar-Jonah had administered. He was sure Zach was dead and dragged him out to the water just beyond the cabin. When he placed the board in the sand, the boy began to fight with all he had left. The policeman had his way with Zach already—he was ready to teach him the ultimate lesson. The policeman began stabbing Zach repeatedly with his hunting knife.

The policeman lost control and couldn't stop. He went all the way through the boy's body and down to the board, leaving tiny triangular marks behind. There were speckles of Zach's blood all over his face, getting in his multi-colored eyes.

When Bar-Jonah cut the boy's throat, he relaxed a little bit. The older man would not win in *this* lover's quarrel. Nobody would have Zach. He wanted to keep Zach for himself, even in death. He began to cut the boy into pieces. He filleted the boy all afternoon in the cabin. Nobody had seen him. The grounds were a barren wasteland in the winter. Getting each piece of Zach to his satisfaction, Bar-Jonah carefully placed his fillets in plastic bags and walked out of the cabin the same way he came in. *It was all going way too perfectly*, he thought.

Sherri had no idea what to think of the policeman's story. She had known Bar-Jonah for a short time and he had seemed like such a nice, Christian man. He had a vivid imagination. *Perhaps he was on drugs*, she thought. His eyes seemed so fixated during the story that she thought he was in a trance. Sherri had no idea he was confessing. *Every word of it may have played out that way*, Sherri thought, *that he was at the very least insane and probably dangerous.*

At some point, Nathaniel Bar-Jonah realized he had crossed the line with Sherri. Like most predators, he was itching to talk about his crimes. He couldn't tell his best friend, Doc Bauman. *Doc would eventually get tangled up with the law*, he thought. The chances where Doc might have a chance to roll over on him and talk. Sherri was nonthreatening enough that Bar-Jonah chose her to make his confession. It wasn't long before he confessed to Sherri that it was time for her to leave. He handed her a handwritten eviction note.

As soon as she made her escape from his apartment, she called Detective William Bellusci and told him that she had some information about Zachary Ramsay. Bellusci eventually met with her before she left Great Falls and she recounted the policeman's story to him in vivid detail. He listened intently to every word and thanked her for her time.

The detective never followed up with Bar-Jonah about the "policeman."

It wasn't long before the children who would be Nathaniel Bar-Jonah's downfall moved into his apartment building. In the winter of 1998, Lori Big Leggins moved upstairs with her two boys, and they were Nathaniel's ideal victims. They were of Native American heritage with dark complexions and dark hair and eyes. He immediately recognized that the boys would be easy victims to isolate. Lori was an irresponsible mother who often let her kids run crazy on Great Fall's streets. Bar-Jonah would flatter the kids with toys and snacks after school. Lori felt lucky that such a nice man lived downstairs. Sure, his apartment stunk most of the time. The smell would almost knock you over when you opened the door.

Bar-Jonah was a hunter, he told her. He was always in the process of butchering meat and storing it in his freezer. Lori bought that excuse; *he looked like a hunter*, she thought. This was one of the rare cases of a predator grooming victims with a father present. Lori's husband, Gerald, worked long hours and money was always an issue in their household. The family did accept welfare but it was hard for them to keep up on a day-to-day basis, so Bar-Jonah filled a lot of those monetary gaps. He fed the boys often and even took them out for extravagant birthday dinners. He had pinned Lori and Gerald as absent parents who much preferred to drink beer at the casino than be home parenting their children.

Bar-Jonah often said to his buddy Doc Bauman that he was in real luck that these kids moved upstairs. Doc's preference was also for dark-skinned young boys. He immediately offered Bar-Jonah the opportunity to visit with him as well. Doc claimed he was always concerned about Bar-Jonah's violent streak.

Doc was a true boy lover; he didn't have a sadistic bone in his body and Bar-Jonah wasn't like him, he thought. Bar-Jonah loved the boys but he enjoyed inflicting pain on young boys even more. In his more lucid moments, Doc would often tell himself that Bar-Jonah did not love boys the way that he did. He was a phony. A fraud. Doc was concerned for these new neighbors' well-being. Doc offered his apartment to Bar-Jonah and the boys for a sleepover a few times, but Bar-Jonah always declined. He was going to be selfish with these kids this time, not like Zach. Bar-Jonah had wormed his way into the boys' lives so much that he eventually convinced Lori and Gerald it would be easier if their oldest boy lived with him. I cannot fathom parents allowing their child to move in with a man they have only known for a few months. Lori readily agreed, however. She had no idea the hell she was allowing her son to walk into. The oldest boy loved Bar-Jonah and considered him to be his best friend; he had convinced the boy that he was an officer, working in federal law enforcement as a US Marshal. He promised he would train the boy and teach him the ways of a marshal's service. The boy was over the moon about his luck. Bar-Jonah was a real-life US Marshal and he gave him his undivided attention.

The older boy didn't mind when Bar-Jonah took him out for his little excursions. He would park with the boy in his idling vehicle and take pictures of school kids while they were on their lunch break. Bar-Jonah needed the pictures for his fledgling toy business, he told the boy. He was a willing sidekick hanging out with a US Marshal who moonlighted as a toy retailer. It all made perfect sense. The three-hundred-pound Bar-Jonah obviously would never have gotten through the first physical fitness exam prospective marshals are administered. It was all a complete front to gain the young boy's trust and, of course, take advantage of him sexually.

On the brutally cold morning of December 13, 1999, Detective Robert Burton of the Great Falls Police Department was making the same drive from his home to work he had made for nearly ten years. Like most, the Great Falls detective knew Nathaniel Bar-Jonah's back story. He knew he had abducted children back in Massachusetts, so Burton always kept his eye out for the obese man with the scraggly beard. He was concerned that morning when he saw Bar-Jonah, clad in black or dark blue, walking just mere blocks away from the local elementary school. Burton knew Bar-Jonah had gotten off easy on his last case—fondling a boy—in 1994. Bar-Jonah was always on his radar. After the detective's gears started turning, he recalled he had seen Bar-Jonah twice that very week near the elementary school.

What the hell was this guy doing? Burton thought.

He needed a patrol officer to make contact, so he radioed dispatch about a suspicious male near the elementary school. Great Falls Patrolman Steve Brunk was the first on the scene and contacted Bar-Jonah at the 400 block of 27th Street South. Bar-Jonah was out early in the cold. It was still dark at that time of the morning in December and the patrolman had to shine his spotlight to see him. Bar-Jonah had on a dark, police-style jacket, along with a winter cap. Brunk wanted him to remove his hands from his pockets for officer safety. Bar-Jonah was known to be violent and was a mammoth of a man, and Brunk wanted to exert control immediately. He commanded Bar-Jonah to remove his hands from his pockets but the request was ignored.

At that time, a second officer, Patrolman Badgely, arrived on the scene and asked Bar-Jonah if he had something he was hiding in his pocket. He confirmed he had what he described as a stun gun in his pocket. The officers immediately placed the predator against the vehicle and searched. Police found pepper spray, the stun gun, another replica toy gun, and a police badge. The police officers reviewed Montana's concealed weapons laws and radioed to their higher command back at the unit. The shift commander at the Great Falls Police Department advised the officers to release Bar-Jonah, but a report would be filed, and a detective would be following up. Detective William Bellusci got the report; Bar-Jonah was back in his clutches again.

Detective Bellusci consulted the district attorney, who thought that Bar-Jonah should be charged with impersonating a public servant, but the DA needed more evidence. Bellusci applied for a search warrant to get into Bar-Jonah's apartment, listing the items he was looking for: replica handguns, pepper spray, and any attire that looked like police or law enforcement. The search warrant was authorized without a hitch. Two days later the detective executed the warrant on the apartment and found an array of items—a silver police badge, a blue police coat, a Stun Master stun gun, and two albums with cut-out pictures of children. Police also found undeveloped film and disposable cameras.

They had found what they were looking for on the impersonation charge but the film and the cut-outs had roused their suspicion. Knowing Bar-Jonah's history of offenses against children, Bellusci thought he should apply for another search warrant and dig a little deeper. The language in the second search warrant application specified searching the undeveloped film Bar-Jonah had in his apartment. Bellusci also needed to prove why Bar-Jonah dressed as a public servant and to show the courts that Bar-Jonah's motivation for impersonating law enforcement was to stalk children.

During the second search, police seized Bar-Jonah's writings, bulletin boards, twenty-eight boxes full of miscellaneous newspaper clippings, and pictures. Bellusci knew that Bar-Jonah had been caught that cold morning just before he was about to kidnap a child. He knew deep in his soul that, unlike 1994, he had Bar-Jonah this time and he wasn't going to let him go without a hell of a fight.

Detective Bellusci was also unnerved by a piece of paper he found in a drawer. The paper had some bizarre code on it. It looked like gibberish. Names were written backward and sideways. He took it anyway. FBI agent James Wilson of the Great Falls office joined the detectives when they served the search warrant. The FBI was heavily interested in Bar-Jonah and the agent became completely obsessed with his crimes. The agent found a piece of paper with the title "CATCH A LITTLE FISH AND A LITTLE BOY POPS OUT" scribbled on top in Bar-Jonah's handwriting. Agent Wilson had no idea what the hell to make of it but he took it anyway. He immediately sensed that there was way more to Nathaniel Bar-Jonah than just a guy who dressed as a police officer to impress kids. He knew he wasn't dealing with a run-of-the-mill predator.

He began to dig into Bar-Jonah's background. He immediately wrote to Bridgewater and requested every record they ever had on David Brown/Nathaniel Bar-Jonah. Wilson wrote that Bar-Jonah was now being investigated for dressing as a public servant, just as he had in 1977 when he abducted the two boys in Shrewsbury. The agent stressed that time was of the essence. They had just served two search warrants on his apartment, and he possessed police badges and replica weapons.

Agent Wilson was hoping to develop a profile on Bar-Jonah to better get inside his mind when it came time to question him. They were also developing a film they found in Bar-Jonah's possession. Lab technicians were completely unnerved by the negatives. There were pictures of Bar-Jonah nude from the waist down, which was long before the days of selfie sticks. Due to the angle of the pictures, he had to have asked someone to take the pictures for him, Bellusci figured.

He also had pictures of young Native American boys in various poses. In some pictures, the boys' shirts were up, and in others, they were naked from the waist up. Bellusci recognized the children. He had seen them around town running crazy. He knew the boys had very little supervision. He also knew they had lived upstairs from Bar-Jonah. Bellusci immediately radioed other detectives to track down Nathaniel Bar-Jonah and arrest him. Bellusci also tracked down the boys' mother, Lori Big Leggins. Bellusci questioned Lori about Bar-Jonah's relationship with her children. Bar-Jonah had completely duped her; she was under his psychopathic spell. Lori stood up for him, telling Bellusci that Bar-Jonah was a great friend to her boys and they were lucky to have him as a babysitter.

Detective Robert Burton caught up with Bar-Jonah that day and advised him he was going to be placed under arrest for impersonating a police officer. Burton radioed that he needed a uniformed officer there with him in case the three-hundred-pound suspect resisted but Bar-Jonah went quietly. He had a can of pepper spray on him, supposedly, for protection. He likely would never have believed it at the time—he had beaten every rap the cops had put on him in Great Falls—but this arrest would be the last time Nathaniel Bar-Jonah saw the light of day outside of prison walls.

Detective Bellusci executed a third search warrant on the apartment after his arrest. This time, authorities found a rope fashioned into a noose and twenty boxes of pictures and cut-outs of children. He had noted the awful smell in the house on the prior searches. He assumed Bar-Jonah had terrible hygiene and the place was a disorganized mess. Bellusci opened the refrigerator at one point and noticed the awful rotting meat staring at him in the face. He didn't bother to take samples of the meat. Why would he? There's no way he could have known Bar-Jonah had human remains in his refrigerator. Years later, the detective would beat himself up over that chance encounter in the freezer. Maybe he could have broken the Zach Ramsay case wide open right there if he had been quick enough on his feet.

At that point, Bar-Jonah's mother wasn't aware the police had been searching for her son. Tyra thought that her son had finally gotten his life in order. She thought he was a misunderstood and persecuted man and so she was aghast when her son called her after being booked into jail.

Nathaniel Bar-Jonah demanded his mother get over to the apartment immediately and clean it up. The cops had searched it twice and he was concerned about its status. Tyra went immediately to Bob. Bob Brown went to the apartment and enlisted the help of the young boy who lived upstairs. Bob had no idea the police had pictures of that same boy in suggestive poses. The boy didn't bother to tell Bob he had taken the pictures of Bob's brother. Bob wanted the place cleaned and the little boy needed to help him. Bob used this time together to make sure they knew that Bar-Jonah passed along a message: keep your mouths shut.

Bob Brown enabled his brother to commit crimes his entire life. Now, he was obstructing justice by interfering in a criminal investigation. He was extremely culpable in covering up his brother's crimes against children in Montana, and what was about to happen would accentuate that point. He would coach the oldest boy on what to say if the cops came around asking questions. He *knew* Bar-Jonah was a predator and he continued to cover for him and run interference.

On December 18, Bob arrived to clean up the apartment.

Bob was instructed to save nothing. Everything needed to go. It took him a few hours to rip through the small apartment. He tossed everything in the giant dumpster outside the apartment complex. He scrubbed everything. Bob cleaned the refrigerator too. He took the foul-smelling meat out of the freezer and double bagged it. That too went in the dumpster. Bar-Jonah would often tell friends and even random people he encountered that Zach Ramsay's body would never be found. He had good reason to believe it. Zach's body had been in his freezer and Bob threw him out with his brother's junk a week before Christmas.

Sergeant John Cameron of the Great Falls Police Department could never get Nathaniel Bar-Jonah out of his mind. He took over the case in February 2000 from Detective William Bellusci. The case nearly killed Bellusci and cost him his marriage and his sanity. I contacted Sergeant Cameron numerous times during my research. I got the sense he never wanted to talk about Bar-Jonah ever again. He had ridden the monster from his psyche and hoped to never get back to that place. That is the effect Nathaniel Bar-Jonah had on most people who encountered him.

It wasn't until well after the first version of this book was released that Sergeant John Cameron finally reached out to me. I sat through a thirty-minute orientation on a serial killer named Ed Edwards whom Cameron believed was responsible for everything from JonBenet to the Zodiac Killer who haunted Northern California in the late 1960s. I walked away believing Cameron was either insane or had cracked the biggest case in history. During the meeting, I made a promise to myself that if he started to talk about Jack the Ripper, I would just fake a heart attack and call an ambulance to get me out of there. In all seriousness, I think Cameron is heroic for his work on Bar-Jonah. We both had the same feelings about the case: Bar-Jonah had skated on murder and there were more bodies out there.

When he was assigned to the Bar-Jonah case, Cameron immediately ran into the all-too-common politics that run many organizations. Lieutenant Corky Groves, who oversaw and outranked Cameron, immediately started complaining to Cameron that the Bar-Jonah investigation was wildly mismanaged and he needed to get to some finality on Bar-Jonah, now. He gave Cameron a month to wrap it up. Cameron thought Groves was a moron and the detectives who were focusing only on Rachel Howard were incompetent. He was convinced that this was a stranger abduction case and wanted to explore the Nathaniel Bar-Jonah angle in depth. He immediately dove into all of Bar-Jonah's bizarre writings and paperwork obtained in the searches.

He zeroed in on something that took place on February 6, 1996. Cameron found a receipt Bar-Jonah had for the urgent care center across the street from his apartment. He had visited the clinic at 2:20 p.m. that day for a sore leg and a jammed finger and thumb. Cameron found it curious that on the day of the disappearance, Nathaniel Bar-Jonah had been injured. Cameron was a seasoned investigator. He often found suspects visiting medical facilities on days they committed crimes. Injuries happen when you physically assault someone because people fight back.

Cameron was locked in on that note from the doctor and the piece of plywood they found in Bar-Jonah's apartment. He studied that plywood repeatedly. There were triangular holes in the wood like someone stood over it and stabbed it repeatedly. He knew the board was an important piece of physical evidence. Another piece of physical evidence that struck Cameron was Bar-Jonah's handwritten notes—a piece of paper on which more than a dozen names had been scribbled. The names of the boys found on his negatives were printed on the paper. Another name that showed up was Zachary Ramsay, the missing boy from 1996. The investigation reached a new level of intensity when

Cameron found the list of names. He immediately rounded up everyone he could find who was connected to Bar-Jonah. Tyra Brown was sick of the whole thing. She moved from Great Falls back to Massachusetts. She never saw a minute of what was to come for her son whom she had doted on his entire life. She was eighty-two years old and tired of his antics.

Sergeant Cameron connected with Bob Brown to talk about his brother. He found Bob to be odd but an honest broker. Bob even suggested some sites the police may investigate for Zach Ramsay's body, to think how his brother may have thought. He suggested rivers and the city dump. Did Bob know more than he let on about Zach's disappearance? Probably not. Bob knew that his brother was a predator capable of lashing out at children at any moment. He still fought to have Bar-Jonah released and even welcomed him to Great Falls. There was no way Bob could be shocked the police were coming to him about a missing boy and his brother's involvement in the boy's disappearance.

Cameron continued to study the bizarre and cryptic writings. He would stare for hours at the handwritten codes in the pedophile's notebook. The code went like this:

NIQASUTSEHEDARKNIAEDEDSLOEBNXETANHL-
JEAAPC MAAITRNITL OAEWNVIDITMBHYARZROI-
JATOSTNTLAEEHDM DCIAHDVLDILEDDSPLSAIE
UTRLTT8LREOBWONYLSUTNECW HBARBEGELPEN-
PRAISEGREENHANGEMH IGHHAPPYHALLOWEENC
ASRLSOSFPGOSETRESUSNSESICEETISLTLOYOPEEI EA
SAOERATDIRATDUKYOPADTWMNMAPEITEBPTISPNSSR
EUMFECFIDIAAS XRLEMSRBTNSCIGHLTLOYPHSNSCI
YMYRNHREKDNLEOASXAATAIGUKNTEI TEBSEIADUKN
GTRFNLNTEITEOADIIGIOREAAHUKNHRNEVANFRHF
IDYODI GHLTLBYNGVNHMHRBTFCISEIHRGIADTEN

He knew the key to the Zach Ramsay case—and maybe other missing children—lay right in those mysterious codes. Even the best cryptologists from the FBI could not make heads or tails of Bar-Jonah's writings. During one of his many struggle sessions with the notebook, Cameron started to draw a snake-like line around the letters and nearly jumped out of his chair. A small sentence jumped out at him: "*Little Boy Pot Pie.*"

He immediately shrieked, "My god, he ate him!" Cameron's colleagues immediately joined him, helping draw the lines.

Before long, the following phrases became clear:

Penises are yummy.
French-fried kid.
Little boy stew.

The investigation was now galvanized and Cameron believed he had a cannibal on his hands. He felt he had solved the mystery of what happened to Zachary Ramsay's body—Nathaniel Bar-Jonah had eaten him. John Cameron thought that Zach Ramsay's bones could still be out there. He needed to obtain search warrants for everywhere and anywhere Bar-Jonah touched. They also needed his DNA and hair samples pulled immediately. Tyra Brown's Toyota Corolla, which was in Dudley, Massachusetts, also needed to be searched. Cameron thought he had Bar-Jonah dead to rights.

John Cameron quickly drew up search warrants for the Corolla because it was the sole means of transport Bar-Jonah would have had on February 6, 1996, and Bob's garage at 1216 1 Avenue South in Great Falls. The warrant was approved in no time. In early April, Cameron and company arrived in Nathaniel Bar-Jonah and Wayne Chapman's old stomping grounds. The early April chill of New England was nothing to the grizzled Montana lawman. He found the

Massachusetts State Police completely useless in getting Tyra's vehicle to the state police barracks. An agreement was made ahead of time that the state police would facilitate the Browns getting the vehicle from Dudley to the Worcester barracks. The duty officer at the barracks refused to let Cameron search the vehicle. A mass of confusion ensued. Eventually, after many phone calls back and forth from Montana to Massachusetts, the vehicle was searched. The irony was not lost on him that the confusion between the two states years earlier was exactly the reason this scenario even played out at all. Massachusetts dumped its garbage on Montana and the Montana authorities would have to scramble to pick up the pieces.

When he arrived back in Montana after the bizarre Massachusetts debacle, Cameron immediately served the search warrant on Bob's property, which commenced in the early hours of April 18. He focused on the garage where Bar-Jonah used to do his Mr. Popcorn Head puppet shows for the neighborhood kids. Authorities, along with archeological students from a nearby university, quickly hit pay dirt after breaking ground in the garage. The searches started to unearth bone fragments. Some were short, some long, and they came fast. Cameron's pulse was starting to pound watching the students sift the dirt. *Had he solved the Zach Ramsay case? Or were there other victims buried underneath this garage?*

His hunch about Bob's property was spot on. The search party was running out of time. They excavated as much dirt as possible and stuck it into bins. They would bring the dirt back to the gym adjacent to the Great Falls Police Department and sift it there, where they had endless time. The bones they turned up were not full. They were sawed-off chips. The bones had clearly been sawed and cut and buried there. Cameron knew he had enough fragments to test against DNA technology. He immediately went and saw Rachel and pulled a blood sample for the technicians to test against the fragments. He sent the fragments to scientists to be tested and held his breath.

When the DNA test results came back, Cameron was shocked to learn the bone fragments didn't match Rachel Howard's DNA. The bone fragments did not belong to Zach Ramsay like he had been sure of. They belonged to someone else. Cameron was chilled to the bone by this revelation. *Just what had this monster been doing right under his nose? If the bone fragments were not Zach Ramsay's, whose were they? Did John have other missing kids on his docket?* He would have to crosscheck in every state Nathaniel Bar-Jonah had been in.

The sergeant was getting political pressure again as well. His lieutenant was putting heat on him to close the case. The investigation into Nathaniel Bar-Jonah was a waste of money that produced very little, Lieutenant Groves told him; Rachel Howard was the real culprit, he told Cameron, but he knew the man was a politician who was utterly clueless about what Cameron was on to. The political pressure and his crumbling home life were taking a major toll on the investigator. By then, Cameron had interviewed Bar-Jonah's neighbors pictured in his stash of film. The boys admitted that Bar-Jonah had molested the oldest boy, whom Cameron was planning to have testify. He was hoping to send Bar-Jonah away forever on that case.

In July, Cameron stopped by Nathaniel Bar-Jonah's jail and served him the indictment on the molestation charge. He had been "lied about by little brats yet again." He was completely indignant that those boys had turned on him and lied to the cops. He had taken care of the boys when their absent parents were off drinking at the casino. Bar-Jonah had taken the oldest boy out for birthday dinners and paid attention to him like nobody in his life ever had. He felt completely betrayed.

Cameron also knew his department had totally blown the Bar-Jonah investigation early on and a shit storm would eventually gather. Detective Bellusci should have tracked Nathaniel Bar-Jonah down right away. The Rachel Howard focus was completely off base and should have been tossed aside immediately. Also, the mere fact that Bar-Jonah was able to enter the state of Montana at all befuddled him. He talked to everyone he could in Bridgewater about Bar-Jonah's time there. The documents painted a disturbing picture of an animal that should have been caged forever. *That alone*, Sergeant Cameron thought, *was enough to cost a lot of people their jobs.*

He found correspondence with Doc Bauman in stacks of papers. One thing jumped out to Cameron: Doc Bauman had thanked Bar-Jonah at the end of one letter by writing, "Thank you for the dear meat." Cameron believed then that Doc Bauman knew what had happened to Zachary Ramsay. While Cameron knew Doc was a predator with a long history of molesting children, he had not known that Doc and Bar-Jonah were acquainted. The "dear meat" was no mistake. It was an inside joke. Doc knew exactly what had happened to Zach. He had consumed Zach Ramsay, just like Bar-Jonah had. *God damn it,* Cameron thought. *Bar-Jonah was serving Zach Ramsay around the neighborhood to his pedophile friends*, and he was livid. Livid that Nathaniel Bar-Jonah was allowed to enter his state. He was angry at the system and his department.

He immediately went to shake down Doc Bauman. He had no evidence outside of the notes back and forth between the two, but he tracked Doc down at his apartment. Doc lived in complete filth. Eventually, his place would be condemned. He had dozens of cats that defecated in the house and he didn't bother to clean the place. The stench was overwhelming. Cameron was disgusted by the old man's living quarters but he was a man on a mission. He needed to know about the "dear meat" and he was in no mood to screw around. He cut right to the chase with the aging predator and asked Doc what he knew about the meat in the letters he and Bar-Jonah had traded. He explained that he had read their correspondence and he suspected he knew about Zach Ramsay's disappearance. He was struck by how much Doc acted like a frail, naïve man.

But Cameron knew it was bullshit. Doc was a pedophile who knew quite well how to act around police, especially when guilty. Doc denied knowing anything about the Ramsay case. He didn't bother to mention he was set to leave with Zach that very morning and head to Canada. He also didn't go into the fact that Nathaniel Bar-Jonah was an aggressive sexual deviant who sometimes scared even him. He simply denied knowing anything and told the sergeant that if he thought of anything that may help, he would call him promptly. Cameron knew Doc was lying. He decided to relent a little bit and turn the heat down. He made a mental note to turn the heat back up on Doc soon. He was certain Doc was the key to the Zach Ramsay case. He left and headed home, to presumably burn the clothes he was wearing.

***

John Cameron was so obsessed with Zach Ramsay's case that his wife often asked him if he set a place at their dinner table for Nathaniel Bar-Jonah. I know the feeling. It was around the time of my Montana reporting that I started to fall into the dark hole myself. I took my first Montana trip in 2016. The flight was long and particularly turbulent. I arrived and walked down the exact alley where Zach Ramsay took his last steps. I did it fifty times on my first day there.

The flight was a disaster coming in; the weather was brutally hot and sticky. It reminded me of my time in Afghanistan only a few years prior. Great Falls was easy to navigate. The town is set up like a square grid and the streets interconnect through a series of alleyways. At that time, I was so desperate to make the connection between Nathaniel Bar-Jonah, Wayne Chapman, and Doc Bauman. I was convinced that somehow Doc and Bar-Jonah collaborated on Zach's disappearance. *Had they done it decades prior? Were the disappearances of Zach Ramsay, Andy Puglisi, and David Louison all connected?* Of course they are. I fell so far down the Nathaniel Bar-Jonah rabbit hole that by the time I got to Montana, I was clinically depressed. I knew I had to understand Bar-Jonah to understand Chapman but it was so unnerving to work daily on this kind of depraved subject matter. My memories of childhood sexual abuse were triggered as I walked and talked on the streets of Great Falls. I wasn't showering or shaving. Sometimes, I would walk for hours a day and realize I didn't put on socks with my boots. I was singularly focused.

My blisters ached but I just kept thinking the answer would be around the next corner. One more question to the right person and I would solve the puzzle.

***

Sergeant John Cameron focused on Doc Bauman and Nathaniel Bar-Jonah's plethora of bizarre writings in his apartment. He had written stories—perhaps works of nonfiction—mostly about torturing children and eating their bodies. Cameron thought Bar-Jonah had made confessions in his writings and it added a macabre undertone to the investigation. The suspect was talking through his writings to Cameron. He called the health inspector in Great Falls and made a report about Doc's awful living conditions, believing that the cats and squalor he lived in were a public health threat. Shortly thereafter, the health department showed up at Doc's door.

At the very least, the health inspector told Doc that the cats needed to go. He could keep a few but dozens of cats living in one house were against safety protocols for the city. Cameron was bringing the heat down and wanted Doc on the run. If he couldn't nail Doc yet on his involvement in Zach Ramsay's disappearance, at least he could make him uncomfortable. He also thought the children of the neighborhood would be safer if Doc didn't have a base to stay in every night. Doc had obsessed over his first meeting with Cameron. He thought John Cameron was tough and wouldn't stop coming after him until he got what he wanted.

Doc was a sickly old man. His time was almost up. Doc took almost a dozen different medications a day just to stay upright. He had problems with his leg, which would often swell. When his leg acted up, he was completely immobile. On his best days, he needed a cane to get around. Doc started thinking that he should just tell the cops what he knew about his dear Zach's disappearance. Nathaniel Bar-Jonah had stolen the boy from him. What did he care if Bar-Jonah fried? Doc started making plans to tell Cameron everything he knew. Doc had other pressing issues; the health inspector needed him out of his home within thirty days. Doc's place was scheduled to be condemned and bulldozed into oblivion in a month. He and his precious felines were a month out from being homeless.

Around this time, John Cameron had gotten to interview Nathaniel Bar-Jonah's live-in fiancée. Pam told him that Bar-Jonah had often fed her some funny-tasting meat. The meat stunk, she said. When Bar-Jonah would defrost the meat, the stench would hang in the house for days. At this point, he was still rotting in jail while awaiting trial. Bar-Jonah would often state to anyone who would listen, from guards to inmates, that there was no body. He knew nothing would ever stick if the cops charged him with Zach's murder. Like his buddy Charles Pierce told him, *"No body, no crime."* Bar-Jonah genuinely believed he would beat the sexual assault charges against his upstairs neighbors as well. He had beaten Bridgewater and the 1994 Montana case, after all. He was biding his time until salvation came. Nathaniel

Bar-Jonah hadn't given a thought to what his old friend Doc Bauman was thinking on the outside. He was gobsmacked when he received a letter from Doc while sitting in lockup. The letter stated:

Dear Nathan,

I am being bothered by Detective John Cameron. He seems to think that I know something about dear Zach. As I told you many times before, my heart was broken when you took Zach away from me, and even though I have tried, I have never been able to forgive you. I am in the final sunset of my life and I do not want to continue to be hounded by the likes of Cameron. He is forcing me from my home and taking away all that I love. I just found out today that my dear lady friend was found dead. Supposedly she died from an overdose, but I wouldn't doubt if Cameron had something to do with it, just to put pressure on me. You, Nathan, know what I know about Zach going away. But you also know that I am an old man now, who has many medical problems, none the least of which is my poor memory. It would be inconvenient for you and for me if my memory problems were cured. Anything you can do to direct Cameron's attention away from me would benefit us both. I am sure that you are faring well in jail. Somehow it always seemed to me that you handled being locked up much better than I. In some ways you seemed to prefer it. I leave it in your hands to resolve our sticky problem.

It is unclear whether the guards had taken to reading his incoming correspondence while in jail. I am told it was not protocol to open inmates' mail at the Cascade County Detention Center in Montana. Even though Nathaniel Bar-Jonah was a prolific writer, the prison took no pains to keep up with his pen pals. He read the letter and was livid. He cut the letter up immediately and dumped it down the toilet. The guards would almost undoubtedly flip his cell someday soon and read through his stuff. The letter is just more evidence that Doc Bauman knew exactly what happened to Zach Ramsay. Nathaniel Bar-Jonah had confided in him what he did with the little boy. Both these men were complicit in the disappearance. Whether it was before or after the fact doesn't matter. Doc knew and lied to John Cameron at their first meeting at his condemned apartment. Cameron wasn't done with Doc but he had other business to handle.

With the evidence he had, which now included a meat grinder Bob Brown had given him from Bar-Jonah's apartment with traces of human DNA in it, John Cameron had Nathaniel Bar-Jonah formally charged with murder. Sergeant Cameron walked into Cascade County Jail and served him with the murder and kidnapping indictment in the Ramsay case. Bar-Jonah was reeling but kept repeating that it would never stick. "There is no body."

Cameron hated being in Bar-Jonah's presence. When he served Bar-Jonah, he made it quick. His blood went cold when Bar-Jonah walked into the waiting area. He locked his eyes on Bar-Jonah and served the indictment. Cameron swore to himself he would lock this animal away forever so he could never hurt another child. Bar-Jonah was arraigned the very next day and in true characteristic fashion pled not guilty. His bail was set at nearly two million dollars.

Doc Bauman never heard back from Bar-Jonah after firing off his strongly worded letter. He was now out of his apartment and staying at a local hotel. He had read that Bar-Jonah was arraigned for the kidnapping and murder of his special friend, Zach. Cameron bided more time. He was nearly through with Bar-Jonah. He wanted to see the trial through to the end. When Nathaniel Bar-Jonah faced a jury and was served a life sentence, John Cameron could move on with his life. He still read the letters. He thought it would take him years to get through the letters.

FBI Special Agent Wilson also helped sift through the letters. Wilson was struck by a few correspondences in the pile. A man from back East would often write back and forth: a man named Wayne Chapman. Some of the letters went back to 1996, right around the time Zach Ramsay disappeared. There was a letter from late 1995, where Chapman wished Bar-Jonah a very Merry Christmas. *The two have a history*, Special Agent Wilson thought. He needed to dig deeper. Wilson began researching Wayne Chapman's background and was astounded to see the depths of offenses against children in Pennsylvania, Rhode Island, and Massachusetts. Wilson became obsessed with how prolific of an offender Chapman was on the outside. Wilson now knew that Chapman was an inmate at the Treatment Center in Bridgewater. He had been there since the late 1970s and his time had overlapped with Bar-Jonah's. Wilson did the math; they had spent nearly twelve years together on the same unit in the Southeastern Massachusetts town. Wilson had to meet Chapman. Like me, he sensed that the two were intertwined. To understand the depth of Nathaniel Bar-Jonah's crimes and his mindset you need to understand Wayne Chapman's.

In the early months of 2001, seven months before the terrorist attacks of 9/11, Agent Wilson and Sergeant Cameron boarded a plane to Massachusetts. When the plane landed at East Boston's Logan Airport, a few miles away from the Revere house on Mountain Avenue, the men started to formulate their game plan for their interview with Wayne Chapman. They had Nathaniel Bar-Jonah on murder charges. They needed some insight into his mind that a good friend of his could provide.

Cameron and Wilson rented a car and drove from Boston to Bridgewater. They fought traffic down the Southeast Expressway to Route 24. The forty-one-mile drive took forever in the brutal traffic from the city. When they arrived on Administration Road in Bridgewater, they took a long time to look around. They imagined Bar-Jonah walking around Bridgewater's grounds formulating his next move. John Cameron was struck by how far away he was from Great Falls. *How the hell did Bar-Jonah get to my jurisdiction? How did I get here?*

Cameron and Wilson checked in at the front desk and waited for Wayne Chapman to enter the small interview area on the second floor of the Treatment Center. Chapman entered the room after about twenty minutes of waiting. Special Agent Wilson identified himself and Cameron went next. Chapman acted astounded that the FBI and out-of-town detective wanted to meet with him. He knew about the interview and expected the authorities, but he was so deep into his act at that point that he slipped into character immediately. They asked a little bit about Chapman's background and made some small talk. They asked if he was aware of Bar-Jonah's status. Chapman denied ever knowing Nathaniel Bar-Jonah. The lawmen had read all their correspondence with each other. The address of Chapman's letters came from where they were sitting but he still denied everything.

He was a good Christian man; he told the investigators. He didn't know Bar-Jonah and had no interest in talking about his former criminal activities. Cameron and Wilson couldn't figure out where Chapman's accent put him geographically. He sounded like a man with a deep Southern-style slow drawl, even though he had spent his entire life on the Eastern Seaboard. He talked as if he were a possessed Southern man who pieced words together like song lyrics on a sheet of music. Cameron would never forget Chapman's facial expressions and the way he looked at him. It was like he was possessed; some sinister force had its hand under his shirt and was puppeteering Chapman to sound human.

The investigators concluded that Chapman was subhuman. There was just nothing there. The man had no capacity, they thought, to feel human emotions. Cameron and Wilson knew about the Andy Puglisi and David Louison cases. They knew they were looking at a man who may be a child killer himself. He was like a crocodile in the Nile River—he existed only to feed and nothing else mattered. Cameron and Wilson thanked Chapman for his time but the interview was worthless. They knew he was lying; they had the receipts. Chapman had no obligation to talk to them. They left Bridgewater with no more information than when they'd entered. The men took the long flight back to Montana, debating the entire time about who gave them the creeps more, Wayne Chapman or Nathaniel Bar-Jonah? The consensus was that Bar-Jonah was a master psychopath, but Chapman? He wasn't real. He was some sort of demon.

John Cameron came home livid. He thought he had done enough to arrest Doc Bauman on conspiracy charges in Zach Ramsay's disappearance. Even if the charges didn't stick, Doc was old and Cameron thought he could make him crack once he got him back behind bars, even for a short time. He found Doc at the Great Falls motel and issued him an ultimatum: Doc had one week to talk or Cameron would arrest him. He wasn't fucking around anymore. He knew Doc knew something. He told Doc the week ultimatum was "him being nice" and he really should drag his ass down to the police department now. Cameron left and Doc seethed. Doc was now at the decision hour. *Give up Nathaniel?* It was a no-brainer now.

Doc called three days later. He told Cameron that what he knew was somewhat minimal but he thought it could help him. Cameron was over the moon about the phone call. He believed that Doc was the missing piece of the puzzle in the entire case.

I agree.

The two made plans to meet a day later in Sergeant Cameron's office at the Great Falls Police Station on 112 1st Street South. Doc had a plan to tell him straight up about being angry with Bar-Jonah for making Zach disappear. Cameron thought Doc could testify. Doc thought Cameron might be pissed off enough to lock him up on some trumped-up charges like the charges he faced in 1993 with Detective William Bellusci. Doc thought he would simply invoke his Fifth Amendment rights and walk out if the interview started to favor John Cameron. That would give Doc a day or two of lead time to haul ass out of Montana. He made plans the entire morning before the afternoon interview. He looked at bus schedules and planned escape routes out of Great Falls. Doc planned to flee to the Pacific Northwest, Seattle specifically. Doc had a friend out there with a long history of offending children who would be sympathetic to Doc's plight. At seventy-two years old, Doc wanted to find a helping hand to ease him into the last phase of his life. Montana had been great. He had met many boys to love, but with that came trouble. He wore out his welcome in Great Falls. Doc headed off to see John Cameron for their 1:30 p.m. appointment.

Cameron woke up that morning thinking he was sick of the old man's bullshit. Today was the day of reckoning for Nathaniel Bar-Jonah and Doc.

The interview, of course, never took place. Doc Bauman died on the steps of the Great Falls Police Department just a half-hour before the scheduled meeting with John Cameron. His heart, which had been beating for seven decades, just stopped. In a story of incredible coincidences and bizarre Hollywood plot twists, Doc's death on the front stairs of the Great Falls Police Station lobby was a cruel irony. An evil psychopath like Nathaniel Bar-Jonah lucked out again. Cameron nearly had a stroke himself when he was radioed and told the news. He was certain that the staff in the unit were playing a cruel joke. He arrived at the station just as Doc was loaded into the ambulance. Doc was dead on arrival at the hospital in Great Falls.

Doc Bauman died on June 23, 2000, and was buried with full military honors at the Veteran's Cemetery in Helena, Montana. Doc rests in Section A, Row 6, Internment site 43. I have visited Doc's grave twice and I cursed him for besmirching the uniform of the United States Army that we shared for my nearly two-decades-long military career.

I also keenly sense that Doc Bauman knew far more about Zach Ramsay's disappearance than he admitted. Doc is a central figure in this book mainly because he, by his admission, was present during key periods and places. Doc was living in Massachusetts in the 1970s when Andy Puglisi, David Louison, and Leigh Savoie went missing, and he helped form the original NAMBLA contingent. He mysteriously showed up in Great Falls around the same time as Nathaniel Bar-Jonah, then got mixed up with Zach Ramsay—all by his admission. I thought about that a lot on my last trip to see his grave. There were too many coincidences to simply write off. It had to have been by design. In this case, the dead man told no tales. Whatever Doc knew about Zach Ramsay and Nathaniel Bar-Jonah is buried in the Veteran's Cemetery in Helena. I stopped by Doc's old house on my last trip as well. The house was bulldozed and built anew.

The family who lived there at the time had no idea of the events of the late 1990s. It wasn't my place to tell them. I was struck by how many kids were playing up and down the street. Kids were riding bikes and scooters. Games of street baseball broke out. It reminded me of my childhood hundreds of miles away in Massachusetts. Just miles from where Wayne Chapman, Nathaniel Bar-Jonah, and Doc once operated.

The people I interacted with in Great Falls always picked on my Boston accent. "Just what the hell does a guy from Massachusetts care about a little place in Montana?" I was often asked. I had to chuckle. These folks had no idea just how intertwined the two states were. Through a series of miscommunications, missteps, and incompetence, Montana and Massachusetts will forever be inexplicably linked because of these individuals.

It took Sergeant John Cameron a few days to get over Doc Bauman's death. He wished a dozen times the old bastard died an hour later. He went from the highest of highs to the lowest of lows. Nathaniel Bar-Jonah was ecstatic upon hearing of Doc's death. He immediately began singing at the top of his lungs to anyone who would listen that there was a mysterious "old man" who had been stalking Zach Ramsay.

"The police should look into him," he uttered out loud.

He could hardly contain himself. His luck had turned. Salvation was upon him. He turned to his letter writing. His correspondence with Wayne Chapman continued. Chapman gave him tips on how to act in court. The two predators cautioned each other to make sure their correspondence was destroyed after reading. The cops had been down to see Chapman—he was firmly on their radar.

Bar-Jonah laughed off the idea that the cops' visiting Chapman was anything more than desperation. There was no body and he was going to be exonerated on all charges related to Zach. Both men railed against the little brats who lied about them. Chapman had been locked up for decades because of the lying little shits while Bar-Jonah had tasted years of freedom. Chapman was hoping to emulate him and get past the prison walls of Bridgewater once and for all.

John Cameron checked in with Bar-Jonah's neighbors regularly. Their testimony was key to putting him away forever. He knew the murder case was thin. Considering Bar-Jonah's lengthy criminal history, if he were found guilty on the molestation charges, Cameron knew a life sentence was on the table—even if the murder charge didn't stick. When the trial began, his worries melted away. The boys showed incredible strength on the stand. It was clear that Nathaniel Bar-Jonah had done terrible things to these boys. He stole their innocence and smashed their young psyches. He even strangled one of the boys almost to the point of passing out with a crude, homemade noose. After a short trial and a bit of jury deliberation, the verdict was reached. In an incredibly exasperating moment for Cameron and the prosecution, the jury foreperson mistakenly read the verdict as *not guilty* and quickly corrected himself to *guilty*.

Cameron picked his head off the floor and gathered himself while Nathaniel Bar-Jonah was found guilty of three counts of child molestation. The judge sentenced him to one hundred and thirty years in prison. He would never see the light of day outside of prison again. Nathaniel Bar-Jonah never answered for the murder and kidnapping charges in Zach Ramsay's case. The murder charges were dismissed not long after Bar-Jonah was sentenced in his molestation case. John Cameron was livid about the dismissed murder but Bar-Jonah was elated. He was an "innocent man" after all. It was only right that the district attorney sided with him. The decision was monetary as well; Bar-Jonah was gone forever anyway. Why bother spending the resources on a very thin murder case? Cameron never bought it. He knew Bar-Jonah was guilty. He never got the chance to prove it. Nathaniel Bar-Jonah was sent to Montana State Prison and because of his status as a notorious child predator, other inmates earmarked him for death.

Nathaniel Bar-Jonah was sent to solitary confinement to live out the rest of his days. The animal was truly caged. It was mostly bittersweet for John Cameron. Zach Ramsay would never get the justice he deserved.

CHAPTER 9: LATER RESEARCH

A short time after Wayne Chapman and Nathaniel Bar-Jonah were condemned to Bridgewater another little boy came up missing. On September 30, 1978, four-year-old Andrew Amato was playing outside his home with his six-year-old cousin in Webster, the town in which Bar-Jonah lived, and he and Chapman haunted. Andrew was such a sweet, playful boy that the people in town who knew him called him the "goodwill ambassador."

He was playing on a wooded path on the old Route 52, which has since been designated Route 395, just outside the former Ash Street trailer park where he and his family lived. Andrew was wearing a Mickey Mouse t-shirt and had a full head of brown hair, puffy cheeks, and dark eyes. Andrew's parents told their son that the wooded area was off-limits for playing. He and his cousin followed the path along 52 for a few hundred yards. Somewhere along the route, Andrew tripped and lost his favorite toy Weeble. The Weeble was a popular 1970s toy. They resembled a portly little drummer boy with a mop of hair combed to one side. Weeble's came with painted blonde hair or brown hair. The child's toy was small enough to conceal in an adult's hand. Andrew threw a fit as only a four-year-old could. He refused to go home with his cousin until he found his favorite toy.

Andrew's cousin made a decision that would haunt her for the rest of her existence. She left Andrew where he sat to summon Maria Amato to bring her son home. Andrew's cousin ran the fifty or so yards to the Amato home and got Maria to come tend to the screaming toddler. When they arrived back at the tree where she left Andrew, he was nowhere to be found. Andrew's mother and cousin immediately went into a panic. They ran the wood line repeatedly screaming for the four-year-old boy. Andrew's cousin had run so far and so long she had lost both of her shoes in the confusion. Maria and her husband, Andrew's father, Leo, eventually decided to alert Webster Police that Andrew was missing.

Webster Police assumed, like other cases covered in this book, that Andrew had gotten lost and was out there in the woods, scared. It was late September in New England; in the late hours of the day, the weather changes drastically and cold fronts move in. Webster authorities had to act fast to find the missing boy. He would freeze when the sun went down.

A search party was immediately organized to comb the woods. Much like Andy Puglisi's disappearance, the governor put the Massachusetts National Guard unit based in nearby Worcester on active-duty orders to join the search. Soldiers arrived and set up a command center filled with communications equipment inside green tents. Searchers wore red armbands to identify their affiliation. They found no trace of Andrew Amato. Every pile of leaves in the wooded area that Route 395 was kicked over and thoroughly searched. Nothing was found. The first three days of the search were maddening for the Webster authorities. Andrew had seemingly disappeared off the face of the Earth. The first break in the case came when a Burrillville, Rhode Island, man came forward with a story.

The man claimed that he heard about the missing boy through the subsequent search on the CB radio he listened to at home. He rushed down to help in any way he could. This man's name has never been released to the public, so here I will call him "Jesse."

Jesse kicked over some leaves as he blended in anonymously alongside the hundreds of searchers. The search party was going back over the woods they had searched thoroughly the day prior. Jesse, a fifty-year-old who was part of a labor union, had made a discovery. Andrew Amato's Weeble toy appeared under a pile of leaves that was marked as "already searched." Searchers were incredulous.

How the hell did they miss the Weeble toy under the leaves? Authorities were excited that something had turned up. Search dogs had already been brought in and lost Andrew's scent right where he was last seen. Things were becoming bleak until they discovered the Weeble. The search had a new life. Police were starting to wonder though. Some officers had searched that pile of leaves two and three times the day before. Nothing was there. Some officers swore up and down there was no chance in hell they could have missed a child's toy painted bright blue with yellow-blonde hair. Officers began to think Jesse might have planted the toy there.

Webster authorities couldn't shake the notion that the Weeble just "turned up" under the pile of leaves. They started to suspect Jesse. The police grilled him on how the Weeble had gotten under the pile of leaves. They used every interrogation trick in their arsenal to get Jesse to crack. He kept repeating that he was simply a Good Samaritan who heard about the missing boy and arrived on the scene to help. He confessed to police that he had two children himself and he couldn't bear to think that a child could be out in the New England early fall all alone at night. The Webster authorities had no evidence to hold Jesse and he was released after two rounds of questioning.

Webster Police could not keep tabs, after the fact, on the odd man who arrived and found the Weeble. He wasn't even a resident of the city. Webster residents were dumbfounded.

One resident stated, "It was like the hand of God reached down and plucked Andrew out of this world."

Captain James Ruda, the company commander of the National Guard unit assigned to the search, was sure that the area was thoroughly canvassed, and the boy was nowhere to be found. The disappearance slowly faded from the public consciousness and became part of Webster lore. The case got a bump in the late 1990s when Nathaniel Bar-Jonah's writings were being splashed all over the front pages of American tabloids. In one of his rambling, incoherent writings, the words "Lake Webster" appeared.

Lake Webster is a body of water that has a surface area of 1,142 acres. It lies on the border of Webster, Massachusetts, and the Connecticut state line. Webster has bizarre geography even for New England. Go twenty minutes in any direction and you're bound to be in either Rhode Island or Connecticut, so it's easily accessible from multiple states. Lake Webster showing up in Bar-Jonah's writings led some to believe that he might have had something to do with Andrew Amato's disappearance.

Go to Google right now and enter Andrew Amato's name. Many "reputable" missing children's sites tie Bar-Jonah to Andrew Amato's disappearance. It's not possible. He was at Bridgewater a year before Andrew went missing in late September 1978. And the same goes for Wayne Chapman. What does Andrew Amato's case have to do with these main characters? One thing I hope to do is fight the misinformation out there about these predators. The more I see people tying Andrew's disappearance to Bar-Jonah, the less focus is gathered on what happened. As I began to unfurl the years after Andrew's disappearance, I started to think maybe there was some sort of connection.

It is simply speculation but consider this: in 1999, a now seventy-one-year-old Jesse is dying of lung cancer in a Rhode Island hospital. Jesse wants to relieve his conscience before he meets his maker. He starts to confide in his family members that he had not planted the Weeble underneath the leaf pile. There was no need to plant the Weeble, Jesse confided; he had the Weeble all along. Jesse couldn't help himself; he had to interject into the investigation. This phenomenon of murderers interjecting into investigations has been studied in hundreds of cases over the years.

I won't relitigate the mindset behind that here but there is plenty of precedent. Jesse simply pulled the Weeble from his pocket and handed it to the searchers on that fall day in 1978. He concocted the story about finding the Weeble on the way over to Webster from his home in Burrillville. He went on to tell his family that he abducted Andrew and buried his body near power lines in Burrillville. The family had no idea what to make of the confession. This was a man near death, chock full of medications, and he was probably out of his mind.

Jesse passed away shortly after the confession. His family sat on it for nearly four years. Close to the twenty-fifth anniversary of Andrew's disappearance, Jesse's widow decided to go to the authorities in Burrillville. The family recounted the deathbed confession to the police. They stated that Jesse was the man who was present at the search and produced the Weeble. Police had interviewed him two and a half decades earlier and he made a deathbed confession.

The police heard enough and decided they should excavate some areas surrounding Route 395. Police even decided to excavate some heavily wooded areas around Jesse's home. The searches came up with nothing. Police never released Jesse's real name. I became obsessed with this fact and fell into a year-long rabbit hole. I began to convince myself that if I could uncover this mysterious Jesse's identity, perhaps I could tie him to Wayne Chapman and Nathaniel Bar-Jonah.

Remember, these predators are birds of a feather. This man was a Rhode Islander like Chapman, operating in Bar-Jonah's hometown, as Chapman had. I started to think

Jesse might have been just another member of the cadre of men who abused children and ran in the same circles as Chapman and Bar-Jonah. Jesse did not just carry out a crime of opportunity, he had stalked Andrew, he began to fantasize about the crime, and then, when the time was right, he pounced. Andrew Amato, sadly enough, fit the victimology that Chapman and Bar-Jonah preferred—dark eyes and features, much like Andy Puglisi and Leigh Savoie. There are so many bizarre happenings around Andrew's case. Like David Louison, nobody knew at all about what exactly took place around the time of this deathbed confession.

Why was Jesse's identity never released? Why are authors and reporters completely silent on the case? In a world where true crime podcasts, documentaries, and books are the most popular genre with consumers, scant stories exist about Andrew Amato. I am not finger-wagging, though. Nor am I being virtuous. I am just surprised at the relative lack of interest in the case. I have spent years poring over obituaries and records searching for a man who fit Jesse's description who died in 1999. I did come across some names that seemingly were in the age group and had a similar cause of death. I ran all those threads to the ground and came up empty.

As of this writing, I still can't identify who Jesse was and years later, police have yet to release a name. Burrillville and Webster Police have been cordial but the investigations remain open. That designation thwarts the free trade of information on cases. I have done some on-the-ground research in Burrillville; it's close to my home and I have asked around. Residents have little recollection of a dig that happened well over a decade ago nor any recall of a man who died before the turn of the millennium. Everywhere I looked, I hit a wall of nothingness. At the risk of sounding redundant, you may ask yourself, what does this story have to do with Wayne Chapman?

Wayne Chapman was very familiar with the Burrillville area. I know this because the man who investigated him in Providence, Detective Al Mintz, lived minutes away in the town of Gloucester. Burrillville and Gloucester are sister cities. They're so close in proximity that kids often walk between towns to explore the various wooded areas and small ponds that are stocked with largemouth bass. You may remember the story about Chapman stopping Detective Mintz's son in the woods that bordered Gloucester and Burrillville. His young son was hit with Chapman's typical ruse. He asked the boy to help him find his lost dog, Scott. Thinking better of it, the younger Mintz boy declined and Chapman didn't press the matter. Mintz's son walked home and forgot all about the creepy guy with the limp.

In the hours after Mintz got Chapman back in custody in Providence from New York, he was exhausted. He had already been up to Waterloo and interviewed Chapman multiple times. He was so disgusted with him that he thought Chapman needed an exorcism, not a mental hospital.

He secured Chapman a bed at the Adult Correctional Institution in the psychiatric ward. He was ready to go home for the night and take it easy. It was a brutally hot day. Before he left for the night, he slipped Chapman's booking photo into his tweed and black leather briefcase. One thing had been dogging Al. He knew Wayne Chapman was a prolific traveler who haunted Rhode Island like a bad disease. Al wanted to show the kids the booking photo and ask if they had seen the man.

He made the short drive down Interstate 95 South to Gloucester from downtown Providence. He pulled into his driveway, which was set off from the road a bit. He could smell his wife's cooking. *Damn, she is a good cook,* he thought. He stood outside for a few moments and took in the beauty of his surroundings. *How the hell could men like Wayne Chapman exist when there was this much beauty in the world?* he asked himself. He walked into the house and said hello to his wife and kids.

He had been distant lately. They were glad he was home in one piece. Mintz immediately cornered his kids. He didn't wait for dinner; he wanted to get this out of the way. He sat in his recliner chair in the living room. The kids sat on the couch. He unzipped the briefcase and produced the grainy booking photo. He handed it to his son and lowered his gaze on him.

"Have you seen this man?" Al asked his son. The boy stared at the picture for about half a second and replied affirmatively.

The man had been around. He had asked Mintz's son to help him find his lost dog once in the woods close to their home. Mintz asked him again and again if he was certain. The boy was sure that was Wayne Chapman. Mintz knew the ruse. He knew his son had told him the truth. He told his son and daughter if they were ever approached, they should run and scream all the way home. He stopped short of forbidding them from ever leaving the house again but did consider it.

Mintz immediately felt red rage well up under his collar. *It is fucking personal now,* Mintz thought. He stood up, walked past his wife out the door, and got in his vehicle. He gripped the wheel tight to Cranston where Wayne Chapman was temporarily housed. He debated the merits of losing his job over kicking Chapman's teeth back into his windpipe. It was almost worth it. Almost.

Detective Mintz parked at the Adult Correctional Institution and sat there. It was raining now. He stared at the drops dancing on his hood. He looked at the booking photo and cursed it. He showed remarkable restraint of which many, myself included, may not have been capable. He took off and drove south back to his house. He walked in after 8 p.m. His wife asked him if everything was okay, he walked out of there like a zombie, she said. He said it was work. "You know how it is; it's a job that never really ends."

Mintz didn't sleep for weeks afterward. Every time he saw Wayne Chapman after that day, he fought the primal urge to beat him into oblivion. Who could blame him? Mintz is an extremely moral man. When I told him I was reworking the book for a rerelease, he shared a story with me that defined his morality and the corruption that was rampant in Providence. I asked Al why he only spent eight years in the Providence Police Department. He confessed he loved the work but stopped twelve years short of a full pension. Why?

Mintz recounted a story about a bookstore located directly across the street from Providence Police headquarters on Washington Street in downtown Providence. Mintz knew there was some funny business with the store and would patronize it regularly to see what they were selling. Mintz's hunch was correct. One day, he walked in and saw some child pornography on the shelves alongside regular pornography. The detective read the manager the Riot Act and told the owners in no uncertain terms they were now out of the porn business. Mintz told me within minutes he was summoned to a meeting with his superior office (a major, who was later fired) and told that it was best Mintz leave the smut pushers in the city alone. Mintz decided right there and then that Providence Police wasn't a fit for him anymore. He's a man of his word. He hung up his cuffs soon thereafter. Like now, the economy in the city of Providence was reliant on the sex industry; it was best for business if detectives don't meddle.

Armed with the fact Mintz's son positively identified Chapman as being in that neighborhood, I knew I had to chase Jesse's Burrillville deathbed confession if it took.

Wayne Chapman never turned up by accident. He didn't throw darts at the map. When Chapman arrived, it was because he had a friend in the area—one who provided intelligence and a haven if necessary. A friend he could stalk with or who could act as a cameraman when the time arose. Does it strike you as an incredible coincidence that a man from Burrillville, a place Chapman haunted, confessed to taking a boy and murdering him in Nathaniel Bar-Jonah's hometown? It was the same town in which Bar-Jonah and Chapman admitted to taking boys and assaulting them. *Nothing is a coincidence.* It's all there in front of your face. I just have not pulled the block that brings the whole damn house down.

Yet.

***

The 1990s brought no more solace to David Louison's family. Wayne Chapman never spoke about David again and the story faded into complete oblivion. Melanie Perkins-McLaughlin kept Andy Puglisi's name in the public sphere almost singlehandedly. Some stories came out that were interesting as well. Melanie set up a PO box so people could send tips about her friend's disappearance. I did not speak to Melanie. It was her documentary that began my interest in the case but I felt like I needed to make this journey alone. As someone who has put projects into the public that I have worked very hard on, the most annoying thing that someone can e-mail me is something along the lines of "Tell me everything you know!"

I didn't want to do that to Melanie. The whole time I worked on this project, I was also trying to come to terms with own sexual abuse I suffered as a child at the hands of a non-family member. I walked every crime scene in this book, from Brockton to Oil City, but I could not bring myself to visit the Higgins Memorial Pool in Lawrence. I would drive I-93 North and never take the exit. My inner triggers wouldn't allow me to look at that pool. I know—more than anybody—what Andy Puglisi faced in his last moments.

The terror, the confusion, the betrayal the moment an adult turns on you. Andy must have trusted Wayne Chapman for a short time. Kids were taught to respect adults in those days. I cannot accurately describe the dread that overcomes you when your abuser's mask comes off and he makes his intentions clear. My blood is chilled as I type this. I often fought with the notion of a Puglisi family member picking this book up reading my theories on the case and seeing Wayne Chapman's face. My only hope is that this book will get more people talking about the cases and catapult them back into public consciousness.

I was galvanized by the release of the book *I'll Be Gone in the Dark* by Michele McNamara. The book focused on the Golden State Killer investigation. The suspect haunted Northern California from the mid-1970s into the mid-80s. Michelle dedicated years of her life to uncovering the serial rapist and murderer's identity. The book singlehandedly put the case back in the public eye. Social media erupted. The case is now talked about on sites like Reddit and Twitter (aka X).

Michelle introduced a new generation of internet sleuths to the case. Unfortunately, she never got to see Joseph DeAngelo arrested and convicted for his crimes. On April 21, 2016, Michelle's husband, comedian Patton Oswalt (who also pushed the book to completion after her death) found her dead in their Los Angeles home. She had a lethal cocktail of drugs like Xanax and Fentanyl in her system. Michelle's research and writing took a horrible toll on her. She stated in the book that she "had a scream permanently lodged in [her] throat." I sympathize with that statement.

Nearly two years to the day of her death, on April 24, 2018, Joseph DeAngelo was arrested. His DNA profile was pieced together with the help of an ancestry website. Detective Paul Holes found familial DNA matching the suspect's until he zeroed in on DeAngelo. It was a stunning and remarkable victory for justice. He is now serving multiple life sentences and I truly believe Michelle's research pushed the investigation over the finish line.

In 2019, when I was finishing this book's first manuscript, I found myself unable to sleep at night. Wayne Chapman and his cohorts filled my head with awful images. My oldest son was now old enough to sleep in his room on the ground floor of our three-floor condominium. I would religiously come down, usually once an hour, to recheck the locks on our screens and windows. I would snap at my son when he left my sight with his friends in the neighborhood. I was acting so manic that I had to constantly check myself. I would see Wayne Chapman everywhere I went. I would go shopping with my wife and pick out faces in the crowd. *Chapman looked relatively normal to the outside world*, I thought. I was convinced I would be able to recognize Wayne Chapman in my neighborhood when I saw him. I was still working in the jail at that time as well, often assigned to the units that specially housed sex offenders. I never turned down that assignment; I considered it a research project.

That same year, I reconnected with Al Mintz. I pressed the now long-retired detective on his theories about what Wayne Chapman and his accomplices may have done to Andy Puglisi's body. It was my long-standing theory throughout my research that Andy's remains were buried somewhere near where he was abducted. It gave me a small sense of solace that Andy was still home, close to the housing projects he grew up in. Remember, Chapman worked at Miriam Hospital in downtown Providence. Mintz and the Providence authorities maintain that Chapman worked a shift at Miriam the day after Andy's disappearance.

Providence authorities' scenario plays out like this: Wayne Chapman assaults Andy and realizes the boy is seriously injured. He panics. He has hurt the boy terribly and has a problem with his hands. He needs to get rid of the body. Chapman then takes Andy's body and puts him in his van or someone else's vehicle, perhaps Charles Pierce's van.

Chapman then drives Andy's body south down I-93 to I-95 and parks his van outside his apartment on Linwood Avenue in Providence. Chapman waits until the next day and then takes Andy's body down to the Miriam Hospital basement, loads it into the incinerator, puts the incinerator key into the keyhole, and turns it clockwise, burning the body.

Maybe Chapman didn't wait until the next day. Perhaps he went immediately to his workplace on that hot August evening. He would not have gotten back to Providence till around 8 p.m. (at best) after he allegedly abducted Andy. I think this scenario is most likely. There has been much debate on whether he worked the next day. Timecards were pulled and theories have been bandied about for decades. I think it is irrelevant. Wayne Chapman more than likely made a beeline right for the hospital from Lawrence. He got there under the cover of darkness and did his evil deeds that evening.

Who would have questioned him? Chapman's direct supervisor did not work nights and he was often the lone janitor on the swing shift (3 to 11 p.m.). He was completely unsupervised. It wasn't ideal but Chapman would have been desperate. He only meant to assault the boy and take his pictures; things had gotten out of hand. I believe he probably did it alone. Neither Charles Pierce nor any other co-conspirator walked into the hospital with Chapman. It was way too risky. The janitor wouldn't get questioned much for coming to work. Perhaps he was working a short shift or forgot something at work. There are so many excuses for coming to work late.

Coming into work late with your lazy-eyed, carnival-worker friend and hanging around?

Too many questions would be asked. I believe Chapman went alone. If this theory holds up, you must ask the question: if Providence authorities believed this theory, did they have the incinerator tested for DNA or human remains? I have been asked that question many times when I recount this theory. DNA testing as we know it today didn't exist in the mid-1970s. Also, patients' amputated limbs were often burned in that incinerator. The presence of human remains was almost guaranteed if testing had been done. I have been active in many Miriam Hospital social media groups over the years. I have yet to talk to one person who remembers seeing the creepy janitor coming in late on a hot summer night. Many people remembered Wayne Chapman, but not on any specific night. This book can only be based on fact.

I must confess that I searched long and hard for an eyewitness to validate the incinerator theory. I couldn't find one. I still believe it's more likely that Chapman had some luck that night. The staff was so sparse at a later hour that nobody noticed him slip in and then quickly slip out. I think Andy's body would have been found by now if Chapman had buried him in Lawrence. He would have been far too panicked; the burial would have been hasty. The time he would have had on the scene would have been tight. The chances of getting seen by someone in Lawrence would have been far higher than in Providence. It's a good theory and one that many Providence officials maintain.

As always, the investigation is ongoing until Andy or the remains are returned home. I believe Wayne Chapman laid low after he allegedly abducted Andy. He eventually set out for New York State, where he was stopped in Waterloo. You might remember that Chapman had a pair of Andy's sister's socks in the van. There was a pair that Andy's mother Faith Puglisi identified as the socks she saw him wearing when she saw him for the last time. The socks were taken during the stop in Waterloo and booked into evidence. When DNA testing became available in late 1986, it was a game changer for cold cases.

Unfortunately, the socks were never tested for Andy's DNA, or any other of his family members who may have touched the socks. The socks's whereabouts are completely unknown. Providence Police turned them over to Lawrence authorities after Faith Puglisi identified them. Andy's case wasn't Providence's jurisdiction. They had no business keeping the socks. Generations of beat cops and detectives came through the Lawrence Police Department in the succeeding years after Andy went missing. The socks could have been thrown out or taken. It was another missed opportunity to tie the socks to Andy through undeniable DNA evidence, which would almost undoubtedly have sent Chapman away on a life sentence.

The DNA on the socks would have also answered another crucial, nagging question in the case—who was with Wayne Chapman the day Andy Puglisi disappeared?

I contend that Charles Pierce was Chapman's co-conspirator. If it wasn't him, then who was it? That question is by far the most horrifying in this entire story. The thought that someone else is out there who is culpable and got away completely unscathed will haunt me for as long as I live.

There are a lot of myths and urban legends about Andy Puglisi's disappearance. Somewhat reputable media outlets have even reported a few incidents as if they had some connection to Andy. Shortly after Andy disappeared, a school resource officer with Lawrence Police was found in a vehicle with a young boy. The school officer was sexually assaulting the boy. The boy involved lived in the same housing project as Andy. That type of behavior is abhorrent, but the incident with the school officer had nothing to do with Andy's case. That inconvenient fact did not stop outlets like the *Merrimack Valley Patriot*, a paper that serves Lawrence and the surrounding areas, from printing erroneous information that this officer had called in sick the day after Andy's disappearance. There's simply no evidence that the officer involved with the boy did not show up to work. I am not sure how the officer missing work connected him to Andy anyway. Perhaps the implication is the officer called off work to move Andy's body. The officer's behavior was sickening and he was fired from the police force, rightfully, but there is no evidence this officer was connected to Andy. This supposed connection wasn't printed in the immediate aftermath of the disappearance, during the "Fog of War" period. The story ran in 2020, forty-four years *after* the disappearance when countless documents and witness statements were publicly available. The story seemed sensationalized for the sake of getting clicks. This is too often the case in this new world of news where newspapers are essentially dead and all revenue is based on scrollers clicking on stories.

I fought the same battle when I did research in Connecticut. Connecticut authorities are highly interested in Andy Puglisi's case. Charles Pierce confessed to murders in Connecticut. He is a boogeyman figure in the state. Rumors still abound about Pierce five decades later. The most persistent rumor is that Pierce took Andy's body from the pool that day and drove it to Connecticut to bury it. I don't endorse this position, but it's an interesting thought. Did Pierce take care of Chapman's dirty work? The most incredible thing about the Charles Pierce/Wayne Chapman connection is that it was not public until 1998, thirty-two years after Andy's disappearance.

Melanie Perkins-McLaughlin never broke the promise she made to her friend Andy; Melanie never stopped investigating. She was the first person to uncover Chapman and Pierce's unholy alliance. In an internal communication, dated April 4, 1989, Joe Fitzpatrick, who oversaw all Lawrence detectives, recounts a phone call he had with a Massachusetts State Trooper. The state trooper confided in Fitzpatrick that Charles Pierce, an inmate at MCI Norfolk in Massachusetts, wanted to confess to crimes he committed in Lawrence in the 1970s. These crimes weren't petty. They involved murdering children and burying their bodies. The state police told Fitzpatrick that it would be advantageous to Lawrence officials to get to Norfolk and interrogate Pierce before he fell too ill or passed away.

There is no evidence any interrogation ever took place. The state police even wrote a second letter, less than a week later, urging Lawrence officials to come in and talk to Pierce. It was the first time Lawrence officials had even heard the name Charles Pierce. Melanie found the memo nearly ten years after it had been written. By 1998, Charles Pierce was on the brink of death. Prostate cancer had ravaged his body. He was a frail old man by then, nowhere close to his 6'2", two-hundred-pound frame in the mid-1970s. He was wheelchair-bound and required oxygen in his last days. He was balding with thin, closely cropped white hair. His eyes were hollow sockets, with deep bags underneath them. Pierce's face and body looked like the Devil started pecking away at him.

Investigators finally got to Pierce in January 1999. He was confined to the prison infirmary in Shirley, Massachusetts. He began to describe the Lawrence boy he murdered. The physical traits fit Andy Puglisi—olive complexion, dark hair, and eyes. Pierce murdered the boy and kept the body in the back of his van alongside Janice Pockett, whose body he'd also been storing in his van.

Pierce would never name the boy but he went into extraordinary detail about where he buried the bodies of the boy and Janice. He used a spade tool, he said, to dig the holes. He buried the bodies thirty feet apart and the graves were about two feet deep. The burial place was a field in Lawrence marked with pieces of coal. Pierce stopped short of a full confession. When authorities pressed him, he simply became belligerent, throwing his oxygen mask at police and periodically falling asleep. Investigators got fed up with Pierce's nonsense quickly, pressing him every minute of his worthless life for details. Charles Pierce never said another word about the murders.

Janice Pockett disappeared in 1973, three years before Puglisi; even though he was a practicing necrophiliac, it is hard to imagine he kept Janet's body in his van for three years. Pierce admitted to fifteen to twenty-two murders from 1954 to 1978 all over the United States.

When I first wrote this chapter and edited it in 2020, I took a trip to Chicago. I wanted to walk the streets where Billy DeSousa, the Chicago boy who disappeared in 1972, had walked. Charles Pierce confessed to his abduction and murder. I always had the assumption he confessed to abducting Billy to screw with the police. I found out on the Chicago trip that Pierce gave the police information that was not made available to the public. Only the police and the murderer knew the information that he recounted. Pierce found Billy DeSousa at the carnival separated from his parents. He paid the boy three dollars to set up a carnival game and promised there would be plenty of games to set up if Billy was interested in a job. The boy said he was interested in working *for sure*. Pierce suggested to the boy that they go to a local burger joint and grab some lunch and after that, Pierce would drive him home. Billy panicked when Pierce drove away from his home. He claimed he brutally beat Billy and buried his body in a shallow grave. Billy's body was found in 1975 in a wooded area just west of Chicago. Incredibly, Charles Pierce was never charged with the crime. It remains an open investigation.

I was so struck by Billy DeSousa's friends when I visited the Midwest. They never forgot about him and most I encountered had vividly remembered his disappearance. I plan on visiting again and doing more work on Billy's case after being completely galvanized by the community. In the summer of 2023, as I reworked this new edition of this book, I received an email from a Chicago-based private investigator. She explained to me that a Chicago cold case unit was reinvigorated to work on Bill DeSousa's unsolved homicide. I was invited to visit Chicago again in the winter of 2025 and I plan to make that trip. I believe in my heart Charles Pierce abducted and murdered William DeSousa and I am motivated now, more than ever, to find more evidence to prove it.

Charles Pierce was also never charged in Janice Pockett's disappearance. Investigators continue to work on and hope for a break in the case. In 1990, a body turned up in a shallow grave in Southern California that fit Janice's description. The little girl had long blonde hair, just like Janice. Investigators were ecstatic; had they caught a break? Unfortunately, they hadn't. DNA evidence excluded Janice. The same year, a former Tolland, Connecticut, resident murdered a San Diego, California, man. The man was a resident of Tolland in the 1970s and lived in Janice's general area. His murder in San Diego had a similar victimology and abduction method to Janice's. The man would have been fifteen years old in 1973. There was no evidence to connect the murder in San Diego and Janice's. I believe whoever killed Janice Pockett is still out there or has since died. Charles Pierce's preferred victims were little boys. It is not unprecedented, but very uncommon for a predator to stray from his preferred victims. Janice had long blonde hair at the time of her disappearance; it's unlikely Charles Pierce would have mistaken her for a little boy, as Nathaniel Bar-Jonah sometimes did. The fact that Pierce confessed to Janice's disappearance and then quickly recanted is just another bizarre subplot in a story full of bizarre subplots.

In the predawn hours of February 17, 1999, Charles E. Pierce died at the Lemuel Shattuck Hospital in Jamaica Plain, Massachusetts. Whatever he knew about the disappearances of Andy Puglisi and Billy DeSousa went with him. There is no way to underestimate the effect Charles Pierce had on other predators like Nathaniel Bar-Jonah and Wayne Chapman. They were under his wing. A patient master, he taught his students the discipline to commit crimes and what to say after the crimes had been committed.

If Pierce never connected with these other men, things would have turned out much differently for Andy and the other children. I have a hunch Pierce cleaned up the mess Chapman created in Lawrence in August 1976, and maybe even Brockton. You do not get the version of Chapman that haunted the children of Massachusetts without Charles Pierce's tutelage. He was a truly despicable character with zero redeemable qualities. May we never forget this unholy union. If Wayne Chapman was upset when he heard about his mentor's death, he didn't outwardly show it. Chapman wasn't shy about who he was affiliated with behind bars. When Pierce died, Chapman had long since left the friendly confines of Bridgewater. He missed his old friends like Rick Peluso and Frank Damiano.

By 1999, Wayne Chapman was living in protective custody at MCI Shirley, the maximum-security prison, well known as the toughest prison in Massachusetts. Shirley was not a safe space for sex offenders. A singular event that took place in 1997 put sex offenders, and particularly NAMBLA members, firmly under the microscope in Massachusetts.

***

On October 1, 1997, card-carrying NAMBLA members Salvatore Sicari and Charles Jaynes abducted ten-year-old Jeffrey Curley, a boy who knew the two men from the neighborhood in Cambridge. Sicari and Jaynes had spent a good bit of time grooming Jeffrey. He was treated to dinners and toys by the two men, who were just twenty-one and twenty-two years old at the time. They promised to meet Jeffrey on the afternoon of October 1, 1997. The two men had promised Jeffrey a new bike. Jeffrey left his grandmother's house around 3:15 p.m. wearing a red and gold football jersey with the number 32 on the back. Sicari and Jaynes met Jeffrey at a prearranged meeting spot. Jaynes let Sicari drive his 1983 Cadillac Seville while he welcomed Jeffrey into the backseat from the right rear door. The two men and the ten-year-old boy headed over to a grocery store in the affluent suburb of Newton, just a fifteen-minute ride from Cambridge.

When they arrived at a gas station parking lot, Charles Jaynes turned on Jeffrey, grabbing the boy and trying to sexually assault him, but Jeffrey fought back. Eventually, Jaynes soaked a rag with gasoline and put it over the boy's face. All the while, Jaynes screamed, "Don't fight it, boy, don't fight it."

Jeffrey passed out, never to regain consciousness. The two men then drove over to the working-class city of Somerville to buy lime and concrete, then to Bradlees Department Store to buy a fifty-gallon container. The two men headed north up Route 128. Sicari had rented an apartment in Manchester, New Hampshire, under an assumed name. They drove with Jeffrey's corpse for more than an hour to the prearranged apartment.

Back in Cambridge, Jeffrey's parents and friends had begun a full-scale search. Flyers were made quickly and police canvassed the area. In New Hampshire, the two men assaulted Jeffrey's corpse and placed his body in the container after filling it with cement and lime. They then headed to the New Hampshire seacoast to dump the container. In the early morning hours of October 2, the two men dumped Jeffrey's body in the water off Route 101 in Maine. At one point, before his body was dumped, the two men had locked themselves out of their vehicle with the container in the back, visibly out in the open. An employee at a local Howard Johnson hotel helped them get back in their vehicle with the assistance of a coat hanger. When they arrived back in Cambridge, they took note of the intense media coverage and police interest.

Jeffrey's face was all over the place. Sicari and Jaynes weren't smart predators. They had been seen with Jeffrey many times around town before the abduction while they were grooming him. They knew his parents.

Police had been told about them and immediately tracked down Salvatore Sicari and brought him in for questioning. He broke down over the course of four interrogations. He initially told police he saw Jaynes with Jeffrey on the day in question, then flipped his confession, saying he was there with Jaynes and Jeffrey and was merely a witness to the assault and murder. Police already knew who Charles Jaynes was. At the time of the abduction, he had an incredible seventy-five arrest warrants open in various Massachusetts courts. It is astounding that he was even on the street to meet Jeffrey Curley. The pair met the same way Wayne Chapman and Nathaniel Bar-Jonah met decades prior: they were both active in circles where men preferred young boys. History was playing out again in Massachusetts.

Charles Jaynes took no pains to hide his relationship with Jeffrey before the abduction. They frequented the Museum of Science together in Boston's North End neighborhood. People would ask about the relationship. They found it strange that he would hang out with a ten-year-old boy, who wasn't a family member, so often. Jaynes brushed it off; he was a predator doing what they do: grooming victims. Like Wayne Chapman, he was focused. No outside noise could stop him. Other NAMBLA members encouraged their relationship. It was natural they were told. Jeffrey was exercising his right to choose his mate. It was all deranged ideology. Police eventually interviewed Jaynes and got a full confession. The NAMBLA members brought police to the New Hampshire seacoast to search.

Jeffrey's body eventually was found in a shallow river in Maine, on October 7, 1999. His body was nude, and he had deep marks and swelling on his face from the gasoline-soaked rag. His red football jersey with the number 32 was found in Jaynes' possession. He had been known to access the first crude NAMBLA website at public libraries near his home. He owned a NAMBLA membership and had NAMBLA bulletins in a manila envelope in his car's backseat when he smothered Jeffrey Curley.

Charles Jaynes received a life sentence for Jeffrey's abduction and murder. Salvatore Sicari received a second-degree murder conviction and was also given life. Jeffrey Curley's parents, upon learning of the two men's NAMBLA connections, filed a two-hundred-million-dollar wrongful death lawsuit against NAMBLA in 2000. The civil suit claimed that NAMBLA promoted "adult-child sexual relationship propaganda." The lawsuit was thrown out in 2008, but one interesting story developed. Jeffrey Curley's parents found a witness who was willing to testify under oath. The witness was also a card-carrying NAMBLA member who had witnessed someone else encourage Charles Jaynes to murder Jeffrey. This small fact confirmed to me that these men had met and talked about hurting children and one member was willing to go under oath and testify to it.

I believe that also happened in the 1970s when Wayne Chapman was part of the loose group that would go on to christen themselves NAMBLA. The same affiliation that killed Andy Puglisi and David Louison may have also killed ten-year-old Jeffrey Curley. Similar lost boys, decades apart and separated by just miles. Charles Jaynes came up for parole in early 2020 and he explained to the Massachusetts parole board that at the time of Jeffrey's disappearance, he was drug-addicted and battling mental health issues. Jaynes worked hard during prison to better understand what led him to that October day in 1997. The parole board commended him for his actions behind bars, thanked him for his time, and promptly denied his parole. He will be up for parole again in the year 2025.

The lawsuit decimated NAMBLA in Massachusetts. All the founding members like David Thorstad, Allen Ginsberg, and Peter Meltzer had either died or went completely underground. The NAMBLA website is still up and a loose band of pederasts across the globe still post on the message boards. The FBI monitored NAMBLA activity for a decade and even had an undercover agent named Robert Hamer infiltrate. Hamer deconstructed a sex tourism business that was sending NAMBLA members overseas to abuse young boys. The trips were masqueraded as boat cruises with stops at different ports. I interviewed Hamer for this book and he recounted a story of visiting a toy store in Manhattan with a gaggle of NAMBLA members around Christmas time. The gang of creeps were catcalling to young boys and making sexually suggestive comments while families were shopping. Hamer confessed if he had a grenade, he would have pulled the pin and sent them all to hell.

While Wayne Chapman, Richard Peluso, and Nathaniel Bar-Jonah were in Bridgewater in the early 1980s, another scandal involving homemade child pornography was brewing in Massachusetts. A forty-one-year-old named Lawrence Brehaut had been using his position as a Boy Scout leader to sexually assault young boys, and, of course, take photos of them in various sexually suggestive poses. Just like Chapman, who haunted the 4-H members a few years prior in Rhode Island, Brehaut joined the Scouts to get closer to children, specifically young boys. Brehaut was born in 1944 in Wakefield, Massachusetts. Wakefield is centrally located north of Boston, 8.8 miles from Revere, and about twenty-two miles from the town of Lawrence.

Lawrence Brehaut was a studious child. Always at the top of his class, he was class president of his high school and finished near the top of his graduating class. His classmates even voted him "Most Ambitious." I came across his story almost by accident. I was researching the Revere sex ring case in 2018. I kept getting reports about an alleged child pornography ring in the Wakefield area in the early 1980s. I was told the ring was an open secret. Parents at the time talked about it in hushed tones when they thought their kids weren't listening. After high school, Lawrence Brehaut got a job in the Burlington public school system nearby. He also became a member of the auxiliary fire department in Wakefield, coached soccer, and was an influential Scout leader. Brehaut was so influential in the community that when the abuse claims and evidence started mounting up, many of his Scout troop's mothers and fathers publicly defended him.

A short time after his arrest, the community held a vigil for him in December 1984. *There is no way Larry could do this to children!* The temperature was below freezing but Wakefield residents didn't care. Larry was great to their kids, and they were not going to let him go down like this. The police knew that Brehaut was a sadistic pedophile who self-produced thousands of child pornography photos. Like Richard Peluso before him, Lawrence Brehaut would slowly poison Wakefield children with alcohol and marijuana. He would feed the children drugs, hang them upside down, and take pictures. Like Wayne Chapman, Brehaut had a dark room in the basement of a Pearl Street apartment in Wakefield. The elderly couple who rented the room to him was completely oblivious to his activities. Brehaut would use a long table in the middle of the room to develop the thousands of pictures he took of the Boy Scouts in his troop. The room had high ceilings and a black couch that seemed to wrap around the entirety of the room. The men who talked to me about this book remembered the large safes that Brehaut would keep in his downstairs dark room. They later learned that's where he kept his developed pictures. When boys started to come forward about the abuse they suffered at his hands, some adults didn't believe their kids. *Not Larry,* they thought, *he coached a championship soccer team in town.* He was a beloved educator at a well-respected middle school.

Police had heard enough of the complaints and decided it was time to visit Larry Brehaut. Wakefield officials visited him at his parents' home where he lived full-time. He was well-put together, authorities thought. He had a close-cropped flat top with glasses that portrayed the mind of an intellectual. He was single, never married, with no children. Police didn't ask him about his sexual preferences, but they assumed he was gay. Authorities asked if his parents' home was his primary residence. He confirmed he had always lived at home but that he rented a room just a few miles away on Pearl Street.

He vehemently denied any wrongdoing with the boys. He talked in long form about his activities helping children in the community. He loved helping kids. Hell, he was an overgrown kid himself. Police thanked Brehaut for his time and let him simmer for a bit. Authorities agreed there was something weird about Lawrence Brehaut. Sure, he was a pillar in the community, but he warranted more investigation. Massachusetts State Police detectives and Wakefield authorities began to investigate the area around the Pearl Street apartment. When authorities talked to neighbors, a common story started to emerge. Neighbors found it odd that Brehaut would come in and out of the backdoor with young boys.

Sometimes the boys would still be in their Scout uniforms. The man seemed to come and go at odd hours of the night as well. Based on some boys' complaints and neighbors' remarks, police applied for a search warrant for the bottom-floor apartment. They executed the search warrant and were met with literally piles of indisputable evidence. Police found state-of-the-art photo development equipment, cameras, and forty-seven boxes of homemade child pornography. Some of the pictures were of boys from the community, including Scouts from his troop and soccer players he had coached. The police had a hard time identifying about two-thirds of the victims from the pictures. He had been producing child pornography for two decades, completely undetected, all the while displaying the outward appearance of an upstanding community member.

Lawrence Brehaut didn't bother to make much of a defense. The now former Scout leader sat down with police and detailed his child pornography production. Brehaut mentioned to police that he had been sexually abusing children and taking their pictures since the late 1960s. He confessed that he'd sold the pictures for so many years, to so many different men, that it would be hard to name all his customers. The police were very interested in Lawrence Brehaut's accomplices. A seasoned Massachusetts State Police detective had seen enough to know that an operation as large as Brehaut's was hard to run alone.

Scouts who were abused later alleged that he did not work alone and he had a male accomplice who was an active Scouts member. This man was never tried in court nor was he ever named publicly. I spoke with former Boy Scouts who had no problem naming the man. I knew I had to track him down. The operation in Wakefield was so eerily like the Revere sex ring, from the parties to the mounds of pornography, I had a feeling that the Wakefield crew was made up of Revere men who had yet to be caught. As always, I was looking for men who ran in the same circles as Wayne Chapman, hoping I could find the person who may have a sliver of information on Chapman's activities in the 1970s.

In 2020, I tracked down Lawrence Brehaut's unindicted co-conspirator in New Hampshire. There were times in my New Hampshire research that I thought maybe I was going offtrack. Brehaut and Chapman may have just been two pedophiles operating in the same area and were unrelated. Two trains passing in the night. I couldn't shake the similarities, though. If I was going to write this book the right way, I needed the entire snapshot of what was going on in Massachusetts during the period.

I tracked the accomplice with the help of word of mouth and a private investigator. I was horrified to learn that the man was now a school bus driver. I never approached him. After all, he was never charged with any crimes; he had no criminal record. I would never confront an elderly person in broad daylight like I had in Fort Lauderdale. The optics would be hard to explain to any onlooker regardless of the back story. I did make many attempts to contact the man by email, however.

Forty adults, who were once Scouts, told me this man was Lawrence Brehaut's best friend and cohort. The stories never changed and were almost always the same. I was utterly convinced of this friend's guilt. When I did finally get a reply from the man, I had to chuckle. It was a one-sentence reply:

"I NEVER WORKED WITH BOY SCOUTS, AND I NEVER MET LAWRENCE BREHAUT."

Deny it all until the end; Charles Pierce is in hell, nodding in approval, I'm sure.

Lawrence Brehaut pled guilty to multiple counts of sexual assault and corrupting the morals of a minor. He tried like hell to get sent to Bridgewater. His lawyers argued that their client was a very sick man and needed to be evaluated by doctors around the clock. The judge was unmoved by the lawyer's diatribe and sentenced Brehaut to only ten to fifteen years at Walpole Prison. He was not in protective custody during his time at Walpole and he was a constant target for attacks. The story of his crimes was major news locally, and the guards and inmates alike picked on Brehaut incessantly. He somehow survived his fellow inmates, but he couldn't defeat his weak ticker.

Just one year before he would have been eligible for parole, Lawrence Brehaut dropped dead in the prison yard of cardiac arrest at fifty-one. The guards saw him drop and performed chest compressions until the ambulance arrived, but he was pronounced dead at Norwood Hospital at 11:32 a.m. Lawrence Brehaut wasn't interviewed much in prison. My suspicion is he was a major player in the underground child pornography rings that began operations in the mid-1960s north of Boston. I wish he had been pressed more. No stone can go unturned in this investigation. Much like Doc Bauman, whatever Lawrence Brehaut knew, he took to his grave.

CHAPTER 10: THE DOCTOR

Sometime in the summer of 2019, I was looking over my handwritten notes from my work in Wayne Chapman's hometown of Jamestown, New York. My notebooks were withering away on me. My five-year-old and our dog were constantly getting into my stuff, slobbering all over the pages, and doodling. While writing this book, I took six hundred pages of notes in notebooks I purchased Bristol Community College bookstore. One sentence I wrote in 2017 jumped out at me. *"Chapman may have had a connection to the pedophile doctor."* I had been told that a few times in Jamestown. *"Chapman got involved in child pornography in Canada, crossing the border at a young age,"* I wrote verbatim a few times after talking to local Jamestown residents.

My work hit the wall in 2019. I was running in circles and never getting anywhere. My frustration level was at an all-time high. I had the innate sense that Chapman was a part of something so large that nothing was off-limits. By this time, I was certain that Chapman was just a low-level child pornography producer who worked to keep like-minded men flush with new material. He was an entry-level employee. The daytime assaults and child luring were just a part of the job. Sure, he was a pedophile who would have abused children no matter what, but the job gave him his purpose. I widened my net outside Massachusetts.

Back in May 2007, a young Connecticut couple purchased their dream home. The home, located at 155

Griswold Drive in West Hartford, was the culmination of their hard work. It came complete with a stone walk-up to the front door and a garage adjoined the house on the right. The couple busied themselves with projects around the house, which included finishing the enormous basement that looked like it had been neglected for years. That spring, the couple started renovating the basement. They stripped the floors and tore out walls. The new homeowners encountered a bizarre cache after pulling apart a wall at the bottom of the basement stairs. Rolls of film seemed to fall out by the dozen. More film spilled out with every nail that was pulled. It was as if someone opened a toothpaste tube and stomped on it. Slide after slide, roll after roll.

The film looked old. There ended up being more than one hundred rolls and fifty thousand slides. The man examined the film; he knew this would be a day he would never forget. He was repulsed by the images. Some were of children, both male and female, alone in suggestive poses. Others were of children being sexually abused. There were hundreds of different children and hundreds of different men abusing them. He ran up the stairs to the kitchen bathroom, turned on the sink, and stuffed his face under it. He needed to feel clean for a minute. He considered showering and burning his clothes. He was so disgusted with what had inhabited his walls. After he got his bearings, he dialed 911 and told the West Hartford Police they needed to get to his home immediately to see what he had found. Police knew the home.

Dr. George Reardon, chief of endocrinology at Saint Francis Hospital in Hartford, previously owned the home. Dr. Reardon was a native New Yorker who had gone to medical school and completed his residency in Albany in the late 1950s. He immediately started abusing children. He abused a brother and sister as early as 1959. After Dr. Reardon's training ended, he moved to Saint Francis Hospital. He bombarded parents with letters stating he was conducting growth surveys and needed child subjects. Some parents readily agreed to bring their children in to participate in the long-term growth study. Parents noted that a lot of these appointments took place after hours, so late that even his secretary was gone for the night. Parents were not allowed into the room with the children.

They sat outside in a quiet waiting room while Dr. Reardon took the children to be examined. This routine happened hundreds of times in the mid- to late 1960s. Dr. Reardon was prolific and cunning. There, of course, was no hospital-sanctioned growth study. He took the Connecticut children and sexually abused them while their parents waited on the other side of the door. He was an active athlete and would often meet young boys at karate studios and Judo clubs and invite them in for his growth study. Nobody at the hospital was suspicious. He was thought of as a brilliant young doctor. Dr. Reardon was often seen outside the hospital's main doors chain-smoking Lucky Strikes while talking to employees. He cut a gregarious figure around the hospital and was so well thought of that he was promoted to chief of endocrinology in late 1978.

In early 1988, another man arrived at Saint Francis, Father Cornelius Otero. Father Cornelius was ordained in 1948 and had had many assignments around New York City. He also had a sordid predatory history. In 1978, Cornelius was working at a summer camp for boys on behalf of the archdiocese. He took a ten-year-old boy, forced him to strip, and took hundreds of photographs of him. In 1979, he was arrested for attempting to sell child pornography to an undercover detective working for the NYPD. The father was embarrassed. The priest thought his life was over. He was sure his photo would be splattered on the front page of *The New York Post* with an unflattering headline. What came next shocked him. The police offered him a deal: inform him on your pedophile network and you will avoid jail time. The priest took the deal and avoided prison. The NYPD was far quicker than Massachusetts authorities. They knew that if Cornelius possessed child porn, there must be an operation behind it that produced the images and videos.

The bizarre part of his informing is that it is unclear whether his information ever led to any arrests. Who exactly Cornelius informed of is unknown. His whereabouts and assignments from 1979 to 1988 are also completely unknown. Cornelius was not assigned to any archdiocese in the New York area. He simply disappeared off the radar and then popped up again in 1988 when he was assigned as a hospital chaplain at Saint Francis. Saint Francis employees and Connecticut investigators have told me many times over that Dr. Reardon and Cornelius were very close during their time at Saint Francis. Pedophiles always find one another. Almost like they have some kind of secret handshake most people cannot decipher.

Dr. Reardon began to catch heat in 1987, a year before Cornelius arrived. The brother and sister the doctor abused in Albany in the late 1950s finally complained to him. Like a lot of abuse cases, when one complaint is made other victims become galvanized. Complaints began streaming in and eventually in 1993, Dr. Reardon had misconduct charges filed against him. Incredibly, between 1987 and 1993, the hospital allowed him to practice at Saint Francis, despite the allegations. Eventually, in early 1993, the doctor's hospital privileges were revoked, and his medical license was suspended. In 1994, the FBI got involved in the case. Federal officials subpoenaed Saint Francis; the feds were looking for the last five years of patient names. Federal authorities wanted to interview every patient that Dr. Reardon had seen to try to ascertain the breadth of his crimes.

The feds figured if Reardon had victims back from the 1950s that surely, he didn't suddenly stop. The hospital blocked the FBI from seeing his patient list and the interviews never took place. In late 1994, hospital officials concluded that the allegations against the doctor were without merit. He cooled his heels for a bit at home in West Hartford. In the summer of 1995, the medical board served the doctor an order that he needed to sign. It revoked his right to ever seek a medical license in any state again. The order stated that Dr. Reardon confessed to "manipulating children's body parts inappropriately." He signed the order without argument and retired a disgraced former doctor to his home on Griswold Drive.

He was never tried in court for his crimes. The real-life "Dr. Evil" never spent a second in jail for years of abusing children. The former doctor had a live-in girlfriend, who had two sons and left his home to the eldest in his will, whom he had sexually abused for years. George Reardon died in 1998, a victim of his decades-long chain-smoking habit. The full breadth of his crimes came out in the succeeding years and dozens of civil suits were subsequently filed against Saint Francis Hospital. One boy, who grew up to be a firefighter, alleged that George Reardon molested him seventy-five times in the 1970s.

In all, five hundred victims came forward; he may have been one of the most prolific child abusers in American history.

After delving into the Reardon case, I immediately began to draw connections between the doctor and Wayne Chapman. Had he been the guy Jamestown residents referred to when mentioning the "pedophile doctor"? I had to find everything I could out about George Reardon and his unreported activities. The real story is always on the underbelly. I needed to know about the child pornography business he was running and who else was involved.

The first thing I learned was that Reardon had his dark room (stop me if you've heard this before). The dark room was in the very basement where the new homeowners found the pornography stash. The police who investigated him first noted the paper on which he used to print his tens of thousands of images. It was so unique that investigators could recognize a George Reardon image by the width of the paper. Connecticut investigators began the arduous task of filing and categorizing the pictures. It was something the authorities would never forget.

Identifying victims was a tall task. Some of the pictures went back to the late 1950s. At least ten thousand images were not printed. The investigators concluded that Reardon had procured the images elsewhere and held on to them for decades. Investigators were mad as hell for one reason above all: the presence of other men in the photos. Thousands of photos in Reardon's stash depicted other men abusing children. Authorities had an impossible task dumped on them: not only to identify victims but also their abusers. The faces were right there in front of them. No one was hiding but just where in the hell were they and how long ago were the pictures taken?

I visited Connecticut in early 2020. I first viewed 155 Griswold Drive on Saint Patrick's Day. The home had already been sold twice since the young couple had found the pornography. My first order of business was to find the man to whom George Reardon had left his estate. I knew the man's mother had been Reardon's live-in girlfriend for many years. I also knew that Reardon had very little sexual interest in adult women. He brought this woman into his home for the same reasons Wayne Chapman married years earlier: to give the outside world the impression he was living a normal life while secretly getting closer to her two young children. I had strong suspicions that Reardon spent years grooming and ultimately abusing his girlfriend's two sons.

Unfortunately, I never had the opportunity to interview either of them. I talked to various classmates and residents all over West Hartford. The boys had been in trouble most of their adult lives. The men served various prison stints for petty crimes and were known as menaces. I believe the young men were lashing out like only the abused can. They were not menaces, but instead victims of a vicious pedophile who destroyed their confidence and sense of self over many years. George Reardon massacred these young men's minds, and the residents of West Hartford paid the bill.

The civil cases were over by the time I reached Reardon's former stomping grounds, but it was still hard to get people to open up about him. It was an open wound for many. You couldn't go anywhere without meeting someone who was victimized or knew someone who was victimized. Parents were embarrassed they allowed their kids to be involved in his "studies." The detectives assigned to the case were hard-working men and women who were thoroughly disturbed by his activities. Most were uncomfortable talking to me on the record; investigators were hesitant to reopen the wound of abuse for victims.

It was during the off-the-record discussions with investigators that I first learned about George Reardon's getaway home in Upstate New York. He owned a vacation home for decades and escaped there whenever his work schedule allowed. The police raided his Upstate home during the initial investigation. During the search, they found a miniature version of the Connecticut house. The vacation home was complete with a smaller dark room and a smaller stash of child pornography.

George Reardon may have taken time off from work, but he never stopped abusing children and producing images.

When my Hartford research hit a dead end, I immediately turned my attention to Reardon's activities Upstate. The West Hartford community's pain was still so palpable. All these years later, George Reardon haunted the people of this large Connecticut community. It began to drag down my mental health. As always, I was trying to solve the riddle of Wayne Chapman's early childhood activities and forays into pedophilia. Someone or some group of men introduced Wayne Chapman early to child pornography. By that time, I had all but ruled out Chapman's father or any other family member abusing young Chapman. His siblings had ample opportunities on the record to expose abuse if it were happening. None of the Chapman clan uttered a word about sexual abuse. I needed to see if he had ever crossed paths with George Reardon during his formative years. I knew it was a reach, but if I could solve the mystery of his upbringing, I thought more dominoes would start falling.

First, I needed to know exactly where Reardon's New York vacation home was located. I knew he had grown up five hours away from Wayne Chapman, in Albany. Reardon also attended medical school in Albany after a short stint serving in the United States Navy. He was also known to cross the border into Canada in his formative years. Cities like Toronto and Montreal were well known for their gay bathhouse scenes in the 1950s and 1960s. Montreal had a sordid reputation for adult magazine shops that specialized in child pornography. Chapman was always open about consuming child pornography in Canada. His Canadian forays fueled his fantasies and set him on a path that would result in many victims over several decades. Had the two crossed paths? I asked that question at least a thousand times in my research for this book about different men involved in this story.

My reflex was always *no way and* almost every time, that reflex would prove wrong. Spoiler alert: I could never put Wayne Chapman and George Reardon in the same place with hard evidence like photos or witness statements. What I *do* have is incredible circumstantial evidence linking the two.

It turns out that George Reardon's vacation home was located just three hours from where Wayne Chapman was born and raised. Police found thousands of pictures depicting child abuse in his vacation home. Some were printed on his trademark paper. Those children were victims he groomed and had produced the pictures himself. Many were not, however. Police were flummoxed by the pictures. Some were taken outdoors in woodland-type areas. Police knew there was a predator out there who was involved in the production trade and took his victims into wooded areas. The investigators could never make connections.

I can.

Wayne Chapman had to rely on taking victims in public places. He didn't have the cover of a medical practice to lure victims like Reardon did. Thankfully, I have never seen the photos in the cache, and it is certainly possible Chapman was so prolific that Reardon got a hold of some of his pictures. Remember, Father Cornelius Otero, who was Reardon's main confidant, was busted selling child pornography. The priest was heavily ensconced in the underground trade and selling images of abused children. I don't think most people who haven't immersed themselves in this scene can grasp just how massive the operation was and how deep the corruption went.

Most investigators involved in the Reardon case told me that they believed George Reardon worked alone. I couldn't disagree more. One thing I have learned is that these pedophiles are not Lone Wolf-type of offenders. There is always some help. At the very least, because of the pictures and the geographical proximity to one another, I believe Chapman and Reardon connected. We will never fully grasp the depths of the child pornography trade in the Northeast from the 1950s to the late 1970s. The two men were on opposite ends of the deal. Chapman was a foot soldier in the trade and Reardon was a high-level consumer and producer. Both men had their fantasies fueled in the Toronto and Montreal pornography shops long before the Internet made it way too easy to access these images.

Many mysteries surround Wayne Chapman and George Reardon. The one enduring mystery that haunts me is the identities of the boys (now men) in Reardon's images. A few were cropped and released to the public. The images depict men abusing children. Their faces are there for the world to see, plain as day. Yet none of these men have ever been identified. I have been on a two-year journey to identify the men in his photos. I cling to the hope that these men will be identified and prosecuted to the full extent of the law.

Maybe these men can answer some questions for me. If these men were willing to be photographed in such photos, they had to have been deeply ingrained in the community. I must know everything about that community and the period. There are families whose children have been missing for decades and they deserve answers. If these men can shed any light on Reardon and his ilk's activities, then it is worth chasing. Websites like SAVAGEWATCH.COM, a website dedicated to cold cases in the New England area, have spotlighted the pictures of the unidentified men.

I have shown pictures of the men to many, many residents in West Hartford to no avail. Most people I talked to were shocked that the images were cropped and made available to the public. West Hartford detectives who initially worked the Reardon case had long since retired and it is unclear if any active law enforcement official in West Hartford is investigating the unknown men pictured abusing children. It is a case mostly lost to the men and women who worked it when it was current—and that is what truly bothers me.

Dr. George Reardon and the mystery surrounding his crimes deserve a book of their own. I grappled with the idea of touching on this story in this book. It may be a major reach to connect the two and I accept that criticism. I feel the intense need to paint an entire picture for you of just what child pornography production was like in New England in the thirty-year timeframe between 1950 and 1980. While I was never photographed, I was one of those kids whose life was destroyed by sexual abuse at the hands of an older man. Any lead I pick up on will be investigated with detail that is borderline obsessive. The Puglisi and Louison families deserve as much and so do George Reardon's victims.

Father Cornelius Otero, whom Reardon considered his best friend, also died in 1998. Cornelius was a man of the cloth who used his pulpit to abuse young boys. The two were often seen in each other's company at Saint Francis Hospital, and God only knows what destruction they caused together. Years after Cornelius' death, stories started coming out about his activities with young children.

Many civil lawsuits were filed, and money was paid out. He was the point man for the child pornography trade in Brooklyn in the 1970s. Boys would come forward in later years and reported that he would often take pictures of them at a summer camp where he volunteered. As was often the case, these boys came from underserved and broken communities. They were the perfect victims for monsters like Cornelius Otero. It was not just janitors with low IQs who produced these photos but highly respected priests and doctors. The depth of the depravity is impossible to understate.

CHAPTER 11: ONE
LAST MYSTERY

The 2000s brought newfound interest in Andy Puglisi's disappearance and Wayne Chapman. It started with Andy's childhood friend, Melanie Perkins-McLaughlin, and her Emmy Award-winning documentary, *Have You Seen Andy?* which was released in 2003. Melanie never stopped making good on the promise she made to her missing friend—looking for Andy. At certain points, the documentary depicted Melanie talking around a dinner table with her childhood friends from the projects about their lives growing up and their missing friend.

The film is both beautiful and haunting and is the genesis of this book. Melanie visited Wayne Chapman in prison at MCI Shirley, and he denied all knowledge of Andy's disappearance. As always, Chapman denied ever visiting the city of Lawrence, as Charles Pierce always told him to do. Chapman always contended that his link to Andy's case was mostly a media creation. He lived like most offenders do: completely disgusted with his depraved behavior. So much so that I believe he had convinced himself he was not present the day Andy disappeared. Multiple witnesses put him there on the day Andy disappeared.

Chapman pleaded guilty to raping two Lawrence boys just the summer prior, but in his mind, if he denied it enough, it didn't happen. Melanie's steadfast pursuit of the truth uncovered the last real mystery of this story.

The mystery centers around a man I could never really get a grasp on— Peter Haskell. Melanie was alerted to Haskell through a tip. After you put yourself out into the public sphere, you're bound to get information from the public that could be useful. A man who had had contact with Haskell when he was a young boy living in Georgetown, Massachusetts, in the 1970s, contacted her. Georgetown is an affluent community ten miles down Route 133 from Lawrence.

The man had a story to tell and eventually called the Georgetown Police Department from West Palm Beach, Florida, in the summer of 2007. The man told the detective who took the call that when he was five or six years old, he witnessed Peter Haskell commit a murder. The man told the detective he witnessed Peter drop a rock on a young boy's head, whom he estimated to be between the ages of eight and twelve years old. The detectives took the report seriously and wondered aloud why it took decades for the man to come forward, but the man had a reasonable excuse: he was an offender himself and was undergoing therapy for suppressed memories with his psychologist. The man had a revelation in one such therapy session. Peter Haskell, who was his neighbor in his hometown of Georgetown, had abused him. Haskell was very open with the man about his crimes against children. The man estimated Haskell committed this murder in about 1969 or 1970 when Peter was in his late thirties.

The man felt he needed to alert the authorities that Peter Haskell was a child killer.

After he made the call, the police told him they would love to speak with him in person. About a month later, the man came to Georgetown. The police had no idea he was coming when he showed up to make his statement. The man sat down with Georgetown detectives and spun an incredible and horrifying story about what he saw Haskell do. Detectives told the man to speak slowly and expound in as much detail as he could remember.

The man started with Haskell picking him up just near his childhood home. Haskell drove the man, then a boy, over to Baldpate Pond State Park located in Boxford, Massachusetts. The state park is well known for great freshwater fishing and scenic hiking trails. The man estimated it was a bit later in the afternoon when he and Peter parked near the wood line at Baldpate. Haskell shut the engine down, unbuckled their seatbelts, grabbed the boy, and threw him over his shoulders. They shuffled through the woods, while Haskell kicked up the thick underbrush beneath his feet. Eventually, the man said they arrived at a tree where a little boy was tied up. The boy had sandy-brown hair and had a look of terror on his face as and looked at them both. Haskell then picked up a large rock from a pile near the tree and smashed the tied-up boy right behind his left ear, rendering him unconscious.

He turned to his young neighbor and said, "That is what happens to bad little boys."

The boy thought Haskell would kill him right there; he had just witnessed Haskell murder a young boy in cold blood. Haskell didn't kill him. Instead, he confessed to the boy that every rock piled up next to the tree represented a child he had murdered. Haskell confessed to his young neighbor that he had been working on the rock pile for years. Haskell told the boy he had been murdering kids in those woods at Baldpate for longer than the boy had been alive. The now grown man could not recall how the conversation ended or how he got out of those woods unscathed, but he did, and his dealings with Peter Haskell were far from over.

The man from West Palm Beach continued to associate with Haskell after this incident at Baldpate. He became more and more interested in Haskell's home, particularly the cellar Haskell seemed very protective of in the 1970s. The man from West Palm Beach was so curious about the cellar that he broke into Haskell's home when he was ten or twelve years old. Haskell had invited the adolescent into his home many times in the late 1960s and the man was often struck by how protective he was of people coming in and out of his basement. The boy would often open Haskell's basement door and poke his head around. It was almost always dark, and the smell was atrocious. Years later, on a job site, the man from West Palm Beach witnessed an electrical accident that left a coworker with burned flesh. Immediately, the man was transported back to the basement door at the white house on Chestnut Street in Georgetown. He was sure the smell of his coworker's burning flesh was the smell he remembered from Haskell's.

Peter Haskell turned his neighbor into Georgetown Police after figuring out who broke into his home. He would use the break-in as an excuse for why the man from West Palm Beach was making these accusations decades later. I heard the story about Peter Haskell in late 2015. I admit that Haskell was not on my radar before then. After I heard about him and these accusations, I had to get to Georgetown and run the Peter Haskell thread to the ground. My first question was, *"Where the hell did Peter Haskell come from?*

Peter Haskell was born in the summer of 1931 in the same city as Charles Pierce, Haverhill, Massachusetts, and was the only son of Tip and Edith Haskell. His parents affectionately called him "little Pete" and it was a moniker that stuck with him for the rest of his life. Young Haskell was a standout athlete. He was the captain of his high school basketball team and was an exemplary baseball player; he was popular with his high school classmates but didn't have any girlfriends, nor did he attend his senior prom. I interviewed seven of his former classmates from a prep school in Maine. Some of their memories were unclear all these decades later, but former classmates remembered him as very handsome and athletic, a bit aloof. Secretive. Everybody knew of Haskell, but nobody *knew* him. In 1953, Haskell, along with his younger sister Mary Jo, who joined the Air Force, enlisted in the United States Army and served in the Korean conflict as a military police officer.

Peter had an honorable three-year tour of duty in the army and had a spotless service record. He took his combat time and Korea and put it to good use, using the GI Bill to enroll at Boston University. He was a studious pupil at BU's hallowed halls. While he was attending university, he explored his real passion in life: coaching youth sports. Haskell founded a youth soccer league in the nearby town of Beverly and coached baseball and basketball for six-plus decades, including at Riverside Bradford, a Little League Baseball organization in Haverhill. Well into his eighties, Haskell would roam the sidelines on weekends, teaching boys the finer techniques of catching or the proper way to throw the ball in from the sideline in a soccer match.

Peter Haskell was a fixture in the community, much like Lawrence Brehaut in Wakefield, but his personal life was shrouded in mystery. Most of his neighbors saw him as a quiet man, who was friendly enough but kept to himself. He was guarded, even. He never married nor did he have a steady girlfriend or children of his own. Haskell's sexual orientation is something I could never nail down. He did not keep a large circle of friends, outside of Mary Jo and a man who lived in New Hampshire. Nobody knew Peter Haskell, but the man from West Palm Beach claims to know all about his sexual proclivities. He accused Haskell of sexual abuse that lasted for years. The man, as he later admitted, went on to be an offender himself, perhaps from years of abuse at Haskell's hands. Some abused children go on to abuse themselves. It's all they know. The child-adult sexual relationship becomes "normalized" in their minds. Some children, me included, become so disgusted with their past, that they do everything in their power to protect people from it. The man from West Palm Beach said he repressed the memories of Peter Haskell's abuse. It wasn't until he decided to go to therapy that the memories started to flood him—the sexual abuse, the little boy in the woods, whom he saw murdered in cold blood.

The man from West Palm Beach contacted Detective Thomas Dejoy of the Georgetown Police Department on August 31, 2007. Detective Dejoy was a veteran of the department and a hard-nosed "cop's cop." The man was sure he saw his neighbor, who sexually abused him, kill a boy in the woods in 1970.

The man told the detective about the rock pile of "murdered kids" that Peter Haskell told him he had been working on for years. Detective Dejoy listened intently and immediately contacted the Massachusetts State Police Unresolved Case Unit, contacting Lieutenant Elaine Gill. He asked if the trooper had any missing children's cases in the area from the 1969 to 1970 timeframe. Lieutenant Gill made a serious effort to locate any files on missing kids, excited that maybe a case had fallen into her lap, but the veteran lieutenant could not turn up a single file on a missing boy in the area at that time. Perhaps, she suggested, the man from West Palm Beach was wrong on the year? Was it a few years later?

Georgetown officers pressed the man on the year he saw Peter murder the boy. He was adamant it was 1969 or 1970 and would subsequently call periodically to ask how the investigation was going. He would throw in little nuggets like, "Ask Haskell about the basement," or "Tell Haskell one right behind the ear," either alluding to how he remembered allegedly killing the boy or maybe even threatening Haskell himself. The police thought for a short time that the man from West Palm Beach might try to confront Haskell. Police took it seriously enough as a threat against Haskell that they brought the man down to the station to clarify his comments and give him a stern warning: do not make comments like that. He stayed on top of the investigation for another two years or so, never gaining much traction. It was something that happened in 1999, though, that put Peter Haskell under the microscope and turned up the heat on the investigation.

In the spring of 2013, Detective Michael Goddu of the Georgetown Police Department was going through some old files. Detective Goddu had heard the rumors at work about Peter Haskell. Even though it wasn't his case, he was interested in the statement from the man from West Palm Beach and in Haskell's case. Detective Goddu remembered a case that was never solved from 1999. Two thirteen-year-old girls were walking down Lake Shore Drive in Georgetown, just minutes from the Black Swan Country Club and a four-minute drive from Haskell's home on Chestnut Street. A vehicle with two men pulled up to the two girls, who were walking home from school. The driver asked the girls if they needed a ride home, perhaps the girls would like to come back to the man's house. The girls' instincts rightly kicked in and they refused the man's overtures and walked hurriedly in the opposite direction. Making enough of a scene, the two men sped off in the opposite direction towards Lufkin's Brook Conservation Area. The teens were spooked enough that their parents decided to report the incident. Detectives, upon learning that one of the girls was a very talented aspiring artist, asked her to sketch the vehicle's driver. One of the girls also had enough clarity to write down half of the license plate number and give a detailed description of the vehicle. The case languished in purgatory for years with no suspects and no tips. Detective Goddu remembered the case and figured he would look at the sketch one more time and compare it to Peter Haskell's photo on file.

He almost fell over when he looked at the nearly decade-old drawing. Peter Haskell was a dead ringer for the girl's sketch. He couldn't shake the similarities and took the information to Detective Dejoy. They started interviewing Peter's neighbors, who described him as "odd" and "weird." One neighbor even asked the investigators if Haskell was "at it again." Investigators were floored when a man who knew Haskell from years living on Chestnut Street asked plainly if "he likes little boys." Neighbors also statements made about his friend from New Hampshire. They thought Haskell and his friend were a gay couple who may have had an affair with a local priest. Investigators started to see a pattern emerge. Everyone who contacted him seemingly believed he was a very strange man. Another domino was about to fall. Peter Haskell brought his New Hampshire friend to the Georgetown Police Station during initial questioning after his former child neighbor made the allegations. Investigators thought the man was there for moral support and questioned Haskell in private while his good friend waited for him. Police got a good enough look at the man to remember his face. Detectives reached out to the two girls from the 1999 attempted abduction to get a handle on what they remembered. One of the witnesses described the man who was sitting in the passenger seat quite well. The woman, now in her early twenties, remembered almost every detail about the passenger.

Investigators were astounded. The man she described sounded a lot like the man from New Hampshire. Investigators made sense of the partial plate number the girls had written down. It turns out the man from New Hampshire had a sister-in-law who owned a vehicle with the same number. The description the girls gave of the vehicle the men were in also matched the partial plate number. Why Peter wasn't immediately arrested along with his friend is a mystery. Investigators may have believed that there just was not enough physical evidence to link Haskell beyond a reasonable doubt to the alleged attempted abduction. Maybe investigators were waiting to gather more evidence on him, biding their time.

Detective Goddu did not stop working on the Peter Haskell case. He contacted the West Palm Beach man's therapist and spoke to her about her client's repressed memories. The therapist affirmed that many abused children's memories get tucked so far away in the recesses of their minds that it takes years for them to bubble to the surface. The therapist thought her client was not mentally ill; she saw her client as very competent with nothing to gain from making up a story about Peter Haskell. The therapist believed the man wholeheartedly and espoused that view to the detective. He also contacted Mary Jo, Haskell's sister. Mary Jo explained that she and her brother had had a falling out and she wanted nothing to do with him. She never explained why. Like everything in the Haskell story, specifics were fleeting. It had been nearly a quarter of a century since she had seen her brother, Mary Jo told investigators.

Georgetown Police Department knew they had a bizarre man on their hands. Was that it? It is certainly not a crime to be weird, but murder allegations and being identified at the scene of a near-abduction had police on edge.

Investigators had already been in the Haskell home the year prior. In 2012, they stopped by and executed a search warrant. Complete with the state police, canines, and ground penetrating radar, investigators largely came up empty-handed. Investigators asked Haskell when the basement cement got poured. He stated that he had the basement cement poured around 1969 or 1970. Investigators noted that he might have had the basement done over after the man from West Palm Beach broke in and snooped around. Whatever had been there was long since gone. The detectives also noted that Haskell had a very disturbing collection of identification cards that depicted children in their soccer uniforms. A Georgetown detective asked Peter why he did not simply return the ID cards to the kids or destroy them. What happened next solidified the investigator's thoughts about Peter. He became viscerally angry and grabbed the identification cards out of the detective's hands. The search party left with no real evidence of any crimes but was steadfast in their belief that Peter Haskell was hiding something. There was something beneath the surface with him, but they just needed to gather enough evidence to prove it.

It infuriated investigators that Haskell could have been abusing, and potentially murdering, children right under their noses. So many things did not add up with him. Peter Haskell had been coaching kids' sports for nearly sixty-eight years and never once did a child come forward with an allegation like the man from West Palm Beach. Was he able to compartmentalize that well? Could he turn it off? I tend to believe the man's story. There is nothing to gain from making such an accusation. I believe Haskell was a predator who could manipulate as well as any pedophile I have ever studied. I looked far and wide for former soccer and baseball players whom he might have coached. I found many who were shocked by the allegations against their former coach. Some had spent time at Haskell's home in Georgetown watching horse racing videos and eating candy. The man from New Hampshire was also hanging around the house often. Most former players I spoke to found point that to be completely odd. They thought maybe the man was Haskell's boyfriend but didn't dare ask their coach. Some former players knew their coach was weird but managed to keep him at arm's length. When I pressed for details on the behavior, I heard a familiar story. He was just *weird,* but nobody could put their finger on it. As of this publication, I have not found one single victim of Haskell's willingness to speak on the record.

The more damning testimony on Peter Haskell comes from Georgetown residents who lived near him, some for many decades. Getting to know Georgetown residents through social media pages and on-the-ground reporting was both a satisfying *and* horrifying experience. Rumors flew around about the weird man on Chestnut Street. Residents had a keen sense that Haskell was odd and potentially dangerous. It was an open secret that he spent too much time with people who were far younger than him. Most children were told to stay the hell away. Never engage him, and if he ever talks to you, walk away, where the marching orders one parent gave. It is so interesting to me that a man like that was able to coexist when the neighbors were so acutely aware of him. Just imagine that happening today. I feel like social media wouldn't allow for a man like that to remain in town. Parents would run to city Facebook groups to out the man and share gossip. Times were different then. I am happy to say it is a much safer world now for children, even with the advent of the Internet.

Detective Goddu could never link Peter Haskell to the attempted abduction of the thirteen-year-old girls, nor could he ever corroborate the man from West Palm Beach's story with hard evidence. He wanted to believe the man, he truly did. There was just no evidence.

On November 16, 2016, the man from New Hampshire, who called himself Peter Haskell's best friend, dialed 911. After not talking to Haskell for days, he decided to go check on his friend. The man found Haskell slumped over his bed in the master bedroom. He had been dead for at least a few days by the time he was found; he was eighty-five years old. Police and emergency vehicles responded to the scene where his body lay. While medical personnel were busy loading him up, some uniformed officers looked around the master bedroom. The officers, who did not possess a warrant, saw stacks ten high of children's videos. Some titles were Disney-themed movies. Most officers knew about the allegations made against Haskell and found it odd that a man who didn't have children would possess these videos. The presence of a small mannequin up against a wall wearing a soccer uniform from the team that he had once coached so disturbed the officers and EMTs that investigators applied for a proper search warrant. Sergeant Robert C. Labarge of the Massachusetts State Police Essex County Detective Unit based in Salem wrote the affidavit for the search warrant.

In early December of 2016, just weeks after Peter Haskell's death, state police and Georgetown authorities along with the FBI convened on the Chestnut Street home. The FBI's technical hazards response team assisted in the search and ground-penetrating radar was brought in. Chestnut Street residents were surprised to see half the street shut down and men and women with black FBI jackets running around Peter Haskell's house. Rumors swirled. *Everyone knew Haskell was weird, but the FBI.* Georgetown Police Chief Donald Cudmore stated the massive law enforcement presence at the 4 Chestnut Street home but was vague with details. Chief Cudmore stressed that the search party posed no danger to the public. Crowds gathered at the end of Chestnut Street to watch the police, who set up a blue tent in Haskell's backyard. Investigators braved the bitter northeast December cold for four days thoroughly searching the house.

Investigators could never find an actual missing child to corroborate the man from West Palm Beach's story about the child Peter Haskell allegedly murdered in the woods. Officials also were armed with the information that he drove trucks for a living. He traveled the state working for Standard Uniform Services for most of his adult life. The company operated out of the greater Boston neighborhood of Dorchester, just a few miles from the Combat Zone. Haskell could have been anywhere at any time in the 1970s. Because of his job, he was mobile. Haskell also had a Florida driver's license and was known to escape to sunny Florida's warm climate when the winter hit Georgetown. Haskell had spent most winters in Florida for many years of his life. Had he abducted a child from Florida and brought the child to Massachusetts? Is that what the man from West Palm Beach saw? It was all on the table for investigators. They were determined not to let Peter Haskell die with his secrets.

Investigators, with every tool available to them, ripped through Peter Haskell's home for days. At one point, they held their breath as they unearthed bones from the property, which turned out to be from an animal. Investigators quickly got a grip on Haskell's bizarre habit of collecting children's identification cards. Searchers found a plastic tote packed to the top with children's IDs. It was clear he had a complete infatuation with child pictures. Much like Wayne Chapman and Nathaniel Bar-Jonah, Peter Haskell was completely bound to his pedophilia. He also kept a collection of Barbie dolls, twelve in total. One doll was mutilated with the left breast cut off. The plastic breast hung down barely attached to its body. The search party took the mannequin into evidence as well and found another mannequin with its arms bound and the fingers cut off.

Investigators dug up nineteen audiocassettes as well. The contents of those cassettes, which were never released, are particularly interesting. If Haskell recorded his thoughts, as Wayne Chapman did, we would gain a unique insight into a predator's mind. Why the audio tapes were never released is beyond me.

Perhaps there was nothing of note on the cassettes, but I doubt that. Predators keep notes, record their thoughts, and keep trophies. They simply cannot help themselves and need to relive their crimes repeatedly. It's a way to hold themselves over between crimes. The fact that the audiotapes of Haskell's exist bothers me. So little is known about his crimes, but my intuition tells me there is so much to uncover. Investigators came away from the search incredibly frustrated. They knew Peter Haskell was an incredibly odd man but what they were trying to prove, however, was that he was a murderer. Nothing turned up in the search to confirm the latter. Haskell died, with his secrets and his bizarre collections, a complete enigma to investigators.

I have mentioned Peter Haskell many times in my years investigating the period. I spent way more hours in bathhouses of Providence and Boston than I could count. I sought out older bathhouse patrons, those who looked as if they were old enough to have been active in the 1970s. I tried to befriend these men and ask about their experiences in the 1970s in New England. On-the-ground reporting is my go-to type of reporting. You get much more out of people than you think when they believe the conversation only exists at that moment.

Sometimes, I would wait for hours and work for months on specific men who fit the profile. Always keeping it light, I made a lot of headway learning about Wayne Chapman from the gay men who were still active in the community from the 1970s. I would casually bring him up in conversation. Luckily, he was on the news every so often and I was able to bring his name up without arousing any suspicion. I learned there that Chapman was part of a massive underground subculture of gay men who met at bathhouses and adult bookstores all over the region in the early 1970s. A lot of my suspicions were confirmed except everyone I spoke with who remembered Chapman claimed not to have known anything about his crimes against children.

Could I learn the same about Peter Haskell? For two years, I hunted him in every area where men from his age group would congregate. I attended meetings of gay men at bathhouses, bookstores, and adult movie theaters. I befriended many. Most were decent people from what I could see. Nobody had ever heard of Haskell or recognized him when I would casually bring up his photo on Google and talk about his alleged crimes.

I remain equal parts bewildered and sometimes angry with myself over the Peter Haskell case. There is a large part of me that believes there is so much more. Was the man from West Palm Beach wrong? Was it not 1970 when he saw Haskell murder a boy with a rock in the woods at

Baldpate Park? Maybe it was 1974 and that little boy was Leigh Savoie of Revere. I will never be able to shake that thought. I will also never shake the thought that I wasted a lot of time and energy on Haskell. Perhaps the man from West Palm Beach was lying the entire time and Peter was just a harmless weirdo who collected dolls and identification cards.

Maybe the girls who were nearly abducted were wrong in their descriptions of their would-be abductors and Peter Haskell was simply unlucky. No child whom he coached has ever come forward claiming abuse. Certainly, there would have to be some sort of abuse claim if Haskell were a true predator. But what if he was involved with these men, who all seem so interconnected to one another? The men who systematically abused children to feed the underground pornography trade? He could not have operated in that timeframe without being connected.

That is what keeps me awake in the late hours. That is also why I put Peter Haskell's story in this book.

CHAPTER 12: THE
END, FOR NOW

Wayne Chapman lived out most of his retirement years shuttled back and forth between Bridgewater Treatment Center, MCI Shirley, and North Central Correctional Facility in Gardner, Massachusetts. Chapman shed his "sexually dangerous" label with help from psychiatrists Drs. Ober and Sweitzer. He was sent to actual prisons around Massachusetts to live in complete segregation. Leaving Bridgewater represented the first step to freedom for him; the light was there at the end of the tunnel. The predator had seen a lot of offenders and former friends come and go. Richard Peluso, the orchestrator of the Revere sex ring, was released back into the community in the early 2000s. As far as I could find, Richard never had to register as a sex offender. I have attempted to contact him (he is alive and well and in his eighties), but I have stopped short of outright confronting him. Peluso, however repugnant I find him, paid his debt to society and doesn't deserve to have me harass him. He melted back into his community and has lived, as far as I can tell, a very quiet life.

In 2007, Wayne Chapman was civilly committed once again. Massachusetts civil commitments range anywhere from one day to life. He was now facing the very real threat he would die at Bridgewater. The full breadth of his crimes was reconsidered and the civil commitment was declared in April. Chapman had not been participating in sex offender treatment. Instead, he leaned heavily on religious beliefs and faced health issues. His teeth were in awful condition and he still had major issues with his hygiene, a problem for him most of his life. Most prison staff believed Chapman pretended his health issues were far worse than they were. Staffers who spoke to me anonymously did not buy his "spiritual man" act. They saw Chapman as a chameleon, a man who would do or say anything to paint himself in a sympathetic light. He would urinate on himself even when it was clear he could walk to the bathroom on his own. His best chance, he thought, was to prove he was an invalid and no threat to society to get a sympathetic release. Most considered him to be somewhat dumb but very capable of manipulation. Chapman had been locked up for four decades and his only goal in life was to get out of prison. He served out 2007 sick and incredibly disheartened. The light at the end of the tunnel had dimmed significantly.

2008 was an even tougher year for Chapman. Almost a year to the day of his recommitment, his good friend Nathaniel Bar-Jonah passed away at Deer Lodge Prison in Montana. Bar-Jonah had exhausted his appeals and was lived out the rest of his miserable life in solitary confinement. He busied himself writing letters to his vast array of pen pals around the world. On the morning of April 13, 2008, guards found Bar-Jonah unresponsive in his cell. He had had a rough go before his death healthwise. The alleged cannibal already had one leg amputated on account of his diabetes. His habit of eating entire chocolate cakes in one sitting had caught up to him. When guards found the nearly four-hundred-pound man in his cell, he was clammy, grey, and cold to the touch.

Nathaniel Bar-Jonah was gone. What secrets did he take with him? The bones found in his garage were never identified. Some human beings were buried there and then unearthed by investigators. There is a family out there who once looked or still looks at an empty chair at the dinner table and has no answers about why their loved one is not sitting there. Bar-Jonah could have answered those questions. He made no deathbed confessions nor did he write any "read when I am dead" dossier that explained the mysteries of his crimes.

Bar-Jonah lived in severe denial until the very end. His friendship with Wayne Chapman will forever be a match made in hell. He was the perfect yin to Chapman's yang. Chapman was a mildly mentally handicapped, fixated pedophile, but he wasn't a sadist. He got off on inflicting fear on his victims. He was the personification of evil. Those two crossing paths were the very definition of an unholy union. Nobody was sad to see Bar-Jonah exit this world. In a story in his trilogy of books about the offender, Dr. John Espy recounts what the crematory attendant said as he wheeled the body into the crematorium. The attendant knew about him, as did most everyone in Montana, and as he loaded his huge frame into the flames, he waved his hand and said, "Goodbye, fat boy." It was a fitting end to a worthless existence.

Once a year, Wayne Chapman was offered a glimmer of hope when the court reviewed his sexually dangerous status and his civil commitment. If they found him to no longer be sexually dangerous, he would be released to society immediately. By the mid-2000s, Chapman's prison sentence was long over. The civil commitment was the only obstacle between Chapman and freedom. Melanie Perkins-McLaughlin never forgot her promise to Andy Puglisi, so every time Chapman was reviewed, Melanie was there to remind everyone that this was the man who once admitted to molesting over one hundred children. And that he was the main suspect in her friend's disappearance and the David Louison case. Every year, Massachusetts and society were rewarded when Chapman was recommitted.

Wayne Chapman lived out the first decade of the 2000s among a new stable of predators in Bridgewater. Frank

Damiano, the former bus driver who facilitated numerous young boys' abuse and was a child rapist himself, died behind bars. Chapman took Damiano's death hard. They were often seen socializing. Now Chapman was officially an elder statesman. He cooled his heels in the early 2010s. He worked with his hired psychiatrists and dreamt of the day he would be released.

In 2018, his dreams came to fruition. By then, Chapman depended on nurses to bathe him and he was never seen in public without the help of a wheelchair. His lawyer, a man named Eric Tennen, was making very public arguments that his client should be released. At seventy years old and bound to a wheelchair, his lawyer argued Chapman posed no threat to society. His psychiatrists wrote another report for the Court that their patient was no longer sexually dangerous. The Court agreed. Chapman had finally hit the light at the end of the tunnel. Massachusetts Governor Charlie Baker vehemently and very publicly disagreed with Wayne Chapman's release and proposed state legislation to make Massachusetts even tougher on sex offenders. Chapman tripped himself up in the process. He was charged with lewd and lascivious behavior when he allegedly exposed himself and fondled his genitals in front of a nurse in a prison hospital at MCI Shirley. His victims breathed a sigh of relief that the man who tortured them mentally, and sometimes physically, would be put behind bars again.

One victim told *The Boston Herald* that Wayne Chapman was "the Devil" and that he should never be released. Who could tell how many victims stayed silent, watching in horror as their abuser was set to realize freedom? One examiner, a doctor named Joseph Plaud, interviewed Chapman and deemed him no longer a danger to society, but when asked if he would let Chapman watch his young grandkids, the doctor answered with a flat, "No."

Wayne Chapman eventually beat the charges of lewd and lascivious conduct and was released from state custody after the Massachusetts Supreme Judicial Court ruled that if examiners deemed him unlikely to reoffend, then he must be released. Chapman's prison sentence ended in 2004, but he was incarcerated until 2019 because of the impact of the victims' statements, the breadth of his crimes, and activism from folks like Melanie Perkins-McLaughlin. I watched it from my home thirty-five miles outside of Boston.

I kept insisting to myself that there was no way Wayne Chapman would ever be released. There were simply too many lives shattered by this monster to ever have a Court allow him to see the light of day. The media had done a great job covering Chapman's crimes and Melanie's film put Andy's case front and center in the public's mind. Chapman was released to downtown Boston to live at the Southampton Street Shelter. He registered as a Level 3 sex offender and was immediately put on the state's registry board, which is public information. Massachusettsans were rightly outraged by his release, but I saw it as one last opportunity.

I had often dreamed about meeting Wayne Chapman face to face. When I was researching this book, I fantasized about transporting myself to Lawrence or Brockton. I would swoop in at the last moment and stop Chapman, ensuring Andy Puglisi and David Louison lived long lives. Of course, it's all fantasy, but meeting Chapman in person was now a real possibility. I knew the shelter on Southampton Street had a policy where the residents had to leave the facility in the morning and return at a certain time in the afternoon. This policy allowed residents to go out and socialize, find employment, and keep them from hanging around. I knew the area well having worked in the Combat Zone for over a year and growing up twenty minutes from the shelter.

I started taking the train into the city. I didn't want to stalk a senior citizen, but I needed to see the lay of the land. I assumed Chapman was such a high-profile figure that security around the aging pedophile might be extremely tight. The last thing I wanted was to make him, or whoever was providing his security, think I was a threat. I never had any intention to physically confront a man bound to a wheelchair. I simply wanted to look him in the eyes and ask him a question or two. My senses were heightened when I got down near the shelter. I could smell every smell in the city. Every noise from nearby construction jackhammering drilled in my ears. I alternated listening to Boston radio personalities Gerry Callahan and Kirk Minihane's podcasts in my earbuds. I was ready.

The day I encountered Wayne Chapman was already long. The commuter rail train coming from the south of Boston was late. I carried a heavy backpack with my laptop inside. I was exhausted. I sincerely doubted that Chapman would be out and about wheeling around the city. Parkinson's disease had ravaged his body. I posted up across the street from the shelter right next to 232 Union Street and Tiffany's Barber Shop. It was now or never. I waited for the shelter to empty. What I didn't realize at the time was that the shelter was mostly a medical facility. Southampton Street did not operate like a traditional "leave at 8 and be back at 5" shelter. The residents were there because they needed medical treatment. I needed a new plan. The odds of Wayne Chapman wheeling out to begin his day were slim to none.

I waited outside the Southampton Street Shelter every day for what felt like months but was more like three days. I started to pick up the patterns of patients being driven in and out of the back for what I assumed were medical appointments or more specific care elsewhere. I saw scores of residents go out and come back, but I had not spied Wayne Chapman yet. I was getting weary. The only place nearby to eat that fit my paltry budget was a McDonald's. I began to realize eating fast food twice a day was not wise. My energy was drained and I had a consistent feeling of being stuck in the mud. At that moment, it occurred to me that I could catch Chapman coming in and out for his medical appointments from the back of the shelter. I decided to wait behind the building if it took that to see him. I was obsessed with the idea that I could get Wayne Chapman to talk to me. I was under some sort of delusion. I have no experience interviewing pedophiles, never mind alleged murderers. I once heard an interview with true crime author James Renner, who has investigated the disappearances of Maura Murray and Amy Mihaljevic. Renner had a favorite suspect in Amy Mihaljevic's disappearance and tracked the suspect to Florida. He planned to confront the man and call his bluff with a story that he had dirt on the suspect nobody knew. I planned on doing the same with Chapman. I concocted a story that I had heard that investigators had DNA evidence from the incinerator at Miriam Hospital in Providence that may be Andy Puglisi's. In retrospect, it made little sense and he would never fall for it.

On a Wednesday, I finally caught a glimpse of someone who looked like Wayne Chapman. The old man had a confused look on his face, white hair that encircled a nearly bald head, and thick, bushy white eyebrows. He was being wheeled out the back door and into a waiting red van. I made a beeline for Chapman and stopped short a couple of feet in front of the doors. It's hard to recall exactly what the building looked like; my gaze was steady. The man looked like every grandfather who sits quietly alone in the corner at his great-grandchild's birthday party. I had my backpack on and my headphones in; I planned to make it look like I was simply cutting through, a busy man. Maybe I was on my lunch break. I couldn't risk his handlers fingering me as someone who knew who he was.

It was a beautiful spring day and Chapman was clad in a white t-shirt that fell effortlessly over his arms. I remember he was wearing a wristwatch, but I couldn't figure out if it was for fashion or because he was interested in what time it was. He wore brown pants and black sneakers that strapped without laces and had the same floppy mustache he'd always donned since his early twenties. I stopped a few yards from his wheelchair off to my left. I checked the time on my black Zodiac chronograph that my wife bought me for Christmas. It was 10:32 a.m. Chapman was left unattended for a few seconds as care staff propped the van doors open. I was left alone with him. Face to face. I had hunted this man and empathized with his victims for years. I had spoken to anyone who even had the slightest bit of interaction with him. I needed to know what made him tick—not what he was as much as *why* he was. It has always been about the *why*. Always.

I stared deep into his eyes studying him. Everything I ever heard was true. His eyes were blank. It reminded me of looking at dead bodies during my time in Afghanistan. There was absolutely nothing there. It made me cold. I have never felt pure evil the way I felt it at that moment and I have been all over the world. I have been in the presence of Taliban- and Haqqani-network terrorists, most of whom would cut the body parts off of women who dared to cheat on their spouses or throw gay men off the top of buildings for sport.

And I didn't get the vibe from them I got from Wayne Chapman. In those short seconds, I thought about his victims. *Did they feel the same about his presence? Was it a lifetime of being told to "respect adults" that made them agree to go with the man when they were accosted? Or was he that good of a manipulator?* I leaned into Chapman and told him I knew about the DNA at Providence Hospital. I was expecting some deep, introspective answer.

He just stared back. Nothing.

My pulse was racing. I realized later that I perspired through my black Led Zeppelin t-shirt. I was so thirsty and having a visceral, physical reaction to being in this man's presence.

He said nothing.

I studied his face, looking for the scar that was an

identifying marker for police years before I was born. I took a mental snapshot of that face. Oddly, I did not want to forget it. We had a few seconds of a deep stare down and he was taken away. I think I walked off well before the healthcare workers came. I existed in that weird place where all my senses were overloaded. It's like skydiving. You never really remember what the sky looked like when you're up there. Nothing matters. Your senses are pinned and revved at the highest level.

We live in a world of hyperbole, but I am not being hyperbolic—this man had the presence of a reptile. It just wasn't human. Even now when I walk through that day, I get uncontrollable chills. All these years later, I avoid going into Boston at all costs and it's not on account of its horrific traffic.

I went back home to the suburbs that night. Thirty-two miles away from the streets Wayne Chapman was haunting again, all these decades after he congregated on those very streets with like-minded men. The thought of Chapman being deemed well enough to live freely aggravated and horrified me. Regardless of how many times his lawyer repeated the line that he was too sick or old to be dangerous, I knew differently—Wayne Chapman had been behind bars for decades, dreaming about trawling for victims upon his release. In the quiet hours in Bridgewater, Chapman would congregate with his pedophile friends and discuss how he would commit crimes differently if he were ever released. There is no known cure or magic elixir for a man like him, no matter what hired guns like Drs. Ober and Sweitzer believe.

In December 2020, in a cruel twist, Wayne Chapman was eventually moved to Medford Rehabilitation & Nursing Center. He now lived in rehab just a few miles away from Melanie Perkins-McLaughlin. The facility is in the vicinity of a playground and it housed two other Level 3 sex offenders at that time. Chapman was now seventy-three years old and nearly immobile. Six decades after he began his life abusing children, he was still not truly free. The confines of the facility and the staff kept him from doing what he truly wanted: get out and away from the prying eyes of the media, staff, and folks like me who believe he never truly paid for his crimes.

Chapman's move to Medford also coincided with COVID-19. The lockdowns that followed got me thinking that statistically speaking there was some abused child out there locked down with their abuser at home. It was a bone-chilling realization. The Medford Rehab staff were aware of Chapman's sordid criminal history. Most staff who spoke to me discussed Chapman the way most everyone who ever met him did: the man just seemed dead. He looked like a human being, in conventional terms, but there was something else in him. It was like he was an animal. The staff shed no tears when their most infamous resident was shipped out of state.

Some Medford administrators or Massachusetts politicians came to their good senses and got Chapman out. His presence in Medford set off a shit storm, and rightfully so. It was bad enough for the victim but Melanie's neighborhood? Imagine believing a man murdered your childhood friend, chasing him down for decades, and he gets dropped in your neighborhood as a free man. It's more than a cruel twist of fate. It's completely intolerable.

The residents of Rocky Hill, Connecticut, were less than thrilled when one of the most prolific sex offenders in United States history arrived on their doorstep. The facility where Wayne Chapman arrived sits in the shadows of Moser School, which serves elementary-age students. The school is located five hundred feet from the facility's main entrance. Chapman's window overlooked the schoolyard. The notorious child rapist, who took thousands of pictures of school children and recorded his vile thoughts into audio recorders while following school buses, now had a bird's-eye view of his preferred victims. It was downright laughable. The facility had garnered a reputation for taking in out-of-state paroled sex offenders and residents were rightfully pissed. They felt that the facility valued profit over the safety of the community's children.

After word leaked out to the *Hartford Courant* that there were ninety-five beds in the facility and each bed was worth five hundred dollars a day, the financial incentive to take in former prisoners was now public knowledge. One fiery resident made it a mission to take the police chief and local politicians to task and demanded a closer look at why these paroled sex offenders were now Rocky Hill's concern. The town spent nearly two hundred thousand dollars fighting the facility. At the end of a lengthy litigation, the courts ruled against the Rocky Hill argument. The facility had every right to take in whomever they pleased, regardless of their criminal history. Even Wayne Chapman.

The events that succeeded Chapman's arrival in Connecticut were typical and illuminated something about him: every normal, decent person on Earth completely rebukes people like Wayne Chapman. His mere presence at South Hampton Street, then Medford, and eventually Rocky Hill, was enough to put entire cities up in arms. This is why it was so important for men like him to find like-minded predators and gain validation, especially in their formative years.

When you look at the furious reaction communities had to Chapman, it's not hard to understand why these men often flock to one another. They have something awful inside them and having it validated by someone who is like them, is intoxicating. It became very clear to me when I watched the uproar in Connecticut. No matter where Chapman went, at any point in his life, people were disgusted by him and wanted to drive him out. Residents told me that if the local Walmart had sold pitchforks, they would have sold out in hours. The community wanted Wayne Chapman gone.

In May 2021, something happened that caught me by surprise and filled me with some hope for Andy Puglisi's and David Louison's families. A pedophile priest named Richard Lavigne was on his deathbed battling COVID-19. Father Lavigne was the lone suspect in altar boy Danny Croteau's 1972 murder. Father Lavigne operated out of an Archdiocese in Springfield, Massachusetts, and used his position to abuse young boys, most of whom served on the altar. He racked up forty complaints from various boys over his years and was finally defrocked in 1991. He was convicted in June 1992 of sex crimes and was a registered Level 3 sex offender for the rest of his life.

Thirteen-year-old Danny's body was found floating lifelessly in the Chicopee River. The fun-loving young boy played catcher on the local Little League baseball team and was close to his mother and father. Danny's mother, Bernice Croteau, once compared her son to Huckleberry Finn. The family's life was torpedoed on April 15, 1972, when young Danny's body was found. The state police came to Bernice weeks after her son's disappearance and asked if she knew about Father Lavigne's relationship with him. The Croteau boys had assisted Father Lavigne at Saint Catherine's mass in Springfield. He was like a member of the Croteau family, taking Danny on overnight trips and having dinner at the Croteau house often. Bernice didn't realize at the time that when Danny came home from some of these overnight excursions feeling queasy, it was not because he ate too much candy: the priest was feeding Danny alcohol and drugs. Danny was being systematically groomed and victimized by a man he trusted, a man of the cloth.

After Danny turned up dead, the state police developed a theory on why Father Lavigne would murder the young boy and throw his body in the river. Danny was nearing the end of his rope with the priest and was getting ready to talk. As with most pedophiles, Father Lavigne was only interested in keeping himself out of the line of fire. He hatched a plan to meet Danny on the side of the road by the river and smashed him over the head with a rock, dumping the boy's body on an early spring New England day.

Rumors swirled for years about what the priest did to Danny. The district attorney only had circumstantial evidence. For years, Father Lavigne emphatically denied having anything to do with Danny's murder, even going as far as writing a letter in 1994 about Danny's murder, claiming it was from Danny's "real" killer. A handwriting expert looked at the letter and compared it to Father Lavigne's and found that they matched. He had written the letter to himself. Even with that, Father Lavigne was not charged with anything. However, that same year, Father Lavigne pled guilty to molesting two other boys and somehow avoided prison. The priest received probation and was placed on the Massachusetts Sex Offender Registry Board. He lived out the rest of the 1990s, early 2000s, and into the 2010s as a free man in Chicopee, just a town away from Springfield.

When I first read up on Danny Croteau's case, I tried to think of alternate suspects who might have killed him. Perhaps, the three main protagonists of this book, Charles Pierce, Nathaniel Bar-Jonah, or Wayne Chapman could have crossed Danny. No chance. Bar-Jonah did live in the general area, but Danny was far too old to be his (and Chapman's for that matter) ideal victim. Pierce killed boys and girls of any age and physical characteristics at random. I knew it was a long shot, but I didn't discount Charles Pierce.

That was until April 2021, on the forty-ninth anniversary of Danny's death, when a Massachusetts State Police detective visited an extremely ill Richard Lavigne in his hospital room. The detective made a little small talk with the defrocked priest and then approached the real reason he had come to the father's bedside.

The detective asked the former priest, "What's it been, fifty years now?"

Lavigne let out an exasperated exhale. Fifty years of being asked about Danny had worn the pedophile thin.

Detective Michael McNalley was a Catholic school graduate himself and he was not about to let the former priest off the hook without taking him through the night of April 15, 1972, one more time.

The predator made startling admissions over the course of eleven hours over five visits that ended on May 4, 2021. Lavigne admitted to bringing Danny Croteau to a boat ramp adjacent to the Chicopee River and striking him with a rock. He then shoved Danny into the river and returned later to check on his body, which was now completely lifeless and face down in the river. In a cruel irony, Danny was still clad in his Catholic school uniform when Lavigne returned. He admitted to the detective that he was fascinated with seeing a dead body and watched Danny float lifelessly for a few hours. Lavigne then walked the confession back and told the detective he simply heard that Danny was thrown in the river and wanted to go see for himself. He then admitted he was the last person to see Danny alive.

The detective was rightly fed up with the former priest's bullshit and deadpanned at one point, "I know you did this," referring to Danny's murder.

Detective McNalley took the information Lavigne confessed to Hampden County District Attorney Anthony Gulluni. The detective set out to interview other victims to establish Lavigne's patterns for when the inevitable murder charges were filed against him based on his confessions. Detective McNalley agonized over talking to other victims, which included three of Danny's brothers. Richard Lavigne had an estimated two hundred and fifty victims. He was a menace to society who destroyed young lives with no remorse—a true monster. Some of his victims went on to offend themselves, one died by suicide, and almost all had trouble adjusting to adult life. Richard Lavigne, like Wayne

Chapman, destroyed a generation of children; but unlike Chapman, he never spent a day behind bars.

On May 21, 2021, defrocked priest Richard Lavigne died of COVID-19. The district attorney's office called a press conference days later to reveal he had talked to investigators, basically on his deathbed, and murder charges were filed against him just days before he died. After answering the media's questions, the DA declared the case closed. As far as the law was concerned, Richard Lavigne had killed Danny Croteau. He had admitted to striking Danny in the river and coming back later to see the body. The Croteau family gained a small semblance of peace and a sad chapter in the history of Western Massachusetts was closed forever.

The breadth of Richard Lavigne's crimes against children could fill a book of its own. There is confirmed and indisputable evidence that his leaders in the archdiocese knew he molested altar boys and helped cover it up. Lavigne was allowed to operate in total perpetuity while the leaders of the church knew what he was doing. He made one last admission to Detective McNalley during the long interrogation process. The elderly predator told the detective that he was confident he would be going to heaven.

Lavigne's confession and the closing of Danny Croteau's case gave me hope that the now seventy-three-year-old Wayne Chapman might make the same sort of deathbed confession. There is no indication that investigators made their way down to Connecticut to talk to a sickly Chapman about the disappearances decades earlier in which he was the only suspect named. On the morning of October 21, 2021, I was waiting at the drop-off with my son in front of his elementary school. I hadn't thought about Chapman at all until I received a phone call that he died earlier that morning in Rocky Hill, Connecticut. My initial thought was, *the world is a better place*. I even said, "That's good." I soon realized how stupid that response was.

Wayne Chapman no longer had the opportunity to tell the world what happened. He could have given the families some peace if he had had the humanity, to tell the truth on his way out. Had lived in such a state of denial for so long that perhaps he had convinced himself that he didn't commit those crimes, just like Nathaniel Bar-Jonah. The fact that Wayne Chapman took his secrets to the grave is an infinitely sad end to an incredibly frustrating story. I don't have all the answers. I do believe, though, that I am asking all the right questions.

During the arduous eleven-hour interrogation, Richard Lavigne talked in-depth to Detective McNalley. Lavigne even invited the trooper to his home to see his artwork. He loved to collect art and could talk about his pieces for hours to anyone who showed the slightest interest. Lavigne even had his garage painted outside his home. The white garage door was painted over with a sunburst and the French word "*Perche*" on a giant crest that sat at the noon position. It translates to "*why?*" It could not be a more ironic and better question to ask. It is the crux of this entire book.

Why? Or better yet *how?* That has always been my question. How did these men operate under the noses of law enforcement and parents for that matter for so long? Why were these men covered for and protected? How did David Louison's body end up in a random basement in Brockton? Where is Andy Puglisi's body? I will wrestle with the why and the how for the rest of my life. To this day, it keeps me up at night.

I do feel one thing to be true—all these men were connected: Peter Haskell. Wayne Chapman. Nathaniel Bar-Jonah. Charles Pierce. Richard Peluso. Frank Damiano. The priests. The circumstantial evidence is there. I just need the smoking gun—the proverbial *ah-ha!* Evidence that ties this entire mystery together.

I will never stop looking. Ever.

Epilogue

On November 6, 2020, Priest Paul Shanley, who gave sermons on the streets of Boston, died. His speeches were the catalysts for the formation of NAMBLA. Years after his street-preaching days, Shanley did twelve years in prison for raping a boy in a church in Newton. He also destroyed lives for decades and was covered for by leaders of the archdiocese. His death in 2020 and Wayne Chapman's in 2021 represented the last of the predators who roamed the New England region in the early 1970s. Learning of Shanley's death pushed me to continue writing this book after I put it on the shelf for what seemed like the twentieth time.

We can never forget what went on in those days for fear it could happen again. It probably is happening right now. Instead of meeting in bathhouses or theaters, predators now congregate on the Internet. With Operation Pacifier which commenced in 2014, the FBI took down men all over the globe who traded child pornography on the Dark Web. These men logged a supposedly secure message board and traded images of abused children. At least one hundred and thirty-seven cases were brought around the country and one thousand computers were seized. The creator of the site, a man from Florida, got one of the largest prison sentences in recorded history for his role. Pedophiles always find one another, whether it's in adult bookstores, behind prison walls, or on the Internet, and it's far easier now in the digital age.

Very few people still cover Andy Puglisi's disappearance. Melanie Perkins-McLaughlin still operates HAVEYOUSEENANDY.COM and has a podcast coming called *Open Investigation*. Melanie has lived these cases for decades and has incredible insight into them. Albert Mintz, the Providence Police Department sex crimes detective, is alive and well and is living in his hometown of Jacksonville, Florida. He never forgot Wayne Chapman's eyes and contends Chapman was guilty of much more than for which he was convicted.

When I started investigating these cases, I thought it would be nothing more than a dark obsession. As a victim myself, I feel such a kinship with other abused kids. I know the life-crushing consequences of sexual abuse. I needed to write this for cathartic purposes if nothing else. The fact that people may read this book and go talk about the cases on social media or message boards is enough for me. A common buzz phrase is *"never forget;"* it's said about a lot of different events—terrorist attacks, murders, wars. My sincere hope is you put this book on your bookshelf, walk by it every so often, and think about the victims and the innocence that was stolen from them. Think about the families who must sit around the dinner table at Christmas and look at an empty seat, irrevocably shattered. I hope you hug your children a little tighter and a little longer after reading this. That is the greatest gift you could give back to me.

Thank you, dear reader.

November 2021

EPILOGUE II

After the publication of the first version of this book on January 30, 2022. I took a long break from investigating the disappearances of these young boys and girls from the New England area in the 1970s. Once the book was done, it was almost like a weight was lifted off my shoulders. It was cathartic. I started my own Substack discussing anything other than the disappearances. I was a regular guest on YouTube shows discussing politics, military life, and other topics of interest.

In March of 2023, I was moving into a new house in Providence, Rhode Island. I remember exactly what I was doing. I was setting up my bedframe and sweating. I grabbed my phone off the bureau and had a thought. Maybe I should check YouTube and see if any content creators have put out any new videos discussing the decades-old cases I knew so much about. Truth be told, it had been months since I had investigated any of this. My mind only had so much bandwidth, so I had lost my grasp on the basic facts of all the cases. Even after years of preparing a manuscript.

I was so busy with my private investigator work with a large firm and raising my two boys. I had the feeling that I had moved on. On that day I typed in Andy Puglisi's name into the search bar of my YouTube app and the first video was from a small channel called *Yellow Cottage Tales*. The video was a narrative video from a youngish looking guy with an incredibly smooth voice discussing the facts of the Puglisi disappearance. In the comment section, I noted (brashly) that I wrote the book on this case. I got a response from the channel owner that perhaps we should set up a call as he grew up in Lawrence and was interested in the Puglisi case. I asked him if he had read my book on the case, and he replied he had not. After he read the book, we set up a call.

When Kevin Lenihan called me, I sensed instantly that I was talking to one of the most logical and sober thinkers I had ever met. We discussed the cases for an hour and a half, going point for point on my thesis that all these men were connected. Kevin wasn't convinced and I got off the call thinking I had met a new friend who invigorated me. Kevin also confessed to me that he was not the young handsome guy in the video narrating the Puglisi case but was a fifty-eight-year-old man who spent his life in the bar industry but was now battling Stage 4 lung cancer. He told me he lived his life three months at a time and working on screenplays and serial-type videos kept him invigorated and sharp.

Kevin and I are kindred spirits. We both have curious minds and love to deconstruct cases but also deconstruct our notions. After the first call, we talked every day, eventually moving to me being a guest on his show. Our friendship blossomed and eventually, we started covering local cases outside of the 70s stuff that got us together. We moved to do nightly live shows discussing the day's big events in local corruption cases. Once I started getting out there again, the floodgates opened. In the description of each YouTube live show, I put my email and social media links and encouraged people to get in contact with me. The public didn't disappoint. Someone always knows something out there.

In May of 2023, I was contacted by a man in Virginia. The man had read the first version of this book and was galvanized to open up to his wife about the sexual abuse he suffered at summer camp in the early 1970s. It cut right to my heart to text this man every day and hear the stories he told for the first time. I know how hard it is to bear your soul to the people you love the most. Tommy Moore tells me often that I inspired him but victims like him inspire me. That man coming forward, and my friendship with Kevin, ignited my fire to take another look at all this again.

Since the first book was published, many readers have asked me about Maine pedophile Eugene Weir. Earlier on in the book, I talked a bit about how Weir was listed as a friend of Wayne Chapman's and Chapman had floated the idea to the parole board that Weir was willing to let him move in with him upon Chapman's release. All of that comes from Chapman's own words and it was an angle I never got the opportunity to pay off.

In early 2023, I traveled to Cumberland County, Maine, to talk to Weir about his relationship with Chapman. Weir lived on his family farm and proved elusive. I did, however, find his daughter. What I am about to tell you rank among the most horrifying and awkward moments of my life. I found Weir's daughter on Facebook and put together that she worked at a local establishment close to her family's farm. I approached her in the afternoon, right before happy hour. I introduced myself and asked her if I could have some assistance in finding her father, whom I verified was still alive and well. She refused and I pressed her hard that her father had come up in the documents of a former child rapist and alleged child killer and I needed to see him. I told her I had no interest in her father's crimes. I had no idea what her father did, I read the charges he was convicted of, but I had no idea who her father sexually abused. As it turned out, Eugene Weir had been in Bridgewater for raping his daughter. The same one I was pressing for information on his whereabouts. I offered a meek apology and slunk away. I haven't been back to Maine since.

One narrative that has repeatedly been thrown at me is the notion put forward by some journalists that Nathaniel Bar-Jonah was dating Leigh Savoie's mother at the time of her son's disappearance. I have seen this nidicolous rumor on internet message boards like Web Sleuths and Reddit.

Countless readers of the first iteration of this book have emailed me and asked me why I ignored this "fact" in my reporting. I have ignored this rumor for a multitude of reasons I will explain here. Firstly, Bar-Jonah was born in February of 1957. Leigh Savoie disappeared in April 1974. Bar-Jonah had just turned seventeen when Savoie went missing and admittedly had been committing crimes since he was seven years old. The idea that a teenage Bar-Jonah was dating an older woman who lived 52.6 miles away from his home is absurd. There is no evidence that Bar-Jonah ever visited Revere as a teenager or as an adult. Bar-Jonah was not in the address book of Richard Peluso, the curator of the Revere sex ring house on Mountain Ave that operated until the mid-70s.

Secondly, Bar-Jonah was a homosexual man who preyed on young boys. Although it's common practice for gay pedophiles to date and even marry women with young children, there is no evidence to link Bar-Jonah to Delores Savoie. This rumor began with an obituary that surfaced on the internet and has been shared around consistently. The obituary mentions that Bar-Jonah and Delores had dated. You can write anything in an obituary. If I want my obituary to state that I had a long and loving marriage with Pamela Anderson, I can. Newspapers don't fact check obituaries so using that as your "evidence" is faulty. At best. The police in Revere have never heard of the Bar-Jonah connection and have not pursued the angle because there is no real evidence that is anything but nonsense. Sources tell me that the female detective assigned to the Savoie case in Revere is very dedicated to solving the case and pursues all leads. I am hopeful that we may get some closure on a lost boy from decades ago. The dangerous misinformation injected into the public sphere is a roadblock to closure for the family. I take the utmost care to make sure I don't participate in that.

In the few years since I first published, I have taken a long look at my reporting on Wayne Chapman and his crimes. I wanted to perform an autopsy on my preconceived notions and confirmation bias I may have had in my research for the first version of this book. All of which took place between 2015 to 2021. I wholeheartedly believe that Chapman killed Andy Puglisi and David Louison and got away with it due to a lack of evidence and malfeasance on the part of the investigators. Chapman confessed to being on the scene of both crimes. Now I have more questions than answers about what Chapman and company did with Puglisi's body. On August 1, 2023, I went back to the scene of the crime at Higgins Memorial Pool.

Kevin, Melanie, and I walked the theoretical route Chapman would have taken Andy the day he disappeared. I was struck by the undergrowth and sheer vastness of the wooded area that existed in the middle of an urban area like Lawrence. Kevin himself, who grew up in Lawrence, didn't grasp how massive the woods adjacent to Higgins Memorial Pool were. I started to question the theory I offered in earlier chapters of Chapman placing Andy in his van and driving him to Providence to place him in the incinerator. The searches that were performed in the days after Andy's disappearance were thorough but it was impossible to canvas every inch of the vast woodlands in the time they had before it was called off. Remember, the Lawrence Police had made a statement saying that they believed Andy was safe with a family member somewhere just days after he turned up missing. The search was aborted early. *Andy was fine with family and will be home soon,* they thought. The humongous undergrowth there in Lawrence remains to this day at best, partially searched. Maybe even a quarter searched. It's going to take hundreds of volunteers to search that area sufficiently to say that Andy's body isn't there, definitively.

You may ask yourself how, all these decades later, no one has come across Andy's remains in the woods if he's buried there. Surely, someone walking their dog or hiking or jogging would have come across a bone or maybe a skull, right? To answer that question, I would have to tell you to visit this area. It's not a satisfying response to someone who may not be able to make it there or if you're reading this in Arizona and have no trips to Lawrence planned. It is the best answer, however. There are many parts of these woods that nobody is going to hike in or walk their dog. It's the type of treacherous terrain you enter if you want to hide something there, not take a stroll.

Another story that I lend credibility to has come to light in the ensuing years since I first investigated the case of the missing Lawrence boy. A witness came forward with a story to tell about the night of Andy Puglisi's disappearance. This witness observed a Lawrence Police officer accosting a young boy in the Stadium Housing Projects. The witness did not identify this boy as Andy and didn't get a look at this boy, but they did hear the boy. This witness heard the young boy screaming at the police officer something to the effect of he didn't want to enter the policeman's patrol vehicle. The Lawrence resident overheard the struggle and remembered the boys' screams. This is a relevant story because it's known that around the time of Andy's disappearance, a Lawrence patrolman was removed from his job working as a school resource officer after he was found in his patrol vehicle with a little boy. The existence of a pedophile on the police force masquerading as a public servant and the story of a cop in the projects struggling with a little boy just after Andy went missing is enough to keep you awake at night. It also warrants a rethinking of everything I believed around the case. Had Wayne Chapman had help from a pedophile Lawrence officer? Who was that little boy struggling that night? Was it Andy? There is so much to unpack about what was happening in Lawrence in 1976 regarding pedophilia and the porn trade.

On August 1, the very same day we visited the woodlands, we made a stop at a local convenience store just outside the Stadium Housing Projects. I won't print the current name because the current owners have nothing to do with what went on there in the 1970s and I would hate to doxx it but know this: the existence of this store may be the key to unlocking the Chapman/Lawrence connection that is so elusive. As I have said countless times—Chapman didn't go anywhere by chance. When Chapman went to Lawrence to victimize the two boys he was found guilty of raping (and eventually, Andy), it was because he was comfortable there and had the lay of the land.

The convenience store may have been the plug. This was a neighborhood store where patrons could go get their essentials like milk, eggs, and bread. You could also buy pornography. Specifically, child pornography. The men who owned and operated this store drove one hundred and forty-four miles round trip each day to operate this store. They lived in the same town Chapman lived and worked: Providence. It always goes back to Providence. The tentacles extended all the way south down Route 95. Ever since the day in the early 1970s where Roy DeMeo was ordered by his boss Paul Castellano to get out the porn business out of New York and transfer it to Providence. I know this because the FBI notes it in their voluminous files on the Mob killer, DeMeo. That was the first event in a chain that sent Chapman to Providence and may have sealed Puglisi's and Louison's death warrants. Chapman's presence in Lawrence on multiple occasions over two years, coupled with the porn store owners being from Providence, gives me newfound avenues to explore. Why were all these Providence guys in Lawrence? Why were they so comfortable there?

It's been forty-eight years since Andy Puglisi disappeared and his school friend Melanie Perkins-McLaughlin continues to search for answers. She launched a podcast series in fall 2024 called *Open Investigation* that is available on Spotify, Apple, and wherever else you get your podcasts. Melanie discusses the Puglisi case with the knowledge and vigor of someone who lived it. Because she did. Even after nearly five decades have gone by, the story continues to evolve and it's enduring. I still get emails from all four corners of the globe after the first version of this book is released. There's still much more to uncover about Chapman and Lawrence, and that's what keeps my fire burning.

As for Charles Pierce, Wayne Chapman's mentor and cohort. In 2022, after the first books release, I headed down to Florida. As I have noted here, Charles Pierce had a hard time down south for crimes against children in Florida's prison system. When I headed south, I was interested in a case in Marion County, in the city of Ocala in Central Florida. The missing girl's name was Dorothy Scofield. Scofield disappeared from a busy store called J.M. Fields on Silver Spring Boulevard in Ocala. The mall was directly across the street from a Florida Highway Patrol substation. Dee's mother allowed her to go by herself to buy her brother a birthday gift while she went across to FHP to renew her license.

Not a single witness saw Dee leave the mall except for a woman named Cora Mossman. Mossman told police that she saw Dee get into an older grey panel van. A day later, a convenience store clerk told police that she saw a girl who matched Dee's description in her store that same day. The store was fifteen miles from where Dee was last seen at the mall. The clerk told investigators that Dee was crying as she walked around the store and then left with a soda and got into a vehicle with an unidentified man. Charles Pierce also owned a grey panel van and was a Floridian who was known to frequent Marion County. I was tipped off by email that many true crime enthusiasts in Central Florida thought Pierce should be further investigated. What I found in my nine-month stay is that during the month of July 1976, Charles Pierce was in Florida. I know this because he attended court twice during that month for petty crimes.

I interviewed dozens of Ocala natives during my stay who were old enough to remember the disappearance. The neighborhood scuttlebutt was that the perpetrator had out-of-state license plates, somewhere up north. I heard that story repeatedly. It's such a crucial detail that I need to nail it down, it's half the reason I decided to mention this case here. Pierce had a grey panel van at the time and if that vehicle Dee Scofield was last seen walking to had Massachusetts license plates, then we are cooking with gas. Charles Pierce killed many young children. Both boys and girls. Every thread that's handed to me, I will run to the ground. No matter how small. This is not the last time I will write in long form about Pierce. Pierce deserves a book of his own. It's called foreshadowing, folks.

Sometime in late summer 2024, I got a call from a strange number. The area code was from the state of Wyoming. I thought for a few about who the hell would call me from Wyoming before I saw the little voicemail thing come up. I dialed up the voicemail and listened as an investigator from Wyoming asked me to call him back. My immediate thought was: *what crimes would I have committed in Wyoming?* The call came from a private investigator who had read my thoughts on the disappearance of Amanda Gallon, a young girl who had vanished on October 13, 1997, on her way to school in Gilette, Wyoming.

On October 12, 1997, Nathaniel Bar-Jonah made a four-hundred-and-fifty-mile trip to Gillette, Wyoming, from his home in Great Falls, Montana. At the time, Bar-Jonah was under heavy police scrutiny as the main suspect in Zach Ramsay's case. On the evening of the 12th, Bar-Jonah checked into a motel in Gilette at 8 p.m. Bar-Jonah's activities in Wyoming are unknown. He was seen the next day around 2 in the afternoon at an antique mall back in Billings, Montana. Amanda Gallon was last seen by her boyfriend riding her bike at 7:15 in the morning. Bar-Jonah could have committed a crime and gotten back to

Billings by 2 pm. Amanda had a short haircut and was often mistaken for a boy when she rode her bicycle. Bar-Jonah had mistaken a little girl for a boy once in his pathetic life when he was a teenager back in Worcester. Bar-Jonah got so angry at the little girl that he beat her so badly that she urinated on herself. The presence of Bar-Jonah in Gilette on the day Amanda went missing with no good explanation is worthy of review as her case is unsolved. I have a trip planned soon to meet with the investigator and re-interview locals. Like Pierce, Bar-Jonah took a lot of secrets to the grave. It's our job collectively to unearth them.

UNMASKED

In the summer of 2023, Kevin Linehan and I did a live stream on YouTube regarding deathbed confessions. We went over a few national cases and naturally, our discussion landed on the case of Andrew Amato, who went missing from Webster, Massachusetts, in 1978. I mentioned the case in an earlier chapter and discussed how a man confessed the crime on his deathbed and the name was never publicly released. I went over the case in detail on the livestream. I talked about how I researched cancer deaths in the year 1999 in the town of Burrillville, Rhode Island. I knew that the man who confessed to his family had died that year from cancer. I told the viewers how I scoured obituaries and public records for weeks that turned into months trying to come up with names. I did come up with a few and I held them to protect the innocent. All I had were obituaries that fit the timeframe and cause of death. Which amounted to nothing when you're talking evidence.

We spent about an hour on the Andrew Amato case and got off at about 10:30 p.m. that evening. I showered and dried off and grabbed my cell phone. On my phone, I had an email. It was from a woman who I will call "Jenny" here. Jenny had been watching the livestream, as she was obsessed with a case we discussed that evening. She stuck around to hear the end of the show and she nearly fell over when we got on the topic of Andrew.

The discussion triggered Jenny's memory. Years ago, in the year 2006, a friend of hers reached out to her and asked her to fly home to Rhode Island. She needed moral and spiritual support because the feds were coming to dig up her deceased father's backyard regarding Andrew Amato's disappearance. The police thought that Andrew was buried in a wooded area near power lines. How they got that information I could never figure out. Now I knew: the man's backyard ran parallel to power lines in a wooded area of Burrillville. So far it tracked. The woman's father had confessed to the crime on his deathbed years ago.

Jenny, the man's daughter who went by the nickname "Cricket," and I had a three-way call weeks later. The woman explained to me that her father was a brutal man who abused his children, was an adulterer, and kept barrels of acid in his backyard. He was a preacher who often taught the good word at the Adult Correctional Institution in Cranston, Rhode Island, where Wayne Chapman was once held. This man was a truck driver who drove all over New England. The man who I called "Jesse" was a man really named Harold Neal. Neal was from Warwick but settled in Burrillville in his later years. Jenny and Cricket provided photo evidence that they were at Neal's home on the day the feds excavated the backyard.

After the discussion, I confirmed with a law enforcement source that Neal was indeed their guy at the time. He had been on law enforcement's radar since the day Andrew Amato disappeared and had been brought in for interviews but there was not enough evidence to make charges stick. The most bizarre subplot of the Andrew Amato disappearance was the discovery of a paper bag on the side of the road in the town of Woburn, Massachusetts, which is north of Boston. The last person to see Andrew alive told police that Andrew was wearing a pair of dungarees and a Mickey Mouse t-shirt. The paper bag consisted of a Mickey Mouse t-shirt and dungarees. The sizes also matched what would fit a boy of Andrew's age and size. The police were baffled. How the hell did the clothes end up sixty-one miles away from where Andrew disappeared?

I have yet to find a definitive link between Harold Neal and the city of Woburn. Neal was driving trucks up and down the highways all day for work, so it is plausible Neal knew the North Shore area well. I dug into Neal's background immediately after learning of his identity. His daughter was a great source of information. Her father was a bad guy who had many kids and was unfaithful to his wife. I couldn't make sense of him as a killer just based on infidelity. Neal was a ghost with very little criminal history. In my estimation, Neal was just a lone predator who fantasized and stalked young boys.

Murderers don't fit into any box. Some killers are serial offenders. Some, like what we just saw with Richard Allen in Delphi, Indiana, wait until middle age to finally act out on their fantasies. Richard Allen had a precipitating life event. His daughter moved out of the house and Allen was now an empty nester with time on his hands. Life slowed down and the fantasies took over. Something similar happened with Harold Neal. Maybe he lost his dream job as Dennis Rader, aka the BTK killer in Kansas, did. Rader started acting on his fantasies after he lost his dream job at Cessna. It's likely that Neal was in the woods that day looking for targets and fell upon young Andrew and he struck. It was a crime of opportunity after a lifetime of dreaming for Neal. I do not believe Neal had any connections to the other killers featured in this story.

In the lead up to preparing my new material for this book, I looked back on some old emails. I was trying to figure out how Neal could have escaped me during my initial investigation. Years ago, I did a podcast on Apple called *Monster* where I reviewed the cases and talked about where I was with the book research. Searching through my emails I found one dated February 8, 2018, at 2:32 p.m. The subject line simply said "AMATO" and the body of the email read: *Neal. Harold Neal is your man.*

I had discussed the Andrew Amato case a week or so before the note was sent. Someone was listening. The email came from a town email account. I simply overlooked it and when I tried to reply six years later, the email came back undeliverable.

The world is always telling you something. You just need to listen.

Home, sweet home

—2024

For More News About David McGrath,
Signup For Our Newsletter:

http://wbp.bz/newsletter

Word-of-mouth is critical to an author's long-term success. If you appreciated this book please leave a review on the Amazon sales page:

http://wbp.bz/obsessed

www.ingramcontent.com/pod-product-compliance
Lightning Source LLC
Chambersburg PA
CBHW070056030426
42335CB00016B/1906